SHIRLEY
MACLAINE

SHIRLEY
MACLAINE

Michael Freedland

Salem House Publishers
Manchester, New Hampshire

*To my mother
with love and gratitude*

Acknowledgements

It would have been nice to begin these acknowledgements with one to Shirley MacLaine herself. But then, as her agent pointed out to me, a girl who gets $900,000 every time she writes a book herself is hardly likely to want to co-operate with another writer choosing her as his subject.

Yet that was what really got this project going. Shirley MacLaine had written so much about herself that it was worth asking, was that all there was to be said? I felt this was most unlikely. The view one step back is always different from that head on into a mirror. That one-step-back position takes in a view that includes a lot of other people, too.

So that is what this book is – a chance to see the Shirley MacLaine story with the benefit of the people who, one way or another, have been involved in her life; some of them the very people she mentions in her own books, but who have hitherto had no opportunity to tell their side of the story.

Many of the people to whom I spoke, and for reasons I more than understand, want to stay as anonymous in their retelling of events as they have been hitherto. Some of the people I have quoted have offered opinions in the course of research on other matters. Others gave me a great deal of their time just talking for this project. To them all, my grateful thanks – including:

Ray Anthony, Louis Benjamin, Joey Bishop, the late Maurice Chevalier, Jack Cummings, Ivor Davis, George 'Bullets' Durgom, the late Eddie Foy Jnr, John Green, the late Laurence Harvey, Wilfrid Hyde White, Martha Hyer, Perry King, the late Peter Lawford, Jack Lemmon, Dean Martin, Fred MacMurray, Mr and Mrs Vincente Minnelli, Ron Moody, Richard Quire, David Rose, Hal Wallis, Tony Wells and Billy Wilder, all of whom, one way or another, have spoken to me about Shirley MacLaine.

Also my profound thanks to the librarians of the Academy of Motion Picture Arts and Sciences, Beverly Hills, the British Film Institute, and the British Library.

And finally, to my wife Sara who, as always, is everything.

Chapter One

It was at the Wilshire Theater in Los Angeles. One of those buildings that looks as though it has seen better days. If it had, this was one of its better nights.

Theatres in America that are big, are bigger than those anywhere else. This one looked immense – but every seat had been sold and there was I sitting in the balcony, and at the back of the balcony at that. It was the only seat left in the house and as I looked downward to what I believed, with great faith, must have been a stage (it was so far away I could have been told it was a letter-box and believed it) it seemed quite clear that the twenty dollars I had just shelled out would have been better spent on a season ticket for a visiting flea circus. At least the fleas on show would have been fleas. The ones I could see on that stage only looked like fleas. On the best authority, I gathered they were people.

And then those fleas struck up the bars of 'If They Could See Me Now' – and I could see. The figure who pranced out on to the apron of the stage wasn't a flea at all. She wore a slinky black outfit that emphasised curves where no flea ever had curves. There was a smile on her face and I swear from two miles up I could see that smile. There was a twinkle in her eyes and I promise you I saw it glint in the spotlight.

If a seam in her tights had been out of place, I would have noticed that, too. That was Shirley MacLaine in concert. Fifty years old and looking as though she were in the midst of her first love affair. Well, if she looked any older than a high school girl, I'll allow that was something the distance prevented me from seeing.

As for the love bit, I'm prepared to believe that was exactly

9

how she felt. An entertainer doesn't give all, the way that Shirley MacLaine, actress, performer and writer, did that night in 1984, if it's simply work. It's what separates the men from the boys, and Shirley MacLaine from the other girls.

Other performers would have stayed looking like fleas from that spot at the top of the mountain. But she didn't. She made you believe that you would recognise her face from up there, if she didn't have on even a speck of make-up or if her name hadn't been on the programme in front of me.

She came to that theatre fresh from a successful run on Broadway and from seeing her newest film take five Oscars a few months before. That in itself was remarkable.

Others had written that they only knew of Shirley MacLaine as an actress – a serious actress or one who had played so many ladies of the night on screen, she would say the studios never sent her a cheque, they simply left her money on the dressing-table in the morning.

So what would she do? Dance a little? Yes, she had done that before in her films. Sing, too? Of course, she also did that pretty well in *Sweet Charity*.

Tell stories? Well, an actress like Shirley, with three highly successful books to her name, might be expected to be able to turn on narrative much as she was able to twist the taps on her dressing-room basin.

What was remarkable was that here she was, doing all those things. And even more important, the sum total of what she was doing was very much better than any of those individual parts, on their own, would indicate. That was style, too.

For one who has remained in the public eye for so long – and by the very nature of that length of time at the top, one who started so young – Shirley MacLaine remains something of an enigma. She has written a great deal about herself, although what she has written refers to isolated incidents in her life and says practically nothing about most of her career and the events that have shaped it. That is why, more than half a century into the life of the girl born Shirley Maclean Beaty, it is useful to plumb a little deeper, sometimes to get the other side of stories that have become popular currency, occasionally to embellish those tales as seen from the viewpoint of people who have been with her.

Sometimes, when stars like Shirley MacLaine are put on pedestals, all human qualities seem to leave them, as though once having reached Mount Olympus the gods achieve along with sanctification a loss of all other frailties.

It pays these gods no tribute to sustain that impression. Shirley MacLaine is human. Some of the things she has done strike mere observers as not very nice. These are recorded along with the tributes.

None of this will come as a surprise to those who know Shirley MacLaine. But one is always left with the impression that what she really wants is to surprise. Why else would she have taken as her plaintive theme song 'If They Could See Me Now'?

She was born in Virginia, and that says a lot about her and the home from which she came. Virginia people have an opinion of themselves which, while not actually claiming superiority, seems to say that they as sure as hell know that there's no one better.

And with that attitude goes a sense of almost puritan innocence. Mrs Kathlyn Maclean Beaty always kept the house in Richmond spick and span to the point of obsessiveness; the flowered furnishings were always just so; the meals she served conformed to the exact recipes and specifications.

She had done her share of painting and a little acting. Shirley was always to say that Kathlyn thwarted all her own ambitions by getting married – which is why she never foisted the idea of marriage on her daughter.

Her husband, Ira, lived in his own world of Virginian respectability which he carried with him into old age. That didn't mean his definition of a Southern gentleman was someone who needed to conform to the niceties of convention. But he didn't like permissiveness, he was to tell his daughter after she scored yet another of her massive box office successes. What he particularly didn't like was the fact she showed her 'tits'.

There wasn't to be a great deal that Shirley liked about him or the home he kept in the early years after her birth on April 24, 1934.

'My parents never fulfilled their creative potential,' she told *Time* magazine soon after her 50th birthday and when her parents were both 81 years old, a time when they might be expected to live out their old age without sniping from their daughter.

'I grew up surrounded by anxiety and disappointment.'

Like any number of other celebrities, she would say that her parents never really understood her. She has not been afraid in her maturity to criticise them to what some people would say was an unmerciful extent, given her strength and authority and the parents' – who, by all accounts, doted on their successful daughter – inability to answer back.

In those days, it was Ira who did the speaking. He didn't like the way the neighbours talked, objected to Kathlyn strolling around the garden wearing shorts and a big sun hat which Shirley was to write made her look like a walking umbrella.

When her baby brother Warren was born shortly before her third birthday, it seems that both became objects of their parents' desire to mould them in the conservative respectability they craved for themselves.

Shirley has attested that she and Warren were never really close – except that they both appear to have suffered from this desire to keep one stage ahead of the Joneses, almost as though it were part of the Civil War which Virginia never reconciled itself to losing. Outsiders were viewed as if they were part of a fifth column.

Shirley has not tried to hide the other skeletons in the family cupboard. Mr Beaty drank – and, like many white folks in Virginia, didn't exactly fancy the idea of having a black man as a dinner companion.

On the other hand, Warren says that his parents were quite liberal – and encouraged his sister with her early stirrings of feminism. If Warren is being extra kind or slightly hazy in his recollections and it is Shirley with the more accurate memory, then could the MacLaine enthusiasm for left-wing political causes be part of an innate revolt against family mores?

Both Shirley and Warren made no secret of the fact that they were always trying to escape – and succeeded in their early days in escaping to the movies. It was in the rarefied atmosphere of a dark theatre that their own ambitions received their first careful nurturing.

They didn't understand their parents any more than their parents understood them.

The way the Beatys behaved might be better understood when considering the fact that both were involved in education – which in the Virginia of the 1920s and 30s left little or no room for flexibility or imagination. Kathlyn had been a schoolteacher as well as a sometime actress, Ira was Superintendent of Richmond High School.

Not that they had no pleasures in life. Kathlyn, whose mother had taught elocution, used to enjoy directing amateur plays and her husband considered himself quite a talent with a violin. He also had a talent for telling stories that commanded a great deal of attention, particularly from Kathlyn. Seeing them together, Shirley was to say, was sometimes like watching a vaudeville act.

But even vaudeville acts were known to be crusty off-stage, and young Warren was to suffer as much as Shirley from the attitude of their father. All the boy seemed to want in his early childhood was to play with his toy cars which generally – and as most small boys arrange such things – were spread out all over the floor.

Ira Beaty kept complaining about it – and one day feigned a fall over the assembled vehicles. Warren never played with them again. He later spent most of his time at home memorising the plays of Eugene O'Neill and miming to records of Al Jolson – every kid in the late 40s wanted to play Larry Parks playing the central character in *The Jolson Story* and young Mr Beaty apparently managed it as successfully as anyone else, and without any notable parental objection.

Shirley might have been seen to be difficult in her own way, too. If the Beatys wanted to raise what they saw as a normal little girl, then they were to be disappointed.

As she told *Look* magazine in a 1959 article, written at what at the time seemed the peak of her newly-found fame, she had different ideas about fun.

Warren has described her as 'quite an athlete'. An athlete who, at the age of 14, played – left field – for her school baseball team. All the other players were boys, but, in this early demonstration of feminism, she was there with the tough males and in one notable match scored a whole notch of doubles and triples.

Shirley told *Look* that she was simply a 'tomboy' and one who hated dolls and all the other things pretty little Virginia girls were expected to like.

13

(This was never a completely accurate description of her. Shirley likes to remember when she was six years old – and was very much a little girl. She had a multi-coloured gossamer dress, which on a beautiful summer's day she wore on a seesaw. As she went high in the air, the dress flew over her head and she saw the world in a mix of colours, as though her eyes had suddenly become an artist's transparent palette. She saw a butterfly and felt at one with it – until the butterfly flew away and the illusion disappeared with it. It was a happy time and the kind only a little girl would appreciate.)

The only thing that ever made her doubt the wisdom of being a tomboy, she said, was 'I realised that getting punched in the boobs didn't feel too good.'

She even went on record saying that she considered her relationship to Warren as more like that of a big brother than an elder sister – which Mr Beatty has dismissed out of hand. To quote him, that is a ball with which he cannot run.

Nevertheless, Miss MacLaine insists that if she saw little Warren in trouble, she wasn't beyond swinging out with a useful left hook to save the day and her brother's face.

Together they enjoyed their favourite pastime of emptying garbage pails on the front lawns of their neighbours.

If she really was a tomboy, then she was a tomboy who wanted to be a ballet dancer – which might have seemed ridiculous for a girl with the kind of weak ankles her doctor had already diagnosed, but here Kathlyn Beaty had method in her determination.

'I couldn't control (the ankles),' Shirley said when she had achieved the kind of fame her mother never even considered in those days. 'I walked like a duck.' So Kathlyn decided that the best way to strengthen those ankles was to give Shirley ballet lessons.

At the age of three, Shirley waddled into a hall where 25 other girls and three boys were in the midst of one of those lessons which she was about to find were as important to her life as a bowl of ice cream on a hot afternoon.

'I loved it,' she said – and everything she did indicated that it had been a very good idea indeed. Kathlyn had decided that ballet would be an acceptable alternative to leg braces and a gruelling regimen of sessions with an orthopaedic specialist and the exercises that would follow.

She told Shirley that it would be a lot of fun. Mrs Beaty could have had no idea just how much fun. Shirley really did love her dancing. Even more, she loved appearing before a seemingly doting public. At the age of four, the little girl was fast becoming a Virginia ham.

As she herself has said: 'I kept telling Mother, "I want to be a little dancing gal".'

Her first exposure to an audience was at Richmond's Mosque Theater in 1938. She and the bottom of the curtain had a disagreement and little Shirley fell on stage with a large plunk. The audience loved it. When she heard their laughs, she found reasons for falling over for the rest of the show.

'I should have gotten wise and left acting for ballet right then.' More than 20 years later, she would say she must have been a lonely child – she regarded the audience as her friend.

There was also no stopping her ambition – even when the ankles seemingly got a lot better, although her right one wasn't as firm as everybody hoped.

At 11, Shirley changed school – at the same time as the family changed homes. They moved from Richmond to another town in the same state, Arlington, best known for its famous war cemetery – now the resting-place of the two murdered Kennedy brothers – and within walking distance across the bridges of the Potomac River of the Capitol in Washington, DC.

It was in Washington that she joined another dancing school run by a Miss Lisa Gardiner, who had at one time danced with Pavlova. Another teacher, Julia Mildred Harper, Shirley was to say, was 'the reason I don't have muscles in my legs like most dancers' – a very important factor indeed for a young girl who might like to think she'd look great in a pair of fishnet tights 40 years later. . . .

Nobody told the willowy Shirley Beaty at the time, but she was growing perhaps a little too willowy and too tall to be a ballerina. And nobody at Lisa Gardiner's school was really taken all that seriously. The dancing, however, became an obsession.

But she had to fit it in with her work at high school. It was a long hard day – every day of the week. She would get up at six every morning, take the seven o'clock bus which got her to school in time to start work at eight. School usually finished at

12, but that only gave her enough time to grab a snack and go off to the lessons she was taking to be a cheer-leader; a very pretty one indeed who didn't give the slightest impression that she would rather be wearing a helmet and padded shoulders and racing with the ball to the touch line.

That lasted until four, and then she would move on to her dancing school.

When the school gave concerts – Shirley was to write that Miss Gardiner and her younger partner Mary Day ran what was perhaps the best amateur company in America, performing with the National Symphony on occasion – Shirley wanted to be there with the rest of the girls.

Anyone doubting that show business was very much part of Shirley's make-up only had to attend a recital the school gave featuring the young dancer in a Spanish mood.

Shirley was dancing *Malaguena* when she knew one of the buttons holding up her petticoat was breaking away from the rest of the garment. She could hear the popping, but wasn't sure that the audience assembled there that night could, too. So she kept on dancing – with predictable consequences. The faster she danced and twirled, the faster the petticoat swept towards her ankles. The people who had gone to the evening expecting to be bored by every young child except their own suddenly found themselves in the midst of a novel entertainment. Instead of yawning, they laughed – which would have intimidated other children to the point of running off in tears. Not Shirley. She threw down the castanets she was clicking while dancing, picked up the offending garment and twisted it around her middle like a matador's cape. That was thinking on her twinkling feet. It was also showmanship.

At the age of 12, Shirley was five feet seven inches tall and, as predicted, that didn't look all that good on a ballet dancer. (When she got *en pointe*, she was a full five inches taller still.)

Even so, it wasn't long afterwards that people began to realise it looked nice enough on Shirley Beaty. She knew it, too – and was determined to be in the best school shows.

Ira was somewhat less enthusiastic than his daughter – although he wasn't totally the old stick-in-the-mud he usually seemed. For a time he fronted his own band at Arlington, and even school life was beginning to pall on him. He decided to go into real estate. It certainly seemed to offer better financial prospects.

Even Shirley was attracted to that idea. There was, for instance, the time Ira was waiting outside a house he was anxious to sell. He was sitting behind the wheel of his car, a cigar in his mouth. It was a tiring, unrewarding task and with Shirley around to watch both the car and the cigar, he went off to get himself a cup of coffee.

The teenage girl who by now believed that everything was there for the picking (she might not have sung 'Life Is Just a Bowl of Cherries', but assuredly that was what she felt) was doubly tempted that afternoon. She picked up the cigar and began smoking it. Then, when she saw a family drive up to the house her father was trying so eagerly to sell, she decided to pick up the challenge where it lay. The trouble was that by the time she greeted the prospective purchasers as the personal representative of the sole agents, she was coughing and spluttering her heart out. Her face meanwhile had turned the colour of spring lettuce.

That was much less of an act than tripping over the curtain at the Mosque Theater, but it had a similar effect. Whether the people who came to see the house at Arlington that day felt sorry for this plainly sick child who was trying to help her poor father to scratch a living will now never be known. But within two days of exposing themselves to Shirley's salesmanship, they had signed on the dotted line and bought the property. Ten years later, Shirley was saying that she was still waiting for her commission – her father had promised her ten per cent of what he earned if the impossible happened and buyers came to the house after he had left and, even more impossible, she managed to sell it.

Convincing Ira that she was sufficiently talented to play Cinderella was much more difficult. He thought she was not good enough and lost no time in telling her so.

You didn't need a Shirley MacLaine on an analyst's couch to realise that the desire to let the gang see her now was really an intense determination to let her father see how far she could get. After all, he had sneered at her attempts to sing 'I Can't Say No' from *Oklahoma!* at a school concert and now lost no time in telling her it was ridiculous to imagine she could play the title role in their Christmas production of *Cinderella*.

She was so upset, she says, that she vomited. Her father's word appeared vindicated. The school said she was too tall for the part. But there was a consolation in store. She did get the role of the fairy godmother and danced it, high on tiptoe – even though she had a broken ankle.

If anyone would care to read that sentence again, it is worth repeating. Shirley Maclean Beaty, now 16 years old, danced the role of the fairy godmother in the *Cinderella* ballet with a broken ankle.

She had felt the joint – that atrociously weak right ankle – snap in the course of her last-minute exercises before the curtain went up. To outsiders, whose only knowledge of the ballet and the self-inflicted torture that goes with it comes from seeing films about the dance, some of the movements can look extremely dangerous. On this occasion, she wouldn't have been in any greater peril in the midst of a scrum at Twickenham or a scrimmage during an American college football game.

The ankle was swollen by the time she summoned up the courage to look at it. So she bound it, tight as a tourniquet, with her shoe ribbon and went on just the same, conquering the hurt and, it seems, the audience with her. She said she didn't even notice the pain.

When the show was over, she was taken to hospital by ambulance and didn't walk again for four months. Plainly dancing the fairy godmother in *Cinderella* has not become part of the treatment for broken ankles now taught in the world's medical schools.

It was crazy, stupid, dangerous. But it got the message across. Kathlyn understood why her daughter wanted to go off to New York to try to get a job in the *real* world of show-biz, even though she knew she would have some explaining to do to the girl's father.

Shirley was still a student at the Washington and Lee High School in Arlington, but the summers were long and she took them as opportunities to work in seasonal shows in America's biggest city. If they didn't come off, then the budding feminist called Shirley Beaty reconciled herself to being a physicist. She was majoring in physics at school and seemed to be doing well enough at it to make the subject her career. After all, she figured it was the dawn of the atomic age and everyone would need physicists before long. As for herself, she needed a job in show business to prove that she wouldn't have to put that idea to the test. With $25 a week from her father to help her survive in what no one had yet tried to call the Big Apple, she landed herself only the occasional job.

One of the shows was a touring version of *Oklahoma!*

She didn't get to sing 'I Can't Say No'. But if you were in the audience at the time, you might remember the girl who was in the centre of the stage during the ballet. If you do remember her, you were more observant than the director of the show. He contented himself with calling out to her, 'Hey, you with the legs.'

But there *were* people who saw the show as it toured suburban New York that summer of 1950. Among them were its writers, Rodgers and Hammerstein themselves, who were looking for ways of freshening up the cast of the London production which had been running seemingly for ever at Drury Lane and was moving off to Germany.

Would the girl with the legs like to go to Germany?

The girl with the legs said that yes, she would. But the father of the girl with the legs said no, she wouldn't. Once more, it appeared she would be on a collision course with Ira and it would be Mr. Beaty who won. He indicated that she ought to stay on to finish her schooling.

Actually, Shirley didn't fight too hard over that one. As she was to explain: 'I must have realised that I'd have plenty more chances to be in show business, but I'd never have another crack at getting my high school diploma.'

Funnily enough – although this could have been sound psychology – while Shirley was being more flexible, so were her parents. As she said: 'Dad and Mother left the decision up to me but I knew how they felt about it, since they'd both gone to college and Dad had been a schoolteacher.'

When she did graduate from school, she packed her bags and went back to Manhattan – as much to prove to her father as to herself that she could make it.

New York, as she had found out before, wasn't like Virginia at all. There was still an excitement in the air, even though the young dancer with the weak ankles was bright enough to realise that the filthy streets of the city did not have a layer of gold beneath the dirt.

Ira said he would finance her stay, but Shirley, showing the kind of independence he probably recognised, wasn't having any of that and kindly turned down the offer.

At first, she moved into the Ferguson Girls Club – but left it when she couldn't cope with a rule that said members had to be in by 11.30 each night – and another that seemed to indicate it wasn't nice for young ladies to squirt pedestrians walking past the building with water pistols. So she had to find accommodation where the instructions were less severe.

She lived in a tenement with other girls searching for better things – some of them while staring at the ceiling, earning their keep in the oldest way known to woman. There were bugs and rats for company – and not much food.

When she could afford to go out for a meal it was invariably to the neighbourhood Automat. 'In the Automat,' she would explain, 'you could get an iced-tea glass with a lemon in it free.' More substantial food was available, too. 'You could get peanut butter sandwiches on raisin bread for a dime.' It was the iced tea that proved to be the biggest boon, however. The free lemon was always on the side. So Shirley would collect the lemons, get iced water from the fountain and keep herself in free lemonade for a whole evening. 'Of course,' she would later admit,' I had to change Automats pretty often.'

There were occasional jobs, a bit of dancing, singing in the chorus.

'I was conducting a group of youngsters for an early TV show,' orchestra leader and composer David Rose – he wrote 'Holiday for Strings', 'The Stripper' and a host of other numbers – told me, 'when suddenly I became aware of a girl with big eyes and a wide smile whose voice stood out from all the others. I called her to the front. I like to think I was one of the first who spotted Shirley Maclaine.'

She had by then decided that Beaty didn't sound an exciting enough name for someone in show business – Warren would, of course, soon have other ideas, even if he did add a 't' to his name – and took her mother's maiden name of Maclean as her own, but changed the spelling and the intonation to make it seem more interesting.

20

It was too early to start using that name, or at least, *see* the name being used. There wasn't much work and the work that she did get didn't amount to being given a credit.

In Lambertville, New Jersey, Shirley joined a show called the St John Terrel Music Circus. It didn't last long and she was soon back in New York City, singing and dancing whenever she could.

Sometimes the singing and dancing work she got wasn't of the most glamorous kind – like demonstrating refrigerators. Actually, she wasn't selling fridges like the demonstrators who did it every day in department stores. What she was doing was taking part in live shows that were really nothing more than extended commercials.

Refrigerator salesmen – whom she discovered weren't so cold in their approaches to pretty girls as the products they were supposedly selling – would gather at conventions and Shirley and girls like her would dance round the iceboxes looking beautiful. The company figured that if the girls looked attractive – and more than that – the men employed to sell their products would think of the refrigerators as being that, too.

In the business, they were known as 'travelling trade shows', going from one hick town to the next. If the police had discovered that Shirley was under 21 she would have been out on her neck, and out of a job – if not placed in the custody of the local women's probation officer. She was working strictly illegally and giddily. As she said, she had been required to do 55 consecutive ballet turns around the fridges. 'If I'd been connected to it by gears, I could have whipped cream on the inside.'

At the age of 19, she was still taking dancing lessons in between the jobs. 'I suppose,' she said, 'I always had a terrific drive to express myself.'

At the time she was expressing herself in a Southern accent that you could cut with a spoon taken from a mint julep glass. She would never really learn to say ' . . . ing' properly. She was always to do dancin' and a little singin' when she went on stage workin'.

But you didn't stay in New York for long without learnin' to give your vowels that particular nasal intonation common to the Manhattan taxi driver, especially when you went to 'woik'.

*　　　*　　　*

21

She was 'woikin' ' with the best of them, stretching those long, lissom legs that were supporting a 34–24–34 figure. They didn't have much use for hour-glasses in the New York of 1953, but what Shirley MacLaine had made the men who saw her in any of these thespian expeditions forget was their more up-to-date timepieces. She was five feet seven inches tall, had freckles on her face and hands, and her red hair was very, very long.

It was a very attractive sight indeed that she presented, and the young men who tried to date her – and the old ones who would like to have done so had she given them just a chance – were not slow to appreciate it. The only trouble was that this *was* the early 1950s, and young girls out of Arlington, Virginia, were not supposed to know a great deal about the big world which they had now entered.

As Shirley has said, when a boy asked her to go to the movies, she really thought that she was going to see a film. 'Since I was bigger than most of the fellows I met,' she told *Family Weekly* in a piece clearly edited for family reading, 'I was quite safe.'

It seemed, moreover, that her career was quite safe, too. Three times she tried to audition for the chorus of a Broadway show – by Rodgers and Hammerstein again.

She later explained: 'There were maybe ten million people, each expected to sing, dance, do cartwheels and manufacture their own fog.' She was not one of the lucky ones in that ten million.

But you hadn't made the journey from Arlington to Broadway only to be fazed by such mishaps. So she borrowed an Equity card belonging to a friend and tried again under the assumed name. Once more, she was advised it was not necessary to call them, they would call her. But she tried yet again and on this the third attempt, she was lucky. For the chorus of *Me and Juliet*, not the most successful of the Rodgers and Hammerstein productions, the young Shirley MacLaine was employed to dance, kick and look lovely – but not so lovely as to take too much attention away from the stars of the show.

Of course, to her it was the most important event in the world. A regular job in a regular show, and the kind she had most wanted to be part of since she first realised that Broadway was a street in New York and people danced and sang and acted there.

Once in, she was not without problems. Like, for instance, her hair. She wore it in a long bouncy pony tail; so bouncy that the producers decided it was distracting. The audience were watching the girl with the bouncing hair instead of the action – which may have been fine for the girl with the bouncing hair but wasn't good for the show. She was told by the stage manager to have it cut. She refused. But a chorus girl is allowed only so many refusals when she works in the rarefied, privileged environment of a Broadway show. One night before the show, she was waylaid. The hair was cut off forcibly. It may not have appealed to the woman who believed in personal freedom, but it gave Shirley MacLaine an image that would be hers for a very long time – and went some way towards getting her her next job.

Work was without question the most important thing in her life. Certainly, it enabled her to survive her first broken love affair.

A few months earlier, Shirley and a student about her own age had decided they wanted to be married – it *was* the early 1950s – and actually did get engaged. Her fiancé loved her looks, her even then kookie sense of humour – although no one had yet thought of describing it as such – and what could be simply described as her personality. There were, however, hang-ups – for one thing, he didn't much care for a wife who was on the stage. He cared even less for a wife who wasn't on the stage but who was trying to be. It wasn't the sort of life that seemed to him to guarantee a stable home.

Shirley might have gone along with all that and started searching for her physics textbooks if there hadn't been those auditions for *Me and Juliet*. The third lucky try was enough for her to decide that, for the moment, work and its opportunities came first. The romance was broken. A fiancé went away licking his wounds and Shirley MacLaine seemed happier than any time since she toddled into her first dancing class.

There were, however, other things to take her interest, after the curtain went down every night and her time was her own.

Most young actresses of her day used to hang around with other young actresses. None of them had a great deal of money, but there were certain off-off-off-Broadway bars and coffee shops where girls could go for a chat and, if that was what they wanted, leave again having had no more than a chat and a thoroughly convivial evening. None of them had to get up early the next morning, so the night would stretch until the sky grew light and the circles under their eyes grew dark.

It was at one of those theatre district bars, with Shirley alternately giggling about the night's performance and sipping a soda, that she was introduced to Steve Parker.

It wasn't the most auspicious meeting. There she was being introduced by a mutual friend called Lorraine to an actor who was 13 years her senior. As she told *Redbook* magazine, 'I didn't like him. He was good-looking, but he was too old.'

Not that she thought anything would come of it, but that factor seemed to inhibit her. An inhibited chorus girl who still had freckles and red hair probably seemed a very attractive proposition indeed.

But, as she said, he made her, as she sipped her soda, feel like a high school girl. He, meanwhile, was pouring the beer down his throat as though he had just signed off after two years in the crew of a whaler.

Steve had spent his childhood in Japan. That night he seemed to talk of nothing else. He talked and she listened. Too sophisticated, she thought. And that talking . . . too much . . . too much. He had been in Hiroshima soon after the dropping of the Bomb. Even that, moving though it was, wasn't the sort of conversation she wanted to hear.

But despite herself she agreed to see him again. He took her to dinner – the first real meal she had had in six months, as most of her money was going on singing and dancing lessons. And again he talked and again she listened. He made her laugh – always dangerous. And he talked about his own career which somehow gave the impression that he had serious thoughts in her direction.

His big ambition was somehow to get back to the Far East, but he wanted to work there and, more important, he wanted to succeed there. His father had been a diplomat in Tokyo and for part of the time in Bangkok, but Steve had been orphaned at 15 and had had to find his own way back to the States. During the war, he had worked interrogating Japanese soldiers. Only weeks before, he had returned to Japan for the first time, entertaining US troops in the cast of a show called *Room Service*, presented by the show-biz club, the Lambs.

His ambition was to be a film producer, but he was learning

his craft the hard way – acting in military training films, and getting the occasional job in the infant medium of television, which no one considered important enough to be regarded as a serious contribution to a career.

He and Shirley were falling in love, but her career still came first – even if kicking up her heels in the chorus line of *Me and Juliet* wasn't exactly making her an overnight sensation.

Her mother was still not forcing the idea of an early marriage on her, for which she was grateful. Kathlyn was emphasising her belief, however, that Shirley ought still to be a virgin when eventually she did get married. 'Forget about that,' said her daughter – which had Steve known it at the time would have pleased him very greatly.

One has the impression by now that Shirley MacLaine was pretty sure of herself. She tried acting lessons, but gave them up. Not incorrectly, as it turned out, she felt that any acting she would do had to be natural or there wasn't much point in doing it. She was willing to admit she had plenty to learn, but decided that an acting coach wouldn't be much use for the kind of performances she had in mind.

George Abbott, one of the great veterans of Broadway – he was then in his late 60s, and was still working in harness 30 years later – had directed *Me and Juliet*. When he started work on a new show, he thought he would take Shirley with him. She was still going to be in the chorus. But the show would have a much bigger impact on her – and on us. It was called *The Pajama Game*.

Chapter Two

LOOKING BACK now on the Shirley MacLaine career, *The Pajama Game* was just right for her.

In the years that followed the show, Shirley was to embrace a series of causes which in the days when the production first opened on Broadway would have got her hauled before Senator Joe McCarthy's UnAmerican Activities Committee. But this show suited her politics admirably.

The Pajama Game was about labour relations. It was, too, about love. It also had a clutch of marvellous songs in it, like 'Hey There', 'Once A Year Day', 'Hernando's Hideaway' and 'Steam Heat'. That last number was the one that became most important in the life of Shirley MacLaine. But not just yet.

Shirley was not just in the chorus. Using her initiative and tremendous self-assurance, she got herself another job. She convinced Abbott that she would make a much better understudy for the junior lead, Carol Haney, than the girl who had already been picked. How Abbott even listened to her is a matter for speculation. But listen he did and agreed she would make a very good understudy indeed. He probably also thought that since Miss Haney was young and very healthy, there wouldn't be much need for any understudy's services.

Richard Adler, one of the two writers of the piece, thought it was totally unnecessary. 'Honey,' Adler told her, 'why don't you get out there and get ready for the show – instead of worrying about understudies. Who needs understudies?'

In truth nobody thought that they did.

If only given a chance to play it, Carol's was a delightful role for a gamin with short hair, who could dance, throw a bowler hat high into the air, catch it again and sing – all at the same time.

Shirley's salary was $110 a week, which she might have thought was not bad for a girl of her age and experience. But she didn't want to be in the chorus.

Now everybody has read about the understudy who makes an unexpected first appearance and fights against the jeers of the disappointed customers who have come to see the star who has been hitting the front pages for weeks . . . customers who then stay to cheer.

Everybody's heard about it because every now and again the papers on both sides of the Atlantic record such happenings. They've heard about it because Warner Brothers made a veritable industry in the 1930s of telling us about just such a thing, with only the names and occasionally the songs changed to avoid the copyright laws. As a result of those movies, many a chorus girl went to bed with a leotard under the pillow and the strains of *Lullaby of Broadway* ringing in her ears.

Shirley MacLaine had heard the stories, too. It would be safe to say that she was also a little disappointed when it didn't happen to her – at least on that first night and during the first week.

And how *could* it happen to her? Carol Haney had been acclaimed by all the critics. She was not only keen, she was positively brilliant. Performance after performance she only improved and the audience, like a man getting used to a comfortable new suit, was taking to her more and more.

Haney's triumph was all too plainly MacLaine's downfall. After all, how many stars were there in show business? The theatre had a 70 per cent unemployment rate and the lucky ones were those with jobs in the chorus – that was what most people had to content themselves with and when they did, very content they were, too. The trouble was, as Shirley herself has said, she was having to be content with another hit, where she would take a weekly pay cheque for months and possibly years to come – and nobody would ever know she was doing it.

It was a time to be brave. Steve loved her. They were now living together – a demonstration not of the times in which they lived, the Beatys couldn't understand their daughter's definition of morals at all, but of Shirley's attitude to life.

They had to console themselves that Steve was going to want to marry her and he was all set for a wonderfully successful

28

career. What did it matter if she made it or not? It mattered.

When she had a phone call from the producer of another Broadway hit, *Can-Can* – that, too, would later hold a place in the MacLaine story – she made a decision. She would take the producer's offer to understudy the show's lead dancer. It was only an understudy's job again, but at least no one had said how sensational that dancer was going to be and performers do get fed up with arriving on time at every performance.

She not only decided to take the job and give up her stultifyingly successful chorus job in *The Pajama Game*, she was going to tell the management that very night. She scribbled a note, put it in her handbag, went out to eat with Steve and then took a leisurely subway ride to the theatre.

Show-biz is full of seemingly idiotic contradictions. A performer at the beginning of a show is never wished 'good luck'. Traditionally, the wish is 'break a leg'. It is definitely considered *un*lucky to say anything but. Telling someone to go out and break a leg is so patently ridiculous that it can only mean the exact opposite. Well, in this case when Carol Haney's friends told her to break a leg, it was good luck indeed – for Shirley. Carol did break a leg and Shirley had her role.

Not that she had any inkling about it beforehand, however.

Somehow, that night it wasn't quite like usual. So unusual, in fact, that she forgot the note which all the time had seemed to burn a hole in her purse. Outside the stage door, Hal Prince, the producer of the show who had a reputation for making every Broadway show seem if not like a piece of cake then like a slice of buttery strudel, was flapping as though he were Dracula about to fly off to the nearest graveyard.

And graveyard seemed the most appropriate destination. He had been pacing the sidewalk outside the theatre for the best part of an hour – waiting for Shirley, the chorus girl who, remember, nobody had previously heard of.

From inside the auditorium came the sounds that few managements like to encourage – the rustle of papers, the pounding of feet, the shouts from one row to another, the climate of gradual dissatisfaction that tends to become infectious as it passes from one part of the theatre to the next.

Shirley didn't know what the noise was about. Hal Prince did. He was all too closely involved in the pandemonium. She wasn't late, she told the producer. After all, she didn't go on until midway through the second act. That was what she thought.

There was no way of her knowing that Carol Haney had broken her ankle that afternoon and the audience had been told that Miss Shirley MacLaine would go on in her stead. Now, if any audience were told that in the 1980s, they would rush into the theatre in such droves that their safety would be in peril; tickets would change hands at ten times the regular price. In May 1954, the news made the customers very unhappy indeed. Who was Shirley MacLaine?

They were about to find out.

Shirley forgot about her note for Mr Prince. What she did was jump into her dressing-room, try on Miss Haney's clothes – Shirley never bothered to try on dresses she bought for herself, let alone put on the outfits that had been made for someone else – and hear the sound of relief from the assembled management when everything seemed to fit – the tights, the jacket, the bowler hat. The only things that didn't fit were the shoes. Shirley takes size 8; Miss Haney's feet were somewhat daintier. The fact that both girls apparently had weak ankles had nothing to do with the crisis afoot, as it were. There was a pair of Shirley's practice dancing shoes handy and she wore those.

What she couldn't wear quite so easily were all Carol's songs. The male lead John Rait agreed to sing 'Hernando's Hideaway' for her. For the rest, she was on her own.

She went on stage with the sound of booing echoing in her ears. She dropped her hat and when, she reports in her own book, she reacted to the mistake by *whispering* 'shit' there was an audible gasp from the front two rows. Young ladies on Broadway were not expected to know such words, let alone use them.

Before going on stage, she managed to find enough strength – and a finger steady enough – to dial Steve, who miraculously found a taxi when he wanted one and got into the theatre, where he sat notebook in hand, writing down the faults in the performance.

For more than two hours, Shirley MacLaine was on stage and the audience knew that she was. She danced and she sang and she used all the energy she had last called upon the night her own ankle broke before she played the fairy godmother.

This evening, she was her own fairy godmother – although poor Carol Haney, her foot swathed in bandages and her ego more bruised than her ankle could ever have been, had a great deal to do with it.

The shouts from the audience proved that a magic wand of some kind had been waved that night. The boos had turned to cheers and the unknown Shirley MacLaine was the centre of them all.

Hal Prince not only didn't get his letter of resignation, he had forgiven Shirley, covered her in kisses, ordered a dozen bouquets and cheered with everyone else. There was curtain call after curtain call. Shirley MacLaine had become a star. Ruby Keeler had never had it so good in *Forty Second Street*.

The only one who wasn't totally ecstatic was Steve. The person closest to the performer is always their sternest critic, and it was Steve who told her he thought she hadn't been nearly as good as she was led to believe.

All right, he conceded, she had put on a magnificent show out of the blue and both audience and management had reacted to that, almost as if from a sense of relief. But she had to be sure not to drop that hat next performance. She had to know when to turn to face the audience and when not to. She had to know every word of every song – including 'Hernando's Hideaway'. 'Steam Heat', a magnificently hissed number full of jazz and sibilants, set in the pyjama factory's boiler room, had been a sensation, but it wasn't enough. She had to do better next night.

Until six o'clock in the morning, he went over his notes, word by word, line by line, with Shirley at first improvising and then perfecting the faults he had pointed out. It went on for five nights. That was the point when he thought she would be all right – and when he first began to doubt their future together. She was going to make it. But would he be anything more than an appendage? For the moment, he wasn't bothering to find out.

Even if Steve hadn't thought so, the second night was better than the first. . . . Better? It was magnificent. So magnificent that this time the people paying her the biggest tribute of all were those who were now happy to call themselves her fellow stars.

The late Eddie Foy Jnr played the factory manager, the time-study expert. 'It was a performance I'll never ever forget,' he told

31

me. 'I'd been on stage with the greatest of them, including the Astaires in their heyday in the 20s, but Shirley MacLaine that night was something very different – and very, very special.

'She had the confidence of one who had been dancing and singing before Broadway audiences all her life. There was gusto there I'd never seen before. She knew all the lines, she knew all the routines – but when she performed them she was doing so as if she had invented them herself, as if she had written the dialogue and planned the choreography. She was very much better than Carol Haney.'

That was the judgment of a true professional, a man who with his father Eddie Foy senior had been part of one of the legendary acts in vaudeville, The Seven Little Foys – when the family story was told on film Bob Hope played the elder Foy, much to the chagrin of his son. It was tribute indeed. Recalling that night in her book, Shirley MacLaine says that before she went on, Foy sat in his dressing-room, 'throwing up'. It's a pity she didn't know the degree of affection he was to feel for her.

Foy wasn't the only one to think she was great.

The Beatys took 17-year-old Warren to see the show. 'I just thought it was wonderful,' he was to tell *Time* magazine. 'The realisation seemed to come to her in that show that she was more interesting than her techniques as a dancer, about which she had always had a lot of anxieties.'

His sentiments were echoed by the world of show business – a very small community. Word of success spreads almost as fast as that of failure. That week, the business was talking about Shirley MacLaine.

The proof of that talk came from the people who were in the audience for her second performance. Other show people, temporarily resting, came to see and to wonder. They were not to be disappointed. Other managements sent along their spies to see whether this kid was as good as everybody said she was – and then to sign her up, once her understudying was finished and before her price had started to rocket through most Broadway theatre roofs.

There were still other people in the business who thought they could direct Shirley's talents and energies in different directions. Television sent along a handful of executives – although they all realised that none of them could compete with the then senior and much richer medium of the live theatre.

But there was also Hollywood. The film town still liked to think that it knew most about new talent and also reckoned that, some 30 years after the birth of talking pictures, the best unknown musical talent probably could still be found dancing up and down the Broadway stages.

That, anyway, was the thinking of one of the most powerful of all the Broadway names – Hal Wallis, a man who had run the Warner Brothers studios from the 20s up to the time of *Casablanca* and who as an independent producer was now as powerful as any film mogul had ever been.

He saw Shirley MacLaine and made a very prescient decision: she would do very nicely indeed in pictures. Would she like a contract? Just like that. He told me:

'I had no idea what I was going to see that night. I had booked to see Carol Haney. The press reviews had been so great and I wanted to see whether the critics were really right.

'I sat in the theatre, opened my programme and saw a note saying that she wouldn't be appearing that night and instead there would be a girl called Shirley MacLaine. Well, I was sorry, but it happens all the time, a star can't appear and a quite competent understudy takes her place. It was disappointing.

'But then Shirley MacLaine came out and she was so brilliant that the audience reacted in a way I have only rarely seen equalled. They were tremendous.'

So after the show, Wallis went round towards her dressing-room. He caught Shirley mounting the staircase leading to the room she still shared with the other members of the chorus and the bit players.

'I motioned her to come and see me,' he recalled. She descended the staircase and he introduced himself.

'Would you meet me later on?' he asked. Shirley was sufficiently pleased with her own performance to realise that Wallis was on the level and had no ulterior motive.

They met an hour or so later at the Plaza Hotel's Oak Room, a restaurant that in its time has seen many an important deal thrashed out and then signed. They sat in the George M. Cohan booth, a seat not to be treated lightly.

(It had also seen a great deal of food consumed. In her book, Shirley wrote that she and Steve ate huge steaks while Wallis had practically nothing. She said it was because he was inherently mean. 'Not so at all,' the producer told me. 'It was very late and I had had dinner already. Shirley and Parker, though, ate practically everything on the menu. I think I know why. They had never been to a place like it in their lives. I imagine they had only eaten at the Automats before I came along.')

Wallis considered he had had a hunch that was going to pay off. 'I made the deal,' he told me, 'purely on what I had seen on the stage that night. It was the amazing abandon, the spirited dancing and the singing. I knew that if she could do it on a Broadway stage, she'd do it just as well on the screen.'

Actually, that wasn't the end of the story or even the end of the beginning. Before finalising the details, Shirley got herself an agent – itself an episode in her story that was to have repercussions. For the moment, the agent told Mr Wallis that his offer of $200 a week was entirely unacceptable and suggested, by way of a gentleman's agreement, that it be upped threefold. The producer was less than happy with that and said that before he signed for such an outrageous sum, he would demand a screen test.

In the meantime, other film men had come to see her. The Iron Dictator of Columbia Pictures, Harry Cohn, came in person and both MGM and Paramount had their scouts in the audience, enjoying the show and Miss MacLaine in particular. But having met and talked with Wallis she was taking him up on his offer of the screen test.

The test, needless to say, showed that his hunch was going to pay off. Dressed in sweater and shorts – neither of which was big enough to conceal all that was being hinted by her body – she looked sensational, even though there was practically no make-up on her face.

Daniel Mann, at the time one of the leading directors in Hollywood, supervised the test. After it, he asked Shirley what she wanted to make of her career. Her answer was simple and very direct. 'To do comedy,' she replied. 'Comedy with real good acting.'

'And a lot of trouble,' Wallis told me. 'I saw it after only a few days. She was going to be a great deal of trouble.'

Before long, there would be doubts in the minds of both parties to the agreement, but for the moment, Shirley was content to take Mann's prognosis that she had a very exciting career indeed in front of her.

As the director was to tell *Time* magazine: 'That test was animal-like in its naturalness. A searing inquiry with no pretence of being sophisticated.' The sophistication would come in time – and in abundance. But for the moment, Wallis and he were only thinking of the hundreds of roles for an unsophisticated girl that seemed to be waiting for her.

In days, Hollywood was talking about Wallis's new find. At Warner Brothers, Bill Orr who was head of production as well as Jack L. Warner's son-in-law, tried to see if he could beat Wallis – who was, after all, a predecessor in his own office – and had to admit defeat.

'Actually, it was my mother who spotted Shirley,' the now retired Warners executive told me. 'She went to a matinee of *The Pajama Game* and came away ecstatic. She immediately phoned me in Hollywood and said there was a girl called Shirley MacLaine who was absolutely marvellous and we ought to sign her quickly. I told her I'd heard about this girl and that Hal Wallis had beaten us to it. But I went through the motions, but Wallis had her all signed up by then.'

Wallis's move certainly was the envy of Hollywood and it remains one of those stories film men like to talk of, in the class of Lana Turner wearing her sweater in Schwab's drug store and Judy Garland singing with her sisters. Wallis doesn't regret it – even if in the years that have followed finder and found have not been exactly able to see eye to eye. Wallis still admires her talent, recognises he made a shrewd move in 1954. Shirley resents what happened when she took him up on his offer.

Chapter Three

SHIRLEY WENT TO Hollywood with two plus factors in mind. To almost any young performer of her age, the invitation to the film town was a mark of having arrived. Being a star on Broadway was wonderful, but that was not what she had become. She was, still, an understudy; a hit understudy who had gained a certain amount of public attention, but *The New York Times* for instance ignored the event completely and there was every indication that Carol Haney would come back.

So Hollywood was the chance to cement what Broadway was only suggesting. Also, the towering presence of Hal Wallis was a virtual insurance policy for the kind of success which girls like Shirley only dreamed of.

Wallis was producing films that made a great deal of money. After his years guiding Warner Brothers through an era in which the studio flew a banner proclaiming its duty to good films and good citizenship, there was a certain style about a Wallis film. He hadn't lost the knack of knowing what the public wanted, nor had he forgotten the need to bring a degree of quality to his output.

He was at the beginning of the long run of Dean Martin and Jerry Lewis movies which made money and could have been a lot worse in other less sympathetic hands. Before long, there would be the Elvis Presley movies – pictures that didn't please the critics – when Wallis saw the potential of the youngster called 'The Pelvis'.

He believed Shirley MacLaine was one of the group of new performers who had an immense future that he was only too willing to tap. He saw it as a project that was very much to their mutual benefit. He had a sound business investment. She, the very early opportunity to become a big, big star. The problem of what happened after she settled into California for the first time was that she and Wallis had different ideas.

This was the picture presented to her, once she had selected a new agent, looked over the papers and finalised the details.

Shirley envisaged that this was the beginning of a career with Mr Wallis, the near-legendary film man, guiding her every step. She was to be disappointed.

She said that his contract was a deal for seven years with 'loan privileges'; most of those privileges were his.

Steve had a few privileges, too, mind you. In the midst of heady negotiations between a clutch of agencies all wanting to inveigle the long, slim MacLaine fingers around a fountain pen which would then sign her name at the foot of a contract, giving them too a slice of her action, he asked her to marry him. She agreed – once she had started work.

For the moment, she still hadn't said goodbye to *The Pajama Game*. When Carol Haney got better, Shirley went back to the chorus – with the contract with Mr Wallis locked away in the cupboard. And history did repeat itself. Miss Haney became ill and Shirley again deputised for her. This time, another film man was sitting in the audience – and offering the prospect of a contract.

It turned out that Alfred Hitchcock's New York man, the one whose responsibility was to find new talent or a new job for himself, had been deputed to look for something 'unusual'. He decided that the *Pajama Game* understudy with the chopped-up hairdo was just that.

Hitchcock asked Shirley to go to meet him at his suite at the St Regis Hotel. There, obscuring his wife Alma with his bulky form, wedged in one of the hotel's strongest armchairs, he asked Shirley what films she had already starred in. She told him none. But what about movies she had made as a supporting actress? Again, the answer was simple: none. But what about television? Would she send him some kinescopes (the only kind of TV recording then available, dull-looking film shot direct from the tube)? She would have loved to. Except . . . there weren't any. *Me and Juliet* and *The Pajama Game* were just about it. And she was about to leave *The Pajama Game*.

Nevertheless, he told her he had seen enough to suggest that she gather together a wardrobe that she could wear in the film he was about to make.

It was tempting, but she had to point out that she was already committed to Mr Wallis.

Hitchcock said he knew and wanted her to play in *The Trouble With Harry* just the same. He would make the necessary arrangements with Mr Wallis.

'And thus,' she has said, 'began my life in white slavery.' She was only partly joking. Hitchcock wouldn't pay her anything. Her salary would be paid by Wallis – who would get every penny of *The Trouble With Harry* fee.

So Shirley's very first movie was not made for the man to whom she was under contract.

The way she saw things, Wallis was paying her a fairly low amount – which he immediately more than recouped by loaning her out to other companies.

That he was. But the fact also had to be faced that he was the first to see in Shirley MacLaine the potential that made her an investment.

Writing in *Don't Fall Off the Mountain*, she complains of the treatment she received at his hands. There was, for instance, a kiss which she took as being far too friendly for any boss to bestow on an employee. But what really rankled was the money.

It is easy to see why actors and actresses resent that sort of thing happening. Like the buying and selling of sportsmen, it makes them feel they are somehow part of the cattle trade. It was, however, as they say, the accepted practice of the industry.

Hitchcock himself was as convinced he had discovered a new star as Wallis had been.

'Go over and meet this girl,' he instructed a reporter soon after she started work on the film. 'Nobody's ever heard of her, but I say she's going to be a big star.'

Meanwhile, the *Herald Express* was at least one Los Angeles newspaper that took the hint.

'Hollywood,' the paper reported, 'a town not noted for its generosity to unknowns, is gambling $20 million on a rank newcomer, Shirley MacLaine.'

How that figure was arrived at nobody satisfactorily explained, but it didn't matter.

'Shirley,' it went on, 'is a cute young thing who climbed right out of a pair of bedazzled Broadway pajamas into a leading role in her first movie – one of the few understudies to leap from sleeper to stardom overnight. But Shirley is no raw recruit, even though she was only understudy to Carol Haney in *The Pajama Game*.'

A measure of her success was the fact that it was worth writing this before anyone had seen her on the screen. The fact that Hitchcock had discovered her was plainly enough.

The legendary director had long before gone on record as confirming one of Shirley's principal beefs. 'All actors are cattle,' he had said. But Shirley he recognised as having something particularly special. As he told *Time*, she was 'unique', a factor that contributed to the making of a star, 'the rare quality we want'.

Hitchcock, of course, had his own ideas about what constituted that rare quality – and how he was going to get it. Hollywood lore is replete with stories of his team pandering to his requirements – like the writer who explained he couldn't be on the set during a particularly complicated routine 'because I was dreaming up one of those typical Hitchcock touches'.

Shirley found working on those touches more than slightly unnerving, particularly since she had not been on a soundstage in her life before. But he was an unusual man with unusual techniques – like not really directing at all, as far as she could see.

'He just walks around making Cockney jokes,' she was to say.

The biggest joke of all according to her – although she certainly wasn't thinking of it as at all funny in those days – was that he banned Steve from sitting on the sidelines seeing her work.

'He doesn't like husbands,' she went on. 'Some big fantasy thing perhaps.'

But those jokes. They did take some understanding. She couldn't understand why he would look her straight in the eye and say: 'Genuine chopper, old girl.'

She looked back at him equally directly, one of those looks that seemed to say, 'I really haven't a clue what you mean.'

'Do you know a synonym for genuine?' he asked; perhaps, she may have thought, to show that he was a man of culture and education and not just a London boy who knew a thing or two about movie cameras.

She ran through all the ones she could think of. 'Real' finally came up. 'OK,' he said, 'Real. Now what about chopper?' She offered axe. Right, he accepted. Axe. Put the two words together. Instead of genuine there was real. Instead of chopper, there was axe. Real-axe. 'Relax'. She got the message.

Another time he told her: 'Dog feet . . . .' Dog feet? Certainly – 'Pause'.

He was very impressed with Shirley's acting. He taught her, she was to say, how to open her mouth. What really impressed Hitchcock about her was her guts – like those of a bank robber, he said. She had nerves of steel.

Mildred Dunnock, the Hollywood character actress, didn't use that sort of vocabulary. Shirley met her because Hitchcock thought she could be useful in giving his young actress some hints on the art of acting.

They were in the midst of a 'lesson' when Shirley told her she had to stop. It was 2.30. Miss Dunnock was upset. But Shirley was insistent. 'I have to get married in an hour.'

That was when she and Steve finally had their wedding. It was performed by Dr Norman Vincent Peale, the author of *The Power of Positive Thinking*. The date, September 17, 1954.

Before work began on the Hitchcock movie, she again deputised for a star – this time a much more famous one than Miss Haney. Betty Grable was unable to work on a TV spectacular called *The Show of Stars* and Shirley went on in her stead. 'In three minutes designed for Grable,' *Life* magazine reported, 'MacLaine was a last-minute marvel as she changed her dancing pace and pulled on costumes like a veteran.'

But the film she was making for Hitchcock was more important to her and more significant for her career.

The movie, a black comedy about a body that mysteriously won't lie down dead, was filmed mostly on location in New England, with the final wrap-ups photographed in Hollywood.

Hitchcock liked her and she liked him – almost as much as she hated Wallis. And she resented him from the moment he did the deal with Hitchcock.

Wallis gave her an MG car, she wrote, as a belated wedding present. He says it was a combined birthday present and bonus for the work she was doing and the money she was bringing in.

'I bought her an MG,' he told me, 'because I wanted her to

have a share of the deal from Hitchcock, which I thought was only right.'

Shirley at the time, however, couldn't drive. She spent hours searching through the instruction manual looking for the starter button. Unfortunately, there was no manual on how to work with important studio bosses. Mr Wallis was certain when we met that he had been in the right.

And then he went on to emphasise how much he thought he had done with that gift to stress the value in which he held her. 'The car was her own choice. I knew it was her birthday, but I was much more conscious of wanting to pay her a bonus. I thought the birthday was a nice time to do it, to make it seem more personal. I went down to the set that day and told her I knew it was her birthday and what would she like from me for a present. She didn't know what to ask for and joked that an MG would be nice. So I had one sent down to her. She couldn't stop herself both laughing and crying when I handed her the keys.'

In the *Time* interview, Shirley says she was very serious indeed about that request. 'When you're talking to a man with 44 million dollars,' she was quoted as saying, 'you're not joking.'

In his own autobiography (*Starmaker*, written with Charles Higham) Wallis is even more uncompromising. 'The most difficult and unpleasant star I have ever worked with is Shirley MacLaine,' he writes. '. . . She hasn't a grain of gratitude in her. I started her career in films and she refuses to acknowledge that fact.'

It was a festering wound with Wallis. 'Without me,' he said in 1970, 'she would have been a fading chorus girl instead of a fading star.'

The picture wasn't exactly a box office sensation, although it was notable for a film debut that got a sufficient number of people talking.

Her second film she made for Wallis himself, playing with – although not starring with – Martin and Lewis. In *Artists and Models*, Shirley ended up getting Jerry Lewis, which she seems to have thought was a further example of the inhuman way in which she was being treated by a certain part of the Hollywood machine.

(She said she liked Lewis. 'I think he is a real genius. He

taught me so much and was so patient.' Considering the things that have been written about Jerry since then – how he and Dean would cut up the shirts and ties of their producers and cause total mayhem on the set – this is praise indeed.)

She was loudly saying that Dean was the funniest man in the world and he was returning the compliment by describing Shirley as the greatest audience there is – which was obvious to anyone privileged to join them on the set; she collapsed almost every time he opened his mouth and slurred a couple of words.

Anita Ekberg, then at her sexual peak (or peaks, if you like), was in the film, too. Shirley said that she made her feel like John Wayne. Nobody else was under any such illusion.

Steve, meanwhile, had reason to complain about the way life was treating him – even though Shirley was constantly telling anyone who would listen how close they were to each other and how they liked nothing better than going to a drive-in movie to watch science fiction films (the drive-in was preferable to any ordinary theatre; she could shout and scream all she liked from the comfort of their car and no one would notice).

To go with the rented beach house in which they lived in the unfashionable part of Santa Monica bay, they had a second-hand Buick.

Since Shirley couldn't drive, Steve took it upon himself to be both her chauffeur and the man who did the family shopping. It was on one of these expeditions that another motorist drove through a red light and crashed into the Buick, broadside on. Steve landed in hospital for five weeks. Such a disaster could not have helped his frequent but understandable bouts of depression.

Both he and Shirley had made up their minds that Steve would be his own man with his own career. But that wasn't happening. It might have been easier for Hal Wallis if it had. There were now two men who considered they were suffering for Shirley's success.

'She was discontented as soon as she got the sweet smell of success,' Hal Wallis told me. 'She again said – and said it several times – that she was a slave to me.' As a bonus for this film, Wallis gave her a mink coat, which she neglects to mention in her book.

He insists that when Shirley made her third film – hired out again – he increased her salary appreciably. This time, her services were being retained by Mike Todd for the film *Around the World in Eighty Days*.

It was one of those pictures which seemed destined to reach the headlines. Mike Todd, a showman in the Barnum and Bailey tradition, didn't pay a highly-skilled publicity team for it not to do so.

The film, as everyone now knows, starred David Niven. Also, as everyone now knows, it featured a dozen or more top stars in cameo roles. Secure in the knowledge that audiences loved nothing more than a chance to see their favourite performers do anything but perform, Todd retained the top names of the day merely to show up.

Frank Sinatra was a piano player whose face you only saw at the end of the number he was supposedly banging out on a honky-tonk. Charles Boyer, Ronald Colman, George Raft and John Gielgud had equally impressive parts. And Shirley MacLaine played an Indian princess (who from her appearance beneath the jewels and sari had doubtless as a baby been left in a basket by her red-headed freckled parents outside the castle of a maharajah).

To make things even more unlikely, she had to learn an English accent, which to a 20-year-old actress was no more difficult than dancing the juvenile lead in *The Pajama Game*. Why she had to use an English accent and not an Indian one was never explained.

Rumours immediately started flying around Hollywood that she was being 'troublesome' – the favourite word of the time – about the talking business.

'That's not true,' she replied, as angry as she would only be about more serious matters in years to come. 'I was told to play a scene and speak as an Englishwoman. I said I have to study first. It took me years to overcome my Southern drawl and I'm not ready to change it to English without some preparation. So I came home and worked with Steve.'

When Steve was satisfied – and he was no easier to please now than he had been in those *Pajama Game* days when he criticised and monitored her performance from the wings and the orchestra stalls – she knew she was ready for shooting the movie.

It was a chance for Shirley to show that she wasn't entirely in

44

the conventional Hollywood mould. When she arrived for the film's première, she was naturally welcomed with screams and shouts as she walked up the long red carpet to the microphone – where she was interviewed for the radio and television stations. It was all rather like a scene from *Singin' in the Rain* – except that she wouldn't allow herself simply to say that everything was wonderful, a wonderful film, working with wonderful fellow actors, for a wonderful director and she was so pleased to be with those wonderful people who had come to see her. Instead, she burst into giggles.

Did this mean that she was drunk? No, the studios were quick to emphasise, she hardly drank at all – at any time. It was just that she was very happy indeed and that was how she liked to show it.

She showed it on television chat shows so much that programmes in the now burgeoning new medium were quick to offer her anything up to $35,000 an appearance.

For Shirley the film itself had an even greater significance in her life. She spent much of the time she was working on it in Japan. So did Steve.

That was not simply the statement of conventional marital arrangements which it appears to be. It actually records the beginnings of one of the most unconventional marriages even in Hollywood.

Steve was a man of two ambitions, both of which appeared to be stifled by being the husband of a highly promising girl who was considerably more interesting than any starlet. She wasn't yet a star, but she seemed to be on her way.

And that was Steve Parker's problem. Few husbands like to live in their wives' shadows. Still fewer men who have ambitions of their own would relish seeing their plans subjugated to those of their wives – even if their love was as new as was the MacLaines'. That last word needs, of course, to be looked at again. After just two films, Steve was hearing himself called Mr Shirley MacLaine. He was taking a close look at his wife's progress – indeed, it was also a proud look. He relished her success and shared most of her frustrations. But no frustration was as great as his own.

Not only was he seemingly running her career, he was totally neglecting his own. Which brought him to his second dream.

As he told Shirley when they first met, putting on Forces shows was one thing, making films of his own as a genuine, full-blown producer was something else entirely. And, as he also told her, even if he could attain that aim, he wouldn't really want to do it in America.

He yearned to get back to Japan with an earnestness that was close to the homesickness of a small boy in his first days at boarding-school. Only for him, Japan was as much in his blood as if he had had a generous amount of saki injected directly into his veins.

After *Artists and Models*, he told Shirley that he wanted to go to Tokyo. He wanted to stay married. He hoped she would be able to join him when she could and that he would come back to the beach house they had bought themselves on the Pacific Coast outside Los Angeles whenever possible. Without thinking too much about the consequences, or how they would be worked out, Shirley agreed.

Part of the filming of *Around the World* was done in Japan – a chance for Shirley not only to start that transPacific commuting, but to see what her husband had been making all the fuss about.

Her first trip to the Far East inspired her own love for that distant part of the world which until she met Steve had never been more than a place mentioned in the geography books or in the newspapers. He had talked about nothing else since they met – or almost nothing else – and now she could see for herself that he hadn't been far wrong.

The bustling traffic of Tokyo and the quiet serenity of the tea ceremonies: she saw it all. More than that, she became part of it all. The visit was comparatively short, but the women of Japan were at once blood sisters. The architecture, the style of clothes became part of her. If, when the money and Mr Wallis allowed, she could commute between California and Japan, she was going to do it. The sceptics scoffed. The friends she had made since arriving in Hollywood laughed. It was difficult to keep a marriage going in the movie world with husband and wife meeting at six o'clock each evening. But this? They were both going to try to prove everyone else wrong.

The success of *Around the World*, of course, helped. The film was mainly a vehicle for David Niven and the bet he had engineered with his fellow club members. There were jet planes in

1956, but Concorde and all it promised were barely an aeronautics expert's dream. Space travel was as much a fantasy to most people as it had been in the days of Jules Verne. The tale had a piquancy it would not have 30 years later. Shirley MacLaine, on the other hand, looks as pretty in 1986 as she did in 1956. The casting may, in those days, have seemed a little bizarre, but the result was a triumph. Again, one should take issue with Shirley's own writings. She quotes people saying that she had better find herself a new film role quickly or she'd never work again. If it did seem like that in 1956 – and I remember thinking it worked beautifully when I first saw the movie – in 1986, the impression is a little different.

The part didn't do very much for her acting or her prospects of doing even better next time. But it did help her to make contacts. She also got to like Mike Todd – 'Golly,' she wrote to a friend at this time, 'he never came within three feet of pinching me.' But there were those who thought that a blue-eyed Indian princess pinched their fancies.

The Parkers' marriage seemed just as vibrant – even though plenty of people didn't like the arrangement. At least, they enjoyed saying that they didn't. Shirley was to say: 'I learned a lot about life from deciphering the filthy shades of meaning that filled the gossip that flew around me. I was an enigma. I intrigued people. They didn't have a pigeon-hole for me. Tough.'

Steve had married her, he was to say, at a time when he wasn't sure Shirley could make it. Once he was sure that she could, he wanted to be his own man, all the time. Besides, he hated Los Angeles and its environs.

It was at the end of the *Around the World* stay that Shirley felt unwell. They were out, she and Steve, sailing in a junk. Shirley felt seasick. It was a seasickness that lasted for eight days. And for good reason.

She left for home knowing that the marriage had certainly worked in one basic regard. She was pregnant.

Mother laboured in California while father toiled in Japan. He came back to the States in time to accompany Shirley and the baby back to their home.

He hadn't been there when she first realised that the nine months of waiting were over. On Saturday September 1, 1956, he was still in Tokyo. So with the pains coming regularly now,

47

she got into her car, a coat draped over her nightdress, forced her huge stomach between the front seat and the steering wheel and drove herself to Santa Monica's St John's Hospital. Two hours later, she was in the delivery room and after about 60 minutes was up washing her own nightgown. She also said that she was ready to get back to work.

The baby was a girl, which both parents had wanted perhaps even more than most mothers and fathers who dream of pink-coloured nurseries.

Steve had brought back from Hiroshima more than an abiding hatred of war and a continuing love of the Japanese people: the memory of a little girl. He had found the child in the rubble of the devastated atom city and more or less adopted her – more rather than less, as the military authorities had given him permission to take the little girl back to America with him.

Because she couldn't remember her name, he gave her one of his own: Sachiko, which meant 'happy child', Sachi for short. The little girl never reached America. She died of radiation sickness before he could get the papers finalised. Now it seemed only natural that they would call their own child Sachiko, too. A happy child was what they said they both wanted – except that Shirley didn't really seem cut out for being a mother and years later she actually admitted that Sachi had been 'an accident'.

No one doubted that she loved the baby and always would, but from then on, Shirley made a conscious decision not to have another one. She was no more cut out for motherhood then than she would be a generation later. In any case, she didn't call it motherhood. It was 'personhood'.

Shirley was very good at making up names. She wondered whether Sachi might have problems with that name she had. So she gave her an American one, too – Stephanie.

As for her own position in show business, if she were quite the overnight sensation which she had been acclaimed, then the night had been a very long one indeed.

She sent Sachi to Tokyo to be with her father. In the Japanese capital they were reunited as a family. But it wasn't natural and possibly the strain was having its effect on her career. Shirley tried her best not to allow it to do so. When Sachi was home with her again, she even made sure that she wouldn't interfere with her social life.

Invited to a party, she took Sachi along with her in a wicker basket. At one party, she put the basket in a closet. The guests took off for a jazz club and came back hours later. When Shirley said goodnight, she opened the closet door, picked up the basket and took Sachi back home with her.

The trouble was that home wasn't the one she enjoyed living in. In October 1957, she forfeited $1,000 a month for several months, because she cancelled the house's lease.

'I hated to do it, but the place depressed me.' Perhaps she was most depressed of all by the way she thought her work was proceeding.

When Steve came back for one of his brief trips to Los Angeles, they took another house, high on a hillside. And to please them both, they furnished it Japanese style – with low tables from which to eat their meals with chopsticks, while wearing kimonos. Sachi was going to grow up with two cultures as her own. Not that any of that meant that Shirley was forgoing her career for the sake of being a housewife.

'If and when I'm a star,' she said at this time, 'I don't want to be a fad, I want to be someone who'll last.'

That was proof, if anyone needed it, that Shirley certainly didn't suffer from any of the insecurities that were supposed to be part and parcel of the make-up of the average up-and-coming young performers. Occasionally, however, she would allow herself to express uncertainty. As she told one reporter at this time: 'I don't know. I'm not an ingénue and I'm not a character actress. I guess I'm just a character.'

She did a play on the West Coast, *The Sleeping Prince* with Hermione Gingold and Francis Lederer, playing the part that Marilyn Monroe had had opposite Laurence Olivier in the recent film (renamed then *The Prince and the Showgirl*).

Hal Wallis offered her a role in *Hot Spell*, a part that was not nearly as hot for her as the title would have liked to convey. If it was a hot spell – the story was about a man in a small Southern town (Anthony Quinn) who falls in love with a girl 30 to 40 years his junior much to the disgust of his wife (Shirley Booth) and their three children – it certainly wasn't so for the young MacLaine. Shirley played the middle child, a minor part – although *Time* magazine did talk about the young Shirley MacLaine who was 'pretty enough to keep the porch glider occupied almost every night of the week'.

She was directed once again by Daniel Mann, but it wasn't enough either to do much for Shirley's future or her relationship with Hal Wallis.

Wallis was an independent producer whose output was distributed through Paramount. And it was to Paramount that Shirley went next. She played the hat-shop proprietor in Thornton Wilder's *The Matchmaker*. It was the *Hello Dolly* story before anyone had ever heard that strident title song, certainly long before a young kid from Brooklyn called Barbra Streisand had ever seen herself in the role of Dolly Levi or before the notion of Louis Armstrong gravelling his way through the refrain had struck an imaginative film producer. In this picture, Dolly Levi was played by Shirley Booth – a reunion for the two women.

Again, it was a picture that Shirley didn't think did her any good and by no means helped the continuing sourness between her and the man who first placed a contract before her.

Nothing convinces one more of the subjectivity of a bitter relationship than when studying the evidence – and listening to the witnesses.

It must have been frustrating for Shirley. But Hal Wallis would answer that he was in the business of making money as well as movies. And then came the witnesses.

Hardly surprisingly, one of the most effective witnesses for Wallis is his wife – except that she wasn't married to him at the time. Martha Hyer was then best known as an attractive actress in 1950s films who had few aspirations to be either another Bette Davis or a second Marilyn Monroe – even though one writer said he saw her as heiress to the position vacated when Grace Kelly moved to Monaco. She had a very pleasant face and a figure with the right curves in the right places, who did perfectly well all that was expected of her as an actress, but she wasn't aiming for superstardom. Nevertheless, like Shirley, Martha ended up with an Oscar nomination in *Some Came Running*, which provided the most important MacLaine role to date.

Most of the people either involved in the film or seeing it on screen for the first time appear to have been thrilled with Shirley's participation in it. But, according to the now Mrs Wallis, that wasn't the way she herself saw it all.

'I was, I must say, extremely impressed with Shirley at that time,' Martha Hyer told me. 'I could tell when we were making it, she was going to be something special and would produce some of the great performances we have since got used to.

'But one thing struck me as funny. She was complaining and grumpy.

'I didn't even know Hal Wallis at the time, so I didn't take it at all personally, but it seemed strange to hear her complaints. We were sitting on the set one day when she told me what she was getting – salary and a mink coat. That sounded like a fantastic deal.'

Playing the easy Ginny was her introduction to the 'Clan' – run under the joint proprietorship of Frank Sinatra and Dean Martin, her two co-stars in the movie. It was significant, too, because it seemed to confirm Shirley's copyright in the role of the prostitute whose heart valves have been dipped in a solution of liquid gold.

Shirley said that Ginny was someone she understood. She was a pushover, crude, unlettered – but a lady, who wanted to give out with her love and who wanted to be considerate.

She was sure that her father wouldn't have agreed about her being a lady.

The movie was shot on location in Indiana, 'a fun location', as Miss Hyer put it. Sinatra insisted on working from noon to seven instead of having the usual early morning start. 'As an actress, Shirley was marvellous.'

Hal Wallis himself has never disputed that. 'On the set, she was the perfect actress. She gave no trouble at all to any of her producers or directors. The problem was simply one of casting.'

In *Some Came Running*, the problem looked as if it might at last be licked – although not without the now expected hitches. Vincente Minnelli directed the film and, quite rightly, likes to think he had a vital part in fostering Shirley's career.

It was to be, it turned out, a battle between MGM who made the picture and Minnelli, the man who had had such an impact on Hollywood with his musicals and saw *Some Came Running* as an opportunity to strike again, using top musical stars in extremely straight roles.

The story, of a soldier returning to his home town and taking up with both a prostitute and a gambler (Martin, in his first significant serious role) could have resorted to clichés. Minnelli saw MacLaine in the role of the whore Ginny as an opportunity for him to break out of that mould.

Sinatra has told part of the story of how the hunt for the ideal Ginny progressed. Practically every name in the list of Hollywood stars was considered and then abandoned.

'But then one night when we were watching the Dinah Shore show, we saw our Ginny dancing toward us, wearing a tight black leotard and belting a song out in an off-key voice best described as a clamour. It was Shirley MacLaine, but the cuteness, the strength, the humour – everything we wanted in Ginny – was wrapped up in that one package.'

The studio, however, were not at all sure. More than that, they didn't want her. They didn't think she had shown any great dramatic flair in her work to date, didn't feel she looked nearly sexy enough for a role that they believed had to suggest heaving breasts beneath slinky satin dresses – even if the censorship of the time wouldn't allow much more than a mere suggestion. Whichever way they looked at it, Shirley MacLaine, she of the freckles and red hair, didn't strike the cigar-chewing men in the front office in those early post Louis B. Mayer days as the kind of girl they wanted.

'I realised I had to do something to convince them,' Minnelli told me. 'The only way they would be convinced would be to test her for the role – and make her look right.'

Looking 'right' involved making her appear to be the kind of girl a man would pay money to go to bed with. With this thought in mind, Minnelli sent orders to the studio's costume department. He wanted something very slinky. They made her an outfit in black satin – in which she looked like a poodle, but the kind of poodle that would send little boy poodles climbing up lamp-posts in sheer ecstasy. The MGM executives saw the test, directed – unusually, this, as the director of a feature movie usually deputes a second-stringer to make tests – by Minnelli himself and couldn't but agree.

Miss MacLaine also looked very attractive at the 'Clan' functions, even when only paid-up members were in attendance; arranging flowers was a prime requirement, and joining them in their games of gin rummy.

'We're not a tightly knit group,' she said at the time. 'We just like and accept each other and don't ask questions.'

In fact, for a long time Shirley and the other members were denying that the Clan ever existed. 'I've never heard anyone in our group use the term. We don't hold offices or elect officers.' And that went for anything that anyone wanted to call it.

'It's true,' she told the *Saturday Evening Post*, 'that the chemistry between Frank Sinatra, Dean Martin and me is good. It's also fun and it's rare. But there's nothing evil or even questionable about this relationship.'

More important to Shirley was the feeling of mutual respect. 'Not one of these guys ever made a pass at me,' she was to say, which to a young girl in the midst of a group of fun-loving guys, each of whom could make his world a very tasty oyster indeed, was quite vital.

And then there was the soft spot, the one people were most interested in hearing about – how did Frank and Dean and Sammy and the others view the eccentric arrangements under which Mr and Mrs Steve Parker were living?

'Maybe they don't understand my marriage,' she said. 'But nobody says anything. And ours is not the kind of friendship that needs to be nourished. It's there when you want it.'

Everyone was joining in the let's-analyse-Shirley bit. Comedian George Gobel said she had a naturalness. 'She's the sort of girl who can wear a derby with a dandelion sticking out of it and nobody would give it a second thought.'

Other people were detecting in her a profundity of thought that starlets were just not expected to have. There was the interview with *The New York Times* in 1959 for instance (no small accolade in itself) when she said she hated films in which the black star is never allowed to end up with the white girl. (It *was* 1959.) 'Segregation – they should have straightened that out in the 18th century.'

And she hedged no bets about her attitude to money and her work. 'I dig a dollar as much as the next person. But I want to be part of something that's real. I want to make pictures that are an expression of the people, that are authentic. It takes a big star to endorse that kind of picture,' she conceded, but she had no doubt she would be one before long. 'I'll try to do it in that way. If everyone told the truth, then no one would be offended. It's only when half the people don't that the trouble starts. If I don't like something or someone, then I say so and that clears everything up. I'm not what you call part of Hollywood. Not because I don't like them, but because I like what I am better.'

That was the way her fellow actors seemed to like it, too.

On the film set, Frank in particular told how he was captivated simply by her conversation – from books to Japanese art. As he later said: 'It turns out that the egg-beater hairdo is the front for a well-oiled thinking mechanism.'

It was convincing enough for the studio chiefs to give up any idea of having another big name on the credits to match Sinatra and Martin. (Martin himself only got the part because his friend Frank insisted upon it. His own reputation at that time was as the lightweight half of the partnership with Jerry Lewis. His first film on his own, *Ten Thousand Bedrooms*, had been a total disaster and no one had yet seen *The Young Lions* in which he was to do very well indeed.)

Shirley was simply a very good actress.

You believed her, you felt sorry for her, you wanted to somehow walk into the screen and take her away from it all when Sinatra the soldier taunted her and said: 'Why, you don't even know what I'm talking about.'

'No, I don't understand it,' she replied. 'But that don't mean I don't like it. I don't understand you neither, but that don't mean I don't like you. I love you. So what's wrong with that?'

MGM had found a star – but Shirley had found a character who would always be her own.

Years later, Minnelli and his wife were at Shirley's opening night at the Las Vegas Hilton. She ordered the spotlight to focus on the director. 'If it wasn't for him,' she declared, 'I wouldn't be here now.' It was not just a nice tribute to an internationally respected man, it was also the truth.

There were, nevertheless, criticisms of Shirley's work in the film. Some critics suggested that her treatment of the girl Ginny went over the top.

'I don't believe she would have made any impression if I had underplayed her,' she said. 'Most roles must be exaggerated a bit. Let's just say that I was able to put myself in Ginny's place.' That reads now as a highly intelligent and considered judgment by a young girl who by some accounts was still really too green for her words to be taken at all seriously.

Shirley, of course, didn't take her life as seriously as it

appeared. It wasn't easy to put herself in Ginny's place, she admitted, 'when Dean Martin would just happen to tell me funny stories off camera before the big emotional scenes.'

She said that she took no notice of those who liked to acclaim her beauty.

'When I look at some of the pretty girls around I feel like Rin Tin Tin.' If so, she was deprived of some very good dog-catches-thief movies.

To another writer she avoided any pretence that might still be misconstrued: 'I never try to be anybody but me. And if some of the things I say or do come out a bit wacky, whose fault is it?'

The way she saw it, too, this astute businesswoman, it was going to be very much in her favour to be as wacky as she possibly could.

At about this time a friend was quoted as saying: 'Don't try to analyse Shirley. Just be grateful that in this generally sombre world of ours there are creatures like her still around.'

Not long after the film, Minnelli said: 'I don't care what the part is, she can do anything.' Dwight Taylor, the screenplay writer, agreed. (He did *not* write *Running*. That was to the credit of John Patrick and Arthur Sheekman, based on James Jones's novel. But Taylor, son of the famed actress of the 1930s, Laurette Taylor, declared that he could recognise talent when he saw it and wanted to say so.)

He commented at this time: 'There are only a few over the years who can say "I'm going out to buy a can of pork and beans" and find you choking up. Judy Holliday has a lot of that.' (One would suspect that Miss Holliday's mother would have choked, too. Judy was Jewish.) 'Shirley Booth's voice has some of it. But if I had a choice of a performance I'd want my mother to see . . . I'd pick Shirley's (MacLaine) in *Some Came Running*.'

There were rewards aplenty for Shirley after this role. She, however, didn't think they were coming from Mr Wallis. The feud between them continued apace. She was paid $15,000 for her role in the picture – 'the price that was then in operation and a good price,' Wallis told me. 'I don't like being hooked,' Shirley told *Time*. 'I'm a good businesswoman.' She had been so adamant that she knew she was being taken for a ride – and she was not referring to the MG – that she had actually refused to turn up for work on the set of the movie until the day before filming began, which didn't endear her either to MGM or Mr Minnelli. Mr Wallis, who had an investment to protect, could have told them what to expect, but probably didn't.

Now, with the film made, she believed she had a string of good reasons why she deserved better treatment.

For one, she was now accepted as an actress in her own right and was no longer to be subjected to the familiar questions of whether she would be willing to pose for pictures in a somewhat unimaginative bathing-suit. For another, she was nominated for an Academy Award. For a third, she was enrolled as a fully paid-up member of the Clan – although she said her duties were limited to prettying-up the places where the male members were going. Having Sinatra and Martin around on your side was known to scare the daylights out of other business organisations. To her credit, Shirley never tried that. If the 'Clan' existed at all, it *was* just for fun.

For a time no one could be sure what to call the organisation – it was never anything as formal as that; much more a group of cronies who thought they had a lot in common and enjoyed watching people trying to find out how much they really did have. The 'Clan' or the 'Rat Pack'?

Humphrey Bogart had called his set that.

To the other members, Frank was 'Chairman of the Board'. Dean, his recognised deputy, was sometimes the 'Admiral', since his habits owed more to flowing liquid than most of the others. Joey Bishop, Peter Lawford and Sammy Davis Jnr were the recognised followers of their leadership. As for Shirley, if there were any titles going spare, she would have been entitled to take on the role Lauren Bacall had adopted in the days when she was helping to run her late husband's outfit, the Den Mother.

The others paid her the sort of homage one would imagine was a den mother's due. Most of them seem to have adopted her.

Sinatra had no doubts about her. 'We have a kind of trust in each other. If Shirley tells me to read a book, I read it.' Which paid as much tribute to the fact that she was the only Clan member (Lawford apart) to have been to high school as to her membership. 'I trust her taste and knowledge,' said Frank. 'And I think she trusts mine. She's a kind of kook, but very warm.'

When Sinatra said that in 1959 he might not have known that the appellation would stick and would be quoted for the next 20 years at least. A kook had been born. But what exactly was a kook? The accepted wisdom now is that it is short for kookaburra, the Australian bird with a maniacal laugh. Well, Shirley looked prettier than any kookaburra, but the laugh was about right.

Dean Martin saw things from the professional performer's point of view. 'Oh, what a great chick,' he once told me himself. But there were more important factors to her credit as far as he was concerned. 'She's also a great audience. She loves to laugh. I'd be the biggest hit in the world if I only had 500 like her in every audience.'

She was actually the only female member of the 'Clan' and as such excused most of the responsibilities incumbent on a loyal associate. She didn't have to buy a Dual-Ghia car. Nor would she have been expected to buy a $125 white jacket made in seersucker material by Sy Devore, one of Hollywood's By Appointment tailors. She was, however, enjoined to look pretty and take her share in the witty conversation of the hour. Because there were no other women around, the members called her a 'fringie'.

The 'Clan' has since gone down into show-biz history, but it wasn't in existence for very long. True, it was perpetuated by a series of movies that Shirley didn't make, but which featured Frank, Dean, Sammy, Peter and Joe. Once John F. Kennedy was dead, however, the members decided there wasn't a great deal in the world to make them laugh.

As Joey Bishop told me: 'Television came round and we all started doing our own thing. Besides, we've all grown older and I don't think I could keep up with it any more.'

If Shirley wasn't their den mother, she was certainly their mascot. Almost 20 years younger than most of the male members, keeping up the pace wouldn't be her problem even now. But there are not many things a 50-year-old did two decades before that she would like to do now.

Sammy Davis provided the group with an attractive epitaph, however. 'When I'm with the group,' he told me, 'I can relax. We trust each other. We admire each other's talents.'

There were people aplenty who were beginning to admire Miss MacLaine's talents in 1959.

She featured in big-time television, as a guest again on the Dinah Shore Chevy Show. But the director Tony Charmoli wasn't over-impressed by the figure she cut as she walked into the rehearsal studio.

'I bet you haven't spent a nickel for rehearsal clothes since you were in the chorus, have you?' he asked. Proudly, she admitted that, big star now that she was, she was still wearing the tattered, fading leotard that had seen service in *Me and Juliet* and *The Pajama Game*. Why spend money when she didn't have to? In her next film, however, the studio showed how they could spend money on clothes – and then pay her to ruin them.

The Sheepman, in which she co-starred with Glenn Ford, was a Western, which didn't cause nearly as much excitement as her previous picture. It did, however, have a certain impact on Miss MacLaine, mainly because it was the sort of film in which she was expected to wear jeans, check shirts (the kind that showed she wasn't exactly a cow*boy*) and a hat that would have looked cute on a model for a page in *Vogue* – which was partly the trouble. The hat was newly-blocked, her boots looked as if they had been polished for a captain in the British Brigade of Guards and her shirt and jeans had been specially made (and specially pressed) by the best tailors in Hollywood, if by any chance the studio hadn't been able to do a deal with a little man in Savile Row.

George Marshall, the director, spotted this even before Shirley recognised the problem. He put his hands in the soil, rubbed a little of the dirt on her clothes and then watched the rest of the cast thereabouts – she was, as she put it, 'the only gal' in the picture – pull her to the ground and roll her in the earth.

'Now you can play in a Western,' said Marshall.

Shirley had her revenge. She took a bucket of water and threw it over the gentlemen who thought she needed a little preparation. 'Wouldn't you like to cool off?' she asked.

'From then on,' Shirley told *Time*, 'they knew I wasn't a prima donna exactly and whatever they wanted to say, they went right ahead. The language, oh golly!' Now, that might have been the way she saw things in the 1950s or may have sounded just about right for her image. It was not going to be something that would worry her in the years that followed.

The film was made for MGM who were more willing now to

part with the money Hal Wallis demanded (Shirley's salary from him plus a profit for himself) than they had been before Vincente Minnelli presented them with his concept of the new, sexy MacLaine.

Ask Any Girl was a somewhat different proposition; so different, in fact, that quite suddenly people had stopped talking about Shirley MacLaine being a star of the future; a few were taking it unto themselves to invent new words for the English language and award her the previously unknown accolade of superstar, or at least putative superstar.

And that was even when she amazed the studio by turning up in the sort of gear no film star would ever before have been seen dead wearing – like orange capri pants and a red sweater. If that looked odd, she would explain that she was slightly colour-blind in one eye.

Joseph Pasternak, the film's producer, was exceedingly impressed. 'Everything she does is real,' he said. 'The way she picks up a pen or a cup of coffee, the way she eats a sandwich.'

Certainly, there were those who still doubted. But the ones who felt more sure of themselves and their powers of prediction were instantly crying out in exaltation of the find they had before them.

Time magazine was shouting louder and for longer than most.

It described the film as 'a snappy story of what happens when the ancient art of love is improved by the juvenile science of motivational research'. Actually, the tale was a traditional dirty joke, cleaned up and embellished into a 1959 comedy of manners – and with David Niven playing Shirley's boss the manners were very polished indeed.

Shirley was a small-town girl who comes to the big town wishing she knew a great deal more than she really does. How, for instance, to inveigle the boss's younger brother (Gig Young) into helping her explain what she could never understand from watching birds and bees? Since Mr Niven is a motivational research specialist, the best solution to the problem would be through motivational research. All that she was learning smoking cigarettes – Niven's prize account was a cigarette firm – she was going to put into practice in the art of lifeman (or woman)ship. The research was obvious. The fun would be in the motivation.

Time went the nearest thing to crazy in saying how much they approved.

Said its reviewer (in a piece that many a top star would have envied and, had it applied to themselves, cut out and learned by heart): 'She has the face of an idealised Raggedy Ann, the body of a chorus girl, the dead-eyed, wag-jawed delivery of a ventriloquist's dummy and she probably possesses beauty, talent and mass appeal to a greater degree than any cinema comedienne since Carole Lombard.'

The magazine was pleased to note (and Shirley was doubtless even happier to have noted) that a 'somewhat monotonous manner has developed into a supple and imaginative comic style. In *Ask Any Girl*, she practises for the first time a sort of I'm-a-grown-up-girl-now decorum and restraint, so that when at last she does bust loose, the lulled spectator jumps as if a sleeping hose had suddenly come alive and spluttering'.

If a mere lulled spectator had suddenly come alive to the presence of Shirley MacLaine, so then had the media. Quite suddenly – despite all the five years of growing success she had had in Hollywood and all the frustrations she felt under the contract she had signed with Hal Wallis.

Time wrote that review of *Ask Any Girl* in its issue of June 1, 1959. On June 22, the Raggedy Ann girl, looking as cheeky as a child who had persuaded two kind aunts each to buy her an ice cream, appeared on the magazine's cover. It was the supreme accolade. Accolade? For an actress of 25, it was the gathering in conclave of the arbiters of everything important to present her with a golden crown.

Actually, the piece was subtitled 'The New Girls of Hollywood – Talent in Blue Jeans'. Inside, there were potted biographies of Shirley and the others. But apart from one of the contenders for the role of Top Woman Star of the Future, Shirley had it all her own way and was the obvious choice for the cover. The exception was Lee Remick. The others were Carolyn Jones ('a gas'), Inger Stevens ('mostly promise') alas both now dead; May Britt who married Sammy Davis Jnr Susan Kohner, Hope Lange and Diane Baker. But it's Shirley MacLaine's piece all the way.

The magazine said that Shirley was in a new category – 'expert Hollywood status seekers consider her so far out that she is in,

60

way in. Shirley, at 25, is the brightest face, the freshest character and the most versatile new talent in Hollywood.

'Her face, which she can work like a rubber mask, turns from sunny to sad, from Harlequin to Columbine, with imperceptible art. Her lips can tremble like a child's on the verge of tears or curl with three-martini irony; her blue eyes can blink in puppy-dog innocence or wink in complicity with all the world. . . .

'She can also look like a small kitten that has just swallowed a very large canary, a waif who has lost her bus ticket home, a country girl trying to act like a vamp despite her wholesome apple cheeks.'

The girl from Virginia had found herself – if not her husband.

Officially, they had a house now in Encino, a drive away from whatever served as the centre of Los Angeles. It was still too near for Parker, who preferred to stay where he was.

The arrangement of transPacific commuting continued, off and on, with Steve producing shows that were intended for consumption on both sides of the ocean and running events in Tokyo that had the highest patronage – including that of the Emperor, Hirohito, himself.

Meanwhile, Shirley wasn't depriving herself of male company, even if it were only to get a friend to take her to the races. Usually, however, it was more than that.

At the races, the kook's very nature didn't permit her to sit demurely at the side of a man, to talk to him when he wanted to listen, to laugh when he told a joke, even to scream at a horse after her escort had told her he had put a fortune on its back. Shirley heard she was being taken to the races and promptly rang a Hollywood gag writer asking him for ten good racing jokes. She was going to give as well as she could take and if the man didn't think it was very feminine, then he didn't know Shirley MacLaine very well.

She was, Elia Kazan once remarked, a very unusual kind of girl.

'In the old days,' he said, 'with one or two exceptions, Hollywood girls couldn't be both sexy and funny. Nowadays, they insist on being so-called complete women – healthy and natural. The new crop of actresses is dedicated to the proposition that the girl next door can also be sexy. They want to keep one eye on the baby and let the other eye rove.'

61

That was Shirley in 1959, the complete woman. Only she had a great deal more to do – and to prove.

Chapter Four

'I**F** I **DON'T** **LIKE** something or someone,' Shirley had told *The New York Times*, 'then I say so and that clears everything up.'

Hal Wallis couldn't have put it any better. But what seemed to clear everything up better than anything else was the way Shirley was performing on the screen. *Career*, with Dean Martin, was not to be taken too literally. She had no intention of making more movies like this one about the trials of getting a break in show business, nor of figuring too frequently with a fellow card-holding member of the 'Clan'. But it was a serious acting role and helped that ever-broadening portfolio which fitted her curriculum vitae.

Can-Can did even better. Looking at the cast list arranged and published before work on the project began, it seemed set for media attention – most of it attracted by the male stars of the piece. For one, there was Frank Sinatra – another 'Clan' member for Shirley to appear with – to provide the big box office, big show-biz interest. Then Maurice Chevalier was there to add the élan of the Paris of early 20th-century mythology. If that wasn't enough, he was teamed with his partner from *Gigi*, Louis Jourdan, who probably was just about the best-looking man in films of the time. As things turned out – and as anyone who knew anything about Shirley MacLaine might have predicted – it was Shirley who got most of the publicity and acclaim. Or rather Shirley's bottom.

The story was about attempts by the Paris police to break up a performance of the can-can, the wickedest dance known to civilised man; an attempt, as the old roué Chevalier regarded it, at taking most of the joie out of the vie Parisienne.

MacLaine played the principal can-can dancer, doing a

routine that wouldn't have been at all pleasing to the ladies who ran her dancing school in Washington, but which delighted most of the men who saw it.

One of those who feigned disgust was Nikita Khrushchev, Chairman of the Central Committee of the Communist Party of the Soviet Union. Feigned being a not unreasonable term to use in the circumstances, since he was known to be otherwise a very warm-blooded individual – with most of the needs and tastes of the simple man.

Most simple men – and not a few complicated ones too – believed that the sight of Miss MacLaine raising her legs to heaven (legs which started at her armpits) was one of the most pleasant ever seen on a big screen. And then there was that bottom, wearing very, very frilly panties – which Mr K. was reported to have said was a sign of American capitalist depravity.

The Soviet Chairman had gone to America to address the United Nations and then decided he wanted to see something of the country and its industries. He made it clear that above all, he wanted to see Hollywood – which seemed, more than anything else, to prove that the stern days of Stalinism which Khrushchev had condemned so vehemently at home were truly over.

His American hosts looked around for a movie in production that would most interest the Russian leader. *Can-Can* seemed to answer their needs – it was highly colourful, it looked totally non-controversial and it was an example of that then unique American genre, the musical. What was more, Spyros Skouras, the boss of Twentieth Century-Fox, was the least likely to offend Khrushchev.

As it was, the Soviet boss – accompanied by his very, very frumpy wife – saw the dance and clapped enthusiastically. It was only later at the studio lunch that that enthusiasm seemed to wane. Mr Skouras told him that it was only in America that he, a poor Greek boy, could achieve the successes and riches he had won. Mr K. replied that only in the Soviet Union could the people as a whole achieve the great success that they had. Then he complained about the decadence of the dance he had seen.

His annoyance wasn't assuaged by the fact that the dancers, including Shirley and Juliet Prowse, showed no more than their legs and ample supplies of lace on their underwear. In their

64

original guise, the can-can dancers were somewhat more revealing and Shirley had it in mind to tease the Russians that they
were, in fact, lined up to see more than they did. Shirley was
telling everybody she had been busy learning her opening lines
on greeting the Soviet leader.

'How the hell are you, Khrush,' she was telling people she
was going to say. 'I'm goddamned glad you're here. Welcome to
our country and welcome to 20th Century-Fox and I hope you
enjoy seeing how Hollywood makes a musical. We're going to
shoot the can-can number without pants.' Considering all the
fuss that was about to be made, there couldn't possibly have
been more trouble if they had.

Reports in Hollywood were that demands for the Khrushchev
lunch were as high as for an Oscar night awards ceremony. As it
was, it more resembled at most a United Nations celebration, at
least one of the all-star gatherings MGM used to organise on
their soundstages to celebrate important anniversaries.

Among those there were Tony Curtis and his wife Janet Leigh
and Dick Powell and June Allyson – since they were married and
each a star in his or her own right, they were the only ones
who automatically got double tickets. Demand was so high that
other married couples who had not been seen in each other's
company for years were clamouring for admission tickets.

Eric Johnston, President of the Motion Picture Producers
Association, welcomed the Russian leader, and Mrs K. sat next to
Frank Sinatra, close to David Niven and Bob Hope. (It was never
established whether the names meant anything at all to her.)

Skouras told Khrushchev (amid cries of 'Shut up' and 'Sit down')
'Your country is the greatest monopoly the world has ever known'
and Khrushchev complained about the cancelling of a trip to
Disneyland (because of fears for his security). 'We have come to
the town where lives the cream of American art. And just imagine,
I, a Premier, a Soviet representative, when I came here to this city,
I was given a plan, a programme of what I was to be shown and
whom I was to meet here.' As for Disneyland, he queried, 'What
is it? Do you have rocket-launching pads there? I do not know.'

One rocket-launcher pad seemed to be under Shirley
MacLaine who did not say a single 'goddam' or dare to mention
the suggestion that he might glimpse an unpantied bottom, let
alone something altogether worse. But she did learn a speech in

Russian that she hoped would sound a deal more dignified, and stood up ready to deliver it.

The trouble was that her speaking was interrupted by a group of scene-shifters and, as anyone who had got to know Shirley by now would recognise, she was not backward in coming forward to tell them what she felt – precisely what she felt.

'Could you do this later because this is awfully important to me,' she said, and then continued her prepared speech. 'I do hope you'll enjoy these parts of our picture because we very much enjoy the Soviet artists you have sent to this country.'

To some, her speech seemed to smack of going over the top. Even her press agent – a busy man indeed in those early days of her career – appeared surprised. To Shirley, it seemed no more than elementary courtesy.

She explained that there was nothing political in what she had done – or, at least, nothing political was intended.

'I felt it was the only decent thing to do. Here this guy comes all the way from Russia as a guest of our government. I decided it'd be courteous to greet him in his own language. You're supposed to be courteous to your guests, aren't you? So I made up a speech and had a guy translate it for me, then memorised it by playing it over and over on a tape recorder.

'Mr Khrushchev seemed to appreciate it. But Judas Priest! (Her own refinement of a more conventional phrase nice actresses were not supposed to utter, or nice reporters to repeat.)

'The way some of these great LA diplomats carried on, you'd think I'd taken the oath of the Communist Party in front of the television cameras, instead of only trying to be courteous.'

Hal Wallis – loaning out his prize property again – was not consulted either. His views would have doubtless earned a further Judas Priest.

Khrushchev – before he had discussed the matter with his wife – seemed to accept her statement at face value, to say nothing of the can-can. His grin was as wide as it would have been on hearing that a Soviet cosmonaut had reached the moon.

Shirley understood him better than any newsmen who recorded the event were seemingly prepared to do. As she told the *Saturday Evening Post*: 'He seemed to like it very much. He smiled throughout the whole performance, yet he complained afterwards that it had been too risqué.'

She was impressed by that. 'If he thinks *we* were risqué, he should have seen the original can-can. The studio research department told us that in the nineties French girls had danced it without panties.'

Mr K. probably knew more than Miss MacLaine realised – and was doubtless disappointed with the degree of risquéness available to him. But Shirley could well have been right about the reasons for some of the things he later said. The nail was very firmly knocked on the head after Shirley had studied the look on the face of *Mrs* Khrushchev.

'She wasn't smiling and I think that Mr Khrushchev began to disapprove after he saw the frown on Mamma's face. He may bang his UN desk with his shoe, but just like any other husband, he chickens out when his wife catches him getting too bright-eyed girlwise.' In fact, in pictures Mrs K. definitely was smiling!

And to prove how convinced she was that the Soviet party boss really loved her *and* her movie, she had a photograph ready to show anyone who doubted it. The picture, a portrait of Mr Khrushchev, was inscribed in a perfect hand: 'To Shirley, always my best, Nic.'

It didn't require a great deal of arm-wrestling or tooth-pulling to elicit the fact that . . . well . . . 'Nic' didn't exactly write that message himself. But considering the kind of graffiti other Hollywood people had around, it wasn't too bad.

Sinatra seemed as pleased by it all as Mr K. was at that time, and not simply because he was doing his bit at keeping a fellow 'union' member employed.

He gives Shirley credit for talking him out of adopting a phoney French accent for the role of the lawyer François. He had already tried speaking like a Spaniard in the movie *The Pride and the Passion* and the way he said the words in that picture gave pride to no one and doused his passion rating a hundred points.

Shirley reminded him of that. The part had to be played straight and on the MacLaine advice that was how he was going to play it.

Can-Can didn't really live up to the publicity which the Khrushchev visit engendered for it, although Shirley herself got a number of pleasant things written and said about her. On the whole, too, the people with whom she worked were satisfied enough.

Very shortly before he died, Maurice Chevalier recalled being with Shirley MacLaine for me: 'Somehow, it was like being with one of those old-time variety artists, you know, the Sophie Tuckers, the Fanny Brices, the Mistinguetts.' That final name was indeed the supreme compliment. Chevalier and 'Miss' had had a long, highly-publicised love affair. She was the legendary star of the Folies Bergère at a time when long, long legs were more important than shapely breasts.

'Oh, those legs,' said Chevalier. 'Just like Mistinguett's. Wonderful! And when she danced and she sang – there was a punch. Sensational!' Chevalier was in, to quote him, his '83rd winter' but he could still remember Shirley MacLaine with a twinkle in his eye. And that was really what she was doing at this time, no spectacular acting performances but providing plenty of twinkles in the eye.

Her producer Jack Cummings was equally grateful to her.

'We ran into terrible trouble making *Can-Can*,' he recalled for me. 'We were working from one day's script to the next.' And because of that, no one really knew what the writer Charles Lederer was going to provide for them.

'But Shirley really eased things along for us. I couldn't help – and I can't help now – feeling at the time a certain radiation when she was around. She's a darling girl.'

One of the 'darling' things that Shirley did, he recalled, was to act as a bridge between the production department and Frank Sinatra. If the 'Clan' was a kind of mixed-sex freemasonry, then Shirley used every ounce of influence she could to ease things along.

'Mr Sinatra,' said Cummings, 'thinks that he can only shoot a scene his way – and without what most people would consider an adequate amount of rehearsal. She let him know that that wasn't good enough. He had to rehearse. And as for only working from noon till the evening, she told him not to be an SOB.'

Which was not an easy thing to do – even for someone in the 'Clan'. Then as now, Sinatra was very much boss in all he did, but she continued to act as a conduit between the two parties.

'Frankie,' she shouted on one occasion. 'How dare you? You SOB you. Be supportive of this man (Cummings). If you don't, I'll hit you one.'

There were tears in her eyes when she let loose, said Cummings, and tears in his own when he recalled the event.

What really made Shirley cry most of all at this time were the stories about her and Steve. A lot of them were true. It *was* a very funny way to run a marriage.

It was getting harder and harder to explain – except that, as Shirley might well have put it herself, it was nobody else's goddam business. Yet she continued to say it, she had a very happy marriage indeed; a bit unconventional, but undoubtedly very happy.

Steve was going backwards and forwards between California and the various offices he ran in what the Americans were persisting in calling the Orient – the one in Tokyo and another in Bangkok and in various other cities where he needed to set up his operations. He was producing films and his travelling show *Holiday in Japan* seemed never to stop running in Las Vegas and had touring companies all over the United States. Shirley was going from one part to another – which all helped in a ridiculously short time to make hers a name with which people liked to pepper their conversation.

And the gossips were having hotter sessions at the Parkers' expense than they had had for years. Not that Shirley didn't give them good enough reason, even when the conversation was a million miles away from her unconventional marital arrangements. When she opened her mouth, there would be good cause for a shipload of sailors to fall down in a faint.

'People get the wrong impression about me because I don't always conform. So the hell with them.'

She seemed to live on a diet of hot-chocolate fudge sundaes – there were supposed to be four in her diet every lunchtime, together with a plate of snails. So what? 'I need the chocolate for energy and I like snails. It's not all that unusual.'

She worked all day at the studio and loved to go to parties every evening, a regimen that could be guaranteed either to kill most people or drive them to the kind of pills Judy Garland seems to have had with her mother's milk.

Shirley, on the other hand, thrived as much on saying she only needed five hours' sleep a night as she did on actually sleeping. It was as though she had become a top commodity so quickly – even if in her eyes it was Mr Wallis who was getting most of the money and credit – that she had had no real youth. Now, with all the advantages brought by her new status, she was going to enjoy it all to the full. The laughs and the giggles she was seen having on television were there for all to witness at any one of the dozens of more private gatherings she loved attending. But there were those stories about her and Steve wherever she went.

Friends mumbled at the time that her marriage couldn't last. Like a lot of so-called friends, they hoped that it wouldn't. Shirley, for her part, if she didn't reply in gorgeous Technicolor, studiously ignored the gossip. But it was difficult talk to ignore. There was enough truth in the stories to make it all terribly irritating, because plainly this was a crazy way to run a marriage.

She still protested – but the way she did made those who thought about such things wonder whether perhaps the lady wasn't protesting a little too much.

'I have given up expecting people to understand my marriage. Steve has his career in Japan and I have mine here. So of course we are apart, but we love each other and our marriage works. I should hope so. Every week I spend 500 dollars phoning him.'

They came together in Hollywood as well as in Tokyo. One year, Steve flew the Pacific and back 12 times, and on each occasion, he said, he read in an American paper that his marriage was on the rocks.

In 1961, they had travelled to Europe together. In London, Steve said they had come to their arrangement for his own sake. 'It seemed the best thing to do. . . . Otherwise, I would be a Hollywood husband and I'm not the type.

'There was never any doubt in my mind that once she had made her first film, Shirley could never be anything but a big star. So I took the stock of my assets and realised that possibly the only one I had most others hadn't got was the ability to speak and write fluent Japanese.'

Many years later, Steve said: 'Shirley had this drive, this push. She didn't want to be surrounded by a white picket fence. I would be wanting to putter around in the kitchen and she wanted to be in the studio.'

It was the reversal of so many Hollywood wives' stories. Not of the real situations, but of the stories the fan magazines liked dishing up – stories which were frequently being filmed. One after the other the biopics – Hollywood biographies – told of male stars married to women stars who only wanted to stay home to make the dinners, mend the socks and bring up the babies. But that wasn't how it was. A score of such women were go-getters on their own, pursuing careers quite as adamantly – and sometimes ruthlessly – as their men.

Shirley, needless to say, had plenty to pursue – including a little thing called *The Apartment*, which few at the time were in a position to predict would be one of the most successful Hollywood products ever made.

She was superb in a different kind of role. Once more she is a lady who gives rather too much love – although this time she wasn't a whore who allowed her suspenders to show.

But that wasn't by any means all. Her director was Billy Wilder and her co-star was Jack Lemmon, then just about to cross the threshold of becoming one of the most important actors in American films.

These three ingredients gently stirred together proved a heady dish indeed. It was Jack's first departure from unadulterated comedy. It followed on his superb performance opposite Marilyn Monroe and with Tony Curtis in *Some Like it Hot*. In that, the two actors had played Prohibition-era musicians who pose as members of a women's orchestra, both to earn a living and escape the clutches of the gangsters whom they had caught in the act of performing the St Valentine's Day Massacre.

When Wilder offered Lemmon *The Apartment* he was taking a risk – it was asking a great deal of any actor to repeat a brilliant success in the next film he made. It was asking even more of the same actor-director combination to do so. Perhaps Shirley MacLaine was the catalyst both needed to make it happen. That, at least, was how things were to turn out.

Jack was in his usual role – although the laughs had much more than a tinge of pathos in them – the junior member of the team who becomes the butt of everyone else's bright ideas. In this case, colleagues in his office discover that he has an apartment all to himself, complete with a key which he very conveniently is able to lend in exchange for possible future advancement – or at least as insurance against likely dismissal.

Shirley's heart once more glittered and shone, although she

was being cruelly used. The only relationship she and Jack had most of the time was purely professional. She was the elevator operator in the building where he worked. Then, shocked, he realised that to one of his 'customers', she went along with the key. Since that man happened to be his boss (a marvellous performance by Fred MacMurray) there didn't seem a great deal he could do about it.

'I don't think most people who see *The Apartment*,' Shirley told *Newsweek*, 'understand it. I don't think they realise it's as bitter and cynical as it is. The situation seems funny to them, but the reason it seems so funny is it's terribly stark. It's a social comment on ambition . . . .'

Wilder was the kind of director whom she was prepared to accept as a genius who deserved the name. 'He directs every eyelash,' she said years later.

The only quarrel she had with him was over rehearsals. Wilder insisted on rehearsing until every word and every nuance were not only memorised, but were flowing through the very bloodstream of his actors.

Shirley couldn't agree. From her fellow 'Clan' members Sinatra and Martin she had picked up the notion that too much rehearsing cramped spontaneity and freshness. 'We believe the more you rehearse, the less natural the lines sound.'

Both the lines and the actions that went with them seemed very natural indeed from Shirley's *Apartment*.

Most people were exceedingly impressed with Miss MacLaine in that film. 'What a girl!' was how Jack Lemmon put it to me when we discussed her some ten years after making the 1960 film.

That was the way most people saw her. 'She has a unique blend of acting and humour,' said Billy Wilder when we discussed the movie. 'Perhaps that is what is really meant by star quality.'

Fred MacMurray appreciated having Shirley to work with, even if he was very much the villain of the piece and she the hard-used employee-cum-mistress.

'We didn't have too many scenes together,' he told me, 'but she was a wonderful actress – even that young (she was 25 when the film was released). She was highly professional and I have always admired her talents very much.'

Both Billy Wilder and the Mirisch company who produced the picture did, too. But Shirley herself was still getting around $15,000 a time for working on the picture – the money that was being paid as a salary by Hal Wallis, who wasn't doing a great deal with her himself but was proving extremely skilful at renting her out. As he said, she was difficult to cast for his own productions, but with the whole of Hollywood positively lining up outside Wallis's office to make the next loan-out deal, there were plenty of other offers to choose from.

Needless to say, the feuding between Shirley and Wallis continued. But by this time, Hollywood had got used to it and it was being taken as little more than a local domestic squabble. She had a contract with the mogul, which because of various cancellations was gradually working its way up to being a nine-year agreement; except that Shirley wasn't agreeing with it at all. Her second Oscar nomination – she didn't win this time, either – served as some kind of consolation – although she has always thought that she would have got it had not Elizabeth Taylor had her celebrated tracheotomy operation, and knocked *The Apartment* out of the running.

The sympathy vote at Academy Award ceremonies is legendary. So Taylor scooped her and was granted one of the most controversial Oscars in the history of the little bronze statuette. Practically nobody thought she really was better in *Butterfield 8* than Shirley was in *The Apartment*, but win she did. Elizabeth's neck wound was considered more deserving than what Shirley had allowed to be done to *her* body in the Wilder film. It could, though, be argued by anyone who was not in the film business that working on *The Apartment* was reward in itself.

There were others. Both the Venice Film Festival and the British Film Academy gave her their awards for best actress.

It all helped Shirley's frenetic attitude to life – a kind of life that seemed so different from any other star's.

All in a Night's Work was her next film, which more or less confirmed Wilder's dictum that it was asking much, much too much, of any star to expect two consecutive bull's-eyes. This one was more like a sock in the eye – except that Hollywood was becoming a lot more mature than popular legend allowed. The film town was forgetting its old belief that an actor or actress is only as good as the last time on screen and was prepared to accept aberrations in films as par for the course.

This one actually was a Hal Wallis production and once again was a 'Clan' operation, with Shirley sharing her top billing with Dean Martin. Dino kept her laughing and she did her share to make him laugh, too.

But the idea of a film about the heir to a publishing fortune falling for his uncle's mistress was about as tired as Dean's voice sounded after arriving straight from the bar.

How she got herself involved in *Two Loves* – shown in Britain under the title *Spinster* – is a mystery which itself might one day make a decent film: accomplished actress joining with equally accomplished actors to make a film that would give thoroughly amateurish B movies a bad name.

Laurence Harvey, who with Jack Hawkins co-starred with Shirley in this epic which should never have been, told me soon afterwards: 'Every now and then an actor realises that he is in business to make money and you hope you'll draw your cheque without anyone even noticing the film came out.'

That should have been – and generally speaking was – the fate of *Two Loves*. The change of name didn't make this story of a love triangle in New Zealand any better. Shirley played the spinster – a schoolteacher, who showers love on her pupils because she can't stand the advances of a war veteran who is just about as stable as a paper house built on a fault in an earthquake zone.

The original plan was to shoot the entire picture on location, but this was stymied because Laurence Harvey was committed to another film.

But even that couldn't dissuade the *New York Herald Tribune* from saying that Shirley MacLaine 'is looked upon by a great many people out here (in Hollywood) as just about the finest thing that's ever come down the pike. . . . As an actress, she can apparently do no wrong'.

It would be charitable to think Shirley took the role because it was so very different from anything she had done before – and looked as if it would have made her name as a serious actress. She was lucky it didn't make her name as anything else.

Meanwhile, Sachi had gone back to Japan to live with Steve.

Parting had been quite painful, with Shirley going to the airport and kissing her goodbye at the foot of the steps from which the child trundled, leaving Shirley crying until she got home. Then she phoned Sachi for an hour every evening. Judging by the cost of transPacific calls in those days, it would have been cheaper for her to make the journey in person. But, as she also confessed at this time, 'I love what I'm doing. I love making films.'

And she also loved showing people she was doing well at it. When she drove to the airport on her way to join her husband and daughter in Japan in the winter of 1960, the fact that she was wearing a mink coat was not lost on the people who saw her getting in and out of the car – the mink is a Los Angeles status symbol but even in midwinter it is rarely cold enough to justify wearing one. But she had her reasons. 'I'm going to leave in style and arrive in style,' she explained. 'I owe it to my Steve.' That didn't sound like Shirley at all. She was no more interested in fashion than she was ever dependent on her Steve.

This time, it wasn't just going to be a visit to the family. She was making a film in the ancient Japanese capital of Kyoto, called *My Geisha*.

My Geisha was something rather different. Once having played an Indian princess, it probably wasn't asking an awful lot of Shirley to play a geisha girl, complete with contact lenses that prevented her looking the product of some illicit relationship with a Scottish missionary – even if she were twice as tall as some of the ladies in her profession and she wasn't really playing a Japanese at all, just an American trying to deceive her husband.

She hoped that the film would be liked by the Japanese as much as by Westerners, which was precisely why it wasn't being made in Hollywood.

As much as anything else, it was intended to be a marriage cementer.

Steve Parker was her producer. Giving employment to his wife was taken as a very nice thing to do, and so it was. In fact, they were giving employment to each other – making a film for the company they had set up together called, appropriately enough, Sachico Productions. Officially, they were *joint* producers.

It was very much a family affair. Sachi had a small part in the film, too – playing the part of a little Japanese girl who tries to explain the role of a geisha to a mystified elderly American gentleman played by Edward G. Robinson.

75

By that time, the publicists were bending over themselves to point out, she was already speaking Japanese and singing nursery rhymes in the language.

Shirley was engaged in a more delicate occupation.

Her husband – now where did this idea come from? – played by Yves Montand wanted to make it on his own in Japan while she worked in America.

Even playing an American playing a Japanese geisha meant that Shirley had to research the part. She went to the Gion geisha school for lessons, learned how to make tea, please a man and drink saki like a Japanese stevedore.

There were others who gave her tips, too.

Jack Cummings saw Shirley at work at this time – even though he didn't produce the film. She showed him the script and asked his opinion of it. It was he who suggested the contact lenses.

'The trouble with that, I told her,' he said, 'would come when you lost one. You'd have one eye brown, the other blue. If you shut one eye, Yves Montand will think you're winking at him. And unintentionally, it'll work to your advantage.' It wasn't a bad move, even if the film itself in places seemed to justify audiences closing both eyes at the same time.

What the picture did was to confirm for Shirley that she shared Steve's enthusiasm for the Japanese and their country. She learned their customs with an infinite respect, while trying very hard not to seem in the least bit patronising.

She had to learn how to wear the kimono properly. Shirley was intrigued by the fact that although (wrongly) the geisha had a very lurid reputation, her clothes were far more modest than anything worn west of San Francisco outside a nunnery. The art of walking 'from the knees down' and as if she were pigeon-toed (difficult for a girl with size 8½ shoes) was explained in detail. Her instructors were genuine geishas – they placed a handkerchief between her knees to make sure that she didn't overstep the bounds of what they took to be decency.

She thought it was just right. 'You get a firm grip on yourself,' she explained to a *Life* writer. 'You tighten up. You feel all in order and it puts your mind in order.'

There were those who doubted that. 'Can you really get your mind in order?' a friend asked Shirley.

'No more than my kitchen,' she replied.

Working with Steve on the film did not mean, however, that their periods of separation were now over. When filming was complete, they again went their own ways. Once, they thought they would meet in England. When they couldn't co-ordinate their plans, they settled for France. That didn't work out either. They did finally make contact at a première of the completed movie – held in Germany.

What was significant about Shirley at this time was that she was just about the hottest property the magazines of the United States could find, and not just the fan mags. *Life, Look, This Week, Redbook* all did cover stories on her.

Going far beyond a mere press agent's success story, *This Week* achieved the near impossible, by having a signed piece in her honour by Frank Sinatra.

Unless readers were a lot more gullible in 1960 than one hopes they are today, few people were lulled into believing that the Chairman of the Board had actually written the piece – he wouldn't even agree to meet reporters. But it read as a justified tribute to a girl who had quite simply taken the town by storm.

'Writing isn't my racket,' Sinatra, it was claimed, said in the opening paragraph, a disarming way of supposedly proving his bona fides – which therefore became the strongest credentials of all. But he added, 'Let's face it, I'd do almost anything for Shirley MacLaine. I admit I'm prejudiced about that girl. Shirley is one of the liveliest, funniest, most loyal friends anyone could have. But the real reason I'm doing this typewriter bit is that I firmly believe she is the best comedienne in this crazy business.'

Now, he may not have written that highly complimentary testimonial. But ring-a-ding, such words could never have been put in his mouth – or his typewriter – if they didn't measure up to the way he really thought. It was a tribute, the writer said, to a 'combination of talent and heart that's going to keep her on top for a long, long time'.

Life's story concentrated on the *Geisha* film. The cover had Shirley and Sachi together, both wearing kimonos, identical hair-styles and with strings of pearls draped over their heads. 'Sachi,' said Shirley, 'is a ham.'

It was an altogether different world a quarter of a century back, although to those of us who were around at the time, the differences don't automatically seem so apparent. Yet when

Shirley made her first 'official' visit to Britain in 1960, the shock waves positively rippled through London when she was asked how her marriage stayed so successful. 'Because we don't live together,' she replied. A generation later, it would be totally acceptable to reverse the premise – young people lived together without getting married; she and Steve did just the opposite.

It is also difficult now, knowing what both Shirley and Steve have said in recent years, to decide whether things were going well or badly for them in those days. To read what she said at the time is to be convinced that they had found the perfect arrangement – love on terms both of them wanted without the slightest suggestion of straying from the straight and narrow.

Of course, it wasn't quite like that. Nor was the story which emerged, even from the studio-inspired magazine pieces, totally in the form of unadulterated happiness, free from all the tensions. In January 1961, Shirley was actually going into print and asking: 'The only thing I can't figure out is – shall I try to erase the last four and a half lonely, hectic years or shall I always remind myself that that's how I got to be what I am today?'

It was as though she was trying to ease a mistakenly guilty conscience, even if it was her husband who made the initial choice to go it alone, if necessary, to Japan to follow his own career. Shirley, the liberated woman, had meanwhile decided that nothing would be allowed to affect that rocket of a success story of hers. But because it *was* a different world, that wasn't what the magazines wanted to publish. They were full of gushing statements like: 'I've come to realise what's really important in my life – my husband and family. If I never worked again, I'd still be left with a goldmine.'

Well, the real goldmine was still called Shirley MacLaine. When, in August 1961, Shirley declared she was taking a year off from making movies, nobody really believed her – and they were right, despite her pleas that she was 'tired and want to be with my husband and our daughter.'

She was soon back at work at the studio in a remake of Lillian Hellman's *The Children's Hour*, filmed 26 years earlier – with Merle Oberon and Miriam Hopkins – as *These Three*. (Since *Children's Hour* in Britain was the hallowed institution of a young people's radio programme it was called there *The Loudest Whisper*. The loudest whisper of all, however, seemed to be that the picture wasn't really worth making, let alone changing the name.)

We were still some seven years off the really permissive age, but it was, even so, easier in 1962 to talk about the whispers – of lesbianism between two teachers in a girls' school, played by Shirley and Audrey Hepburn. The allegations were, needless to say, way out of line, but the story was a lot less sanitised than the 1936 picture which rather pointlessly had made the rumours nasty stories about teachers carrying on with the nice Mr Joel McCrea.

'In large part, audiences have changed,' Shirley offered at the time. 'They are more curious about life. They are more realistic about stories about life. Then, too, films have progressed. Everything has progressed. Neither the public nor motion pictures can deny the facts that go into life itself. But yet, the motion picture business cannot go beyond the limits of being an entertainment medium. I think we can entertain, yet deal truthfully with meaningful problems. You can't run away from life. You have to face it.'

Shirley was 27 years old, but nobody could say she was running away at that stage of her life.

Every time she signed up for a new film, the studios wanted to do something with a) those freckles and b) her hairdo. She told them that they both helped make up the girl they had hired in the first place – and she must have something. Mustn't she? Faced with an argument like that there wasn't a lot any studio executive could do. He might know his studio, but the gut instinct that told a succession of producers to book Shirley MacLaine seemed to be strong enough.

Unimpressive though *The Children's Hour* was, Shirley's second go at playing a schoolteacher did, in fact, give her an opportunity to play a dramatic part with the benefit of an intelligently-written script. The film, like its predecessor, was directed by William Wyler, whom Shirley described as 'totally inarticulate', not a nice thing to say about one of the big names in Hollywood; Wyler, unlike Michael Curtiz, was a man who made a strong impression without putting his foot in it.

The trouble with Wyler, she would say, was that he wouldn't make up his mind about what he wanted. He did, she went on, 'as much as can be done with a script'. Not a bad thing, you might suggest. That wasn't Shirley's way of looking at him.

'*You* think nothing more can be done with a script, but he will find something. And once you're on the set, that's the beginning. He will try maybe twelve different ways.'

Eminent director or not, he *was* frustrating for an actress who thinks she has arrived and should be allowed to demonstrate a performance the way she feels it should be done. The frustrating thing about Wyler was that he would call for every scene to be done in four different ways – which was just about as hard as being told she couldn't dance in *Cinderella*. She knew she could do it, so what else was there to say? To Mr Wyler, plenty.

'I don't know if Billy Wilder would have done that or not. I tend to think so.I tend to think Billy would have been sure in his mind what he wanted and that would have been that.'

Not that she didn't admire him, and understand what the role of the director was. 'If someone like Wilder, Wyler, Zinnemann, Stevens, some of those people, wanted to film the telephone directory, I'd be apt to say yes, because it's what's in their minds that's important, not so much what is in the script.'

That sounded pretentious and wasn't really what she believed at all. Miss MacLaine was already far too intelligent for that. She was also much more fussy about which scripts she took and which she was ready to accept. It was her right because she was a star – and she knew it.

She also now took it as her right to be scrupulously honest – far, far more honest than most players were about the films they had made, within a decade of making them. No critic liked *The Children's Hour* very much. Nor did Shirley – and she lost no opportunity of saying so, even when being reasonably polite about the director.

It had been a hard role to play, much harder than the one in *Two Loves*. But, she emphasised, it was even harder because it was such a 'bad picture'. Now that was honesty taken to a degree that in a previous age would have had her listed as 'box office poison' by exhibitors who required little more of actresses than that they dressed and looked pretty and pouted at all the right times.

'A bad picture and several of the people in it were miscast,' was her verdict.

*   *   *

80

Previous Page: Almost a star – t
very young Shirley MacLaine.

Left: In those days, they
smiled at each other. Shirley
and Hal Wallis, the mentor
she was soon to accuse of
slave driving.

Below: Everyone said she was
the one to watch. Gary
Cooper was among those who
came to do just that – with
Hal Wallis at left.

Opposite: Shirley and a Hitch
in her career – Alfred
Hitchcock providing a little
shelter with both his hand
and his stomach. At the time
of her very first movie *The
Trouble With Harry.*

Above: If she could play an
Indian princess, the blue-
eyed Miss MacLaine could
play anything. From *Around
The World In Eighty Days* –
with David Niven.

Left: A quiet moment with
Steve in the early '50s.

Opposite: No wonder they
called her the Kook. In
Artists and Models.

Opposite: With Frank Sinatra in *Some Came Running*.

Above: With Juliet Prowse – who could lift a leg higher in *Can-Can*?

Left: The oriental touch. Shirley and chopsticks.

Overleaf: Shirley the charmer – in *Can-Can*.

There was no doubt that Shirley was a very interesting person – if only she had considered the consequences of that marriage of hers. Again and again, that seemed the only thing anyone wanted to talk about.

'I know my marriage is a gamble,' she told *American Weekly*, 'but it will work.'

And she told Hedda Hopper who, predictably, wanted to know more about this strange phenomenon than anything else: 'Distance is no barrier to us. People don't realise how much Steve and I are together – when we are, we don't go out because we have so many things to talk over. But when he isn't here, and I go out without him, people talk about our being apart.' She shouldn't have been surprised. People *did* love juicy stories and strange love affairs, or even marriages, were more juicy than any others.

This was not the only continuing theme in the Shirley MacLaine story at this time. One must not forget Mr Wallis, who, she was suggesting, was now getting something like $750,000 every time he hired her out – while she had been known to pick up, she was later to say, no more than $6,000 a time for her trouble, which was more than the $1,500 she had previously claimed.

She meanwhile declared she was getting no more than the 'gofer' working on the set who was mostly charged with the responsibility of bringing people cups of coffee.

There *had* to be ways of getting her dissatisfaction across. Dissatisfaction? When she had to get to the studio early in the morning – 'I don't stop coughin' until noon' – she would only make up half her face: the half that would face the camera.

When Wallis was, as she delicately put it, 'pissed off' by this, she told him: 'Give me the other $700,000 and I'll make up the other side of my face.'

The arrangement with Wallis would continue for the next two pictures she made.

The first was *Two for the Seesaw*, in which she was cast opposite Robert Mitchum. He played a country doctor. She, appropriately enough you might think, a dance instructress.

Not so appropriately, the girl's name was Gittel. Shirley was supposed to play Jewish. Well, if she could be a Hindu princess, and a Geisha, why not?

Seesaw had a moderately warm welcome from the critics. But that wasn't the greatest significance of the movie. Much more important was that it brought her and Mitchum together – and was the start of a fairly tempestuous affair between them. It was the first proof that those suspicions of trouble between her and Steve were not just a storm in a Japanese tea ceremony.

Shirley told friends at the time that Mitchum was the only lover whom she would like to have married.

But marriage was never on the cards for them. For one thing, she was still legally tied to Steve. For another, Mitchum was still saying he very much loved his wife of 25 years, Dorothy.

The picture was directed by Robert Wise, which apparently was the only reason Mitchum agreed to take the part. It had originally been earmarked for Paul Newman (with Elizabeth Taylor playing the female lead).

The fact that Shirley was to play opposite him swung the deal – although, according to George Eels in his biography *Robert Mitchum*, he had been warned: 'That dame will eat you alive'; a warning intended mainly as a caution against her dramatic abilities rather than her sexual proclivities.

The rumours multiplied to such an extent that there were those who, only having heard stories, would have been willing to testify that they saw the two stars cuddling up out of camera range, holding hands – and then being involved in a huge row in which Shirley and Mrs Mitchum exchanged confidences.

The affair did not continue at high-fever pitch for all that long, but it was enough to kill stone dead suggestions that Shirley and Steve really had a wonderful, if unconventional, marriage.

Irma La Douce followed almost immediately after the *Seesaw* film – with Shirley far enough away from Mr Mitchum for the rumours and counter-rumours to come to an abrupt, if temporary halt.

It was a role which – like *Seesaw* itself – had been earmarked originally for Elizabeth Taylor, but from which she withdrew when the Mirisch company refused to allow her then husband Eddie Fisher to play in the films, too.

Originally, *Irma* had been a small stage musical about the ladies of the Paris streets who weren't really ladies at all. Billy Wilder had decided it would be more effective on the big screen – but without the music.

It was the mere fact that Wilder was directing that persuaded

Shirley to do the film. She signed for *Irma* without having read a word of the script – which with Billy usually appears in dribs and drabs on the set each morning.

'I'd do anything if Billy Wilder had something to do with it. I'd play a man. I'd be John Wayne.' Fortunately, the character she played in the film was nothing like John Wayne, even with cleavage. Why did she keep thinking that she and Duke were somehow inevitably to be compared with each other? Her later life may explain it. But that wasn't something to worry about. Only the film was important.

'I'm playing it like the title – Irma the Sweet,' Shirley declared early on in the filming. So sweet that she had no memory for faces – which Shirley seemed to think was more than reasonable. 'You must remember that Irma was the No 1 hooker on the street. She got more customers than all the others. This was because the men knew they could trust her, they could talk to her.'

All of which were qualities Billy Wilder was convinced Shirley had in abundance. As he told me: 'You know there are many actresses here in America who can be funny, sexy or sad. But I know of only Shirley who can be all three.'

The picture was partly shot in Paris and the rest in the Hollywood studio – although one wag suggested that so much original material had been taken from Les Halles that there wouldn't be anything left of the old place. The studio looked more like Paris than Paris.

Her co-star was again Jack Lemmon, which with Wilder made it a nice reunion. There were no rumours of any romance between these two stars; Jack used his stay in the French capital to marry his fiancée of several years, Felicia Farr, with Shirley joining in with other members of the company in making it a marriage everyone else would remember. (Wilder with Jack's director friend Richard Quine, who was in town for another movie, produced a film of the wedding which became a Hollywood talking point. So did Jack's participation in the wedding ceremony. The star who learned long, long speeches as easily as he remembered his own address forgot the one word he had to speak for the occasion, 'oui'.)

But Jack and Shirley did spend a great deal of time together off the set – all strictly in the line of duty, of course.

Again it has to be explained that once more Shirley played a lady who spent a great deal of her time on her back.

With the help of the madam of the establishment, they studied the various practices of the business as though they were involved in a university project aimed at discovering how an industry could be operated more profitably. And that was really exactly what they were doing.

Using the spyholes normally provided for both the titillation of particularly welcome and favoured customers and for the information of the proprietress, they became informed themselves.

They learned useful facts like the tastes of the clientele – and quite eye-boggling tastes they were; like the kind of clothes the ladies of the night (and a few women of the day, too) wore. This took on a serious dimension: it was more than just how much cleavage was shown, who did and who did not wear bras, and the length of skirts and stocking tops. There were also practical facts, such as it being a great deal easier for such a wearer to get in and out of dresses that were zipped than garments that had lots of buttons.

And there was more – matters which Shirley understood, when one of the girls explained them to her.

'As a dancer,' Shirley told Hedda Hopper, 'I think in terms of line and where I stand.' She saw that applied to her friendly hooker model, too. 'The first thing I noticed was how she walked – her stance and sense of line. She told me that no matter how sexy a girl's walk, there must always be an air of innocence about it. These girls know what's attractive to their customers and what isn't.'

But above all, Shirley said at the time, what she learned was that Irma had to spend a lot of her time talking – which to a kook like MacLaine wasn't a difficult thing to do at all. 'All the research I did in Paris showed that a lot of men come to see these women simply to talk to them.'

The particular girl whom Shirley befriended invited her to follow her progress for several days. Her name was Danielle, and writing in *Don't Fall off the Mountain*, Shirley says that she thought of her every time she herself put on the green stockings worn by Irma in the picture. She didn't say so, but she doubtless thought of her even more when those stockings came off.

It was obviously important research for the part – if only, as the Method school to which she normally felt she couldn't relate might have put it, to help her 'feel' the part. But she also went into the background to it all, particularly the role of the pimp.

Shirley felt sorry for Danielle, bitterly sorry, as only a women's libber who still knew the love of men could feel. But we had reason to be glad that the Method school hadn't taken hold of the MacLaine spirit. We felt sorry for Irma La Douce, too – because of the way she was manipulated and accepted her fate in and out of jail; but not to the point of wanting to take up a fight on her behalf.

Shirley admitted she enjoyed the work. When she collected the Golden Globe award for the part, she said so in public – and had the final words dropped from the television soundtrack. What she said was that she enjoyed it so much, she was giving up acting – for undiluted sex.

Harvard's Hasty Pudding Club – in which her co-star Jack Lemmon had once been involved – was so delighted with her performances of late that its members made her their patron saint, which wasn't at all bad for a lady of the Paris streets.

They made her their 1963 Woman of the Year. The club kindly said that they had 'long held womanhood and acting in high esteem'.

She went to the club's annual show – called this time *Tickle Me Pink* – and experienced fond, admiring caresses and kisses from the cast. Not lost for words at any time, Shirley expected more from such an august gathering on such an important occasion.

'Hey,' she said, 'don't I get to say anything?'

The answer was 'Not a great deal'.

Was she happy? they asked.

'Yesss . . .' she replied tentatively.

'That's a stock answer,' replied the Harvard questioner.

'That was a pretty stock question,' she answered. You had to get up very early to catch Shirley MacLaine out with a question like that.

It was an experience she enjoyed. In fact, she said when she left: 'If I knew college would be like this, I would have come before and put off Hollywood for 10 years.'

Had she done so, she would never have been asked to the Hasty Pudding Club in the first place.

It was *Irma* that enchanted the Hasty Pudding Club so much. Others continued to offer much the same sort of sentiments – although no one dared contemplate what the League of Decency and other censuring bodies might say about it. The prevailing judgment at the time was that they had better get on with enjoying it while they could, because nobody would actually see it in a theatre. (Wilder was to describe the film as 'a nice, clean, warm and sentimental story about the emancipation of the prostitute. We are doing it with taste and feeling.')

Shirley enjoyed the work of making the picture almost as much as she enjoyed that research.

But it mustn't be thought that that research was anything but to teach her how a woman of the kind she played looked as well as worked.

'In this part,' she told *Look* magazine's Joseph Roddy, 'they couldn't have a girl who looks like a hooker who enjoys her work. That's why the standard Hollywood sex symbol in the role would be disastrous. This girl has to be a naive, wide-eyed innocent-looking young thing. Like I am.'

Mind you, playing a hooker had distinct advantages. As she was to say quite a long time afterwards, 'After dancing, it's a lot easier. At least you get a chance to lie down a lot.'

And there was also Jack Lemmon. Again, it was marvellous casting for him. Once more he was everybody's fall guy, but his acting seemed to develop more and more as the film moved on.

He, as well, benefited from the research. He didn't take it quite as seriously as Shirley, not so much to heart. But his eyes popped when hers did at the business in hand.

Those eyes were as big as saucers, he declared at the time. Sometimes, he and Shirley just waited downstairs and watched the girls go off with their clients. There was something of the businessman in Mr Lemmon. What *he* admired most, he said, was the fast turnover of the joint.

The fast turnover in the theatres proved it had been a good move all round. The censors were not very hard on them. Shirley liked it so much that she decided she had now played her last virgin on screen – or, rather, the kind of spinster you were expected to believe was a virgin. As she said soon afterwards, yet again: 'I went that route and from now on, it's going to be just sex, sex, sex.'

The Italians must have liked that. They gave her their own 'Oscar', the 'David', for *Irma*.

It was finally time, however, for Shirley to express in legal terms the dissatisfaction she felt for the turnover of Mr Hal Wallis – at her expense, as she saw it. With the benefit of the best legal advice Hollywood could offer – and that was one commodity that was available in as much abundance in the town as good scripts (perhaps even more so) – she sued.

She took advantage of the California statute which a dozen other performers (notably Olivia de Havilland in her various fights with Jack L. Warner) had used to get out of contracts which had become totally one-sided, very much to the advantage of the employer, not helping a great deal the employee who was worth rather more at the agreement's end than at its beginning.

The studios frequently shielded themselves with the undeniable fact that they had taken the initial risk in bringing under their wings unknown people whom they had converted into top money-making stars. The stars would reply, with equal justification, that they were the ones making the money and earning it, but it was the studios who were banking it in their own accounts.

Shirley charged that Wallis and his associate producer Joseph H. Hazan had entered into the agreement 'with the purpose and intention of evading the provisions of the labour code by enabling them to obtain my services at a time which might occur more than seven years from the commencement of my services under the 1954 agreement.'

What Shirley's lawyer Marvin Gang (not the sort of gentleman to be trifled with in the Californian legal system) was saying was simply this: she had been working for Mr Wallis for too little for too long. She wasn't even claiming damages, just the chance to get out of the contract.

Long before Shirley took the matter to trial, judges had ruled that nobody could be held to a contract beyond seven years from the date employment commenced. Shirley maintained that her nine years were the combined result of the suspensions and extensions which mounted up on top of the original years for which she had signed with Wallis.

Like all the best lawsuits this one was settled out of court. Hal

Wallis agreed to cancel the contract in return for $150,000. It seemed a stiff price, but Shirley justly reckoned she would make more than that from her next movie – and would not have to give a penny of it to Mr Wallis.

When I spoke to him about this, the mogul denied any feelings of bitterness, although he again said how upset he was not to have been shown more gratitude for bringing Shirley to Hollywood.

'It happens with so many people. They are grateful when they have nothing and then when they get money in their pockets they turn on the person who helped them. But you become hardened to such things in this business.'

What Hal Wallis never claimed was that he won the case at Shirley's expense. It was clearly a mutually acceptable arrangement, even if he wouldn't be able to take his share of commission from any more MacLaine vehicles.

But that wasn't what a certain Hollywood columnist said. Mike Connolly of the *Hollywood Reporter* had been getting on Shirley's nerves for quite some time, seemingly enjoying every snipe he was making in her direction. He did it with all the enthusiasm and dexterity of a gunman up a tree taking pot shots at the people below. He hadn't liked her politics much. When he got a whiff of anything which he thought wouldn't do Shirley's career much good, he went into print with what she and many other people considered a haste that was positively indecent.

Now he was saying the worst thing of all: Shirley had lost her court case against Mr Wallis, a man for whom most of the citizens of her neighbourhood knew she didn't have a great deal of time.

The options to Shirley were the obvious ones – get her lawyer to send an angry letter, the kind of warning that can be as frightening as two men at the door holding guns and saying they have been awarded a contract of a different kind from the one Miss MacLaine had just tried to get out of. Or she could have gone into matters more deeply and asked that same lawyer to initiate proceedings for libel, which would result in a great deal of publicity which might not help her cause at all.

Shirley decided on none of these courses. Instead, she went to Mr Connolly's office and slugged him. She herself, with her own fair hands – the ones which more than 20 years earlier she had fought with on behalf of her kid brother and which she only stopped using when she discovered she didn't like being punched in the boobs.

But this case had been too much. The paragraph in question was so simple, it offended her deeply. 'Shirley MacLaine,' Connolly reported, 'told Hal Wallis, "Okay, you win".'

That wasn't what she'd told him, so she took further legal advice.

She put in a call to her lawyer and asked blatantly: 'What's the penalty in this state for assault and battery?' With the answer rounded off for her, she set out to put the advice she had been given into practice. As the attorney had told her, a slap would be just that – a slap. A fist striking at the man's face would be assault and battery.

Like any number of writers who say unsavoury things about people, Mr Connolly took his writings a lot less seriously than Shirley did herself.

He met her apparently warmly. 'Hello, doll,' he said – a form of greeting that didn't exactly entice the 'doll' in question.

Shirley was either there to attack or not. It was not an occasion for pussyfooting, even for a doll such as this.

'Are you in the business to print the truth?' she asked.

'Of course, doll,' he replied – and as one reads the offending words, it is easy to see just how infuriating they must have seemed at the time. If Shirley's hackles had not been rising up till then, they were now on an ascendancy that was virtually rocket-propelled.

With her secretary there as a witness, she took the law into her own *open* hands and slapped the writer's face – twice.

The news got around Los Angeles like a warning of a new earthquake – which in some ways it was. Letters of congratulation flooded in. At Chasen's restaurant, a pair of outsize boxing gloves were waiting on the table as she sat down.

California's Governor Pat Brown sent a message of support. But it wasn't the only one from on high, as it were. The White House joined in, too. President Kennedy wrote to say he thought it had been a very good idea and invited her to take up arms against another man called Wallace, Governor George of Alabama, 'not Hal' as his wire put it.

Mr Connolly himself took it on the chin, if not on the cheek.

After he had soothed his bruised ego, he said that it hadn't been at all damaging.

'She aimed for my head, but it glanced off my shoulder. I'll never wash that shoulder again.' He doubtless thought that he was saying the gentlemanly thing, although Shirley knew that her hand had been the upper one.

But Connolly was claiming moral victory. 'I ducked. What else could I do under the circumstances? I'm just grateful she didn't have brass knuckles.'

All Shirley was saying publicly was that she had 'seen fit to express myself'. And very effectively, too.

Shirley was once again the heroine of California. The film community regarded her in much the same way. With that totally unorthodox tactic she had suddenly taken on the mantle of one who was replying to years of what they considered unjustified attack from a pressman who pontificated from the comfort of the leather chair behind his desk and typewriter.

It was just one of her Causes – to go with civil rights, women's rights and what frequently seemed her one-woman battle against the Vietnam War.

She was also speaking out loud and clear on behalf of Caryl Chessman, the long-time resident of Death Row finally executed for the double crime of murder and rape. Like most of the other things with which she has become involved, it was controversial, to say the least.

'I'm not saying I'm against capital punishment,' she said in 1963. 'For Hitler, yes. For Eichmann, yes. For Chessman, I said "No". What we did when we executed Chessman was to drop cyanide pellets on the world's stage. It was a terrible blight on the American image.'

Madame Nhu, wife of the dictator of South Vietnam, came to America just when a revolution overthrew her husband. Mme Nhu was more than the power behind the Vietnam throne, she propped it up with what were frequently displayed as the best-shaped legs in South-east Asia. She dressed impeccably. She wore make-up which she believed made her look beautiful, although frequently the effect was more like that of one of those sinister Asian spies with which Warner Brothers loved to populate its war-time thrillers. The money to purchase these luxuries was frequently said to be provided by the people of her embattled country.

Shirley didn't like the Madame at all. To Muriel Davidson in the *Saturday Evening Post*, she said: 'She stuck a bow in the hair of her virginal-looking daughter to improve her own image, and she came here to use her feminine wiles to try to convince Americans that she isn't a Dragon Lady – which she is. You know why I'm glad she came here? They got things straightened out in Vietnam while she was gone.'

People had felt much the same about the way she 'straightened out' Mr Connolly. The powerful ones who nevertheless always considered themselves powerless in this field had found a champion – in the very attractive shape of a girl with measurements of 34–24–34.

Chapter Five

SHIRLEY HAD AN Oscar nomination for *Irma La Douce*, but didn't win. For the third time she was a bridesmaid in the Academy Awards, but not the bride.

There was, however, another 'award' for her – and for Lemmon, too. Together, they were invited to preserve their foot and handprints – and also their signatures – in cement in the open-air foyer of Grauman's Chinese Theater on Hollywood Boulevard, joining the rest of what the town liked to call its immortals. Shirley was the 141st artist to be commemorated in this way.

If failing to win the Academy Award yet again mattered to her at all – and the evidence is that it did not – it certainly had no effect on the opinion people had of her. 'Shirley MacLaine – She has style,' declared *Close Up* magazine in a cover story four years earlier and that expressed the general view of her.

She still kept her hair short, almost as though she were wondering whether she would be called in at quick notice to understudy the junior lead in *The Pajama Game* again. She still chuckled, and as anyone who had seen *Irma* would be happy to testify, she still had the most incredible figure.

And she still believed that being funny on screen was the hardest task anyone could be asked to perform. 'You're dealing with millions of separate people,' she explained, 'each of whose emotions are different and their sense of humour is so vastly different and tragedy is easier because our sense of despair is more similar.'

Shirley has always been one for emotions – which doubtless explains why she is the outstanding performer she is. Emotions that vary with the mood and the events that promote that mood.

Jack Cummings saw them all on a trip from Los Angeles to

New York. The man who had produced *Can-Can* and had advised Shirley on her performance in *My Geisha* hadn't seen her for some time when the two, quite coincidentally, booked to travel on the same flight.

To set the mood, Shirley stated the obvious: 'Hey, I guess we're travelling on the same plane.' Having agreed that yes, barring a hijacking or the sudden issue of parachutes they were unlikely to move to any other vehicle between the east and west coasts, they decided to sit together. As the plane neared the airport, Shirley asked him if he had a lift. He hadn't, and she said that since she had a limousine to take her into New York City, why didn't he share hers?

'She had come to conquer the town,' he recalled.

But more than that, she was conquering him, making him laugh, initiating conversation at a rate of knots. As they passed a run-down apartment building, however, things seemed to change.

'I noticed that she had become quiet and had got very pensive,' Cummings told me.

He asked her, 'Who turned off the switch?' Her reply said a lot about her at that moment. 'I used to live in that place,' she said. 'I outlasted my room-mates. I even outlasted the rats.' Somehow it was the bit about outlasting the rats that sank home.

Her next film was *What a Way to Go*, about a woman who is very unfortunate in the number of husbands she loses – one of whom was again Robert Mitchum. Somehow it was safer to remember the rats in New York than the ones who sniped at her affair.

But those days were far, far behind her. Designer Edith Head had by 1962 decided that Shirley was the ideal subject for the clothes she planned for film actresses the way chefs dreamed up exotic gourmet dishes.

'A designer,' she said as she was getting together her wardrobe for *What a Way to Go*, 'is only as good as a star who wears her clothes.' She made Shirley a patent leather outfit stuck together with liquid cement instead of stitching, which would have ruined the line. Shirley, she had decided, despite all the 'kook' reputation, was perfect. The green dress she made for the movie, showing a great deal of Shirley's bosom, demonstrated the fact admirably.

But she was frustrating for a perfectionist like the Academy Award-winning Miss Head – and so very different from a dozen other top stars who were never happier than when playing mobile wardrobes.

'I've never had anyone like her before,' said the designer. 'She can hardly wait to get out of a costume she's fitting.'

It was not a statement with which Shirley was ready to quarrel. She admitted it. 'I hate to try on clothes.'

A bundle on the back seat of her Plymouth station wagon, gradually attracting a generous layer of dust, attested to that. It contained some $250-worth of clothes she had bought a year before without trying on. When she got home, the dresses and skirts she had bought didn't fit. She hadn't yet got around to trying to take them back.

At one time, Audrey Hepburn decided to take Shirley in hand and teach her how to dress. It didn't do any good. Before long, the elegant, ladylike Miss Hepburn had decided there was absolutely nothing she could do. 'But I taught her how to cuss during the process,' said Shirley – as if to demonstrate that all was not lost.

'It only confuses people when I dress up,' explained the MacLaine logic – which was carried a stage further by her posing nude for a magazine layout. It was as if to say that although she couldn't dress properly, there was nobody who looked better undressed – and she was almost right, except she made it all seem like a scene from *Irma La Douce* which the censors would never in a million Paris-while-it-sizzles seasons have allowed through.

'Why should semi-nude calendar art be only for young actresses?' she asked the *Chicago Tribune*, who, like most people in those now far-off days, seemed to think it was not the sort of thing nice women did.

'Those things strike me as humorous,' she replied, 'I wanted to spoof it. When people ask me just what did I have on, I tell them I wore an air of innocence and a cloak of respectability.' Which made a change from Marilyn Monroe's reply to the same question, 'I had the radio on'.

All of this helped Shirley's reputation as not your average young film star. When she was named the Fourth Worst-Dressed Woman in Hollywood in 1960, it was no more than anyone would have expected.

A couple of years later, she would say that it had all become very different: 'If only people would come and see me before writing about how badly I dress,' she said. 'That was long ago. I've changed. People do. I like pea soup now, too.' That was probably more revealing than anything – and slightly disconcerting to the manufacturers of hot chocolate sundaes, to say nothing of the importers of edible snails.

But dressing properly did not mean that she had to travel conventionally, the way Audrey Hepburn did it.

'What a revelation that girl is. I travel around the world with one suitcase I've had since 1958. Audrey and her husband crate up all their possessions and take them with them everywhere. China, pictures, glass, silver, everything. And do you know Audrey lists every item in those crates! If I tried to do things like that I'd be a basket case.'

Of course, she then added casually, she didn't have those sort of items to crate up anyway. Meanwhile, she was demonstrating what she did have to carry. Shirley MacLaine was on her travels.

If anyone was now trying to work out what it was about Shirley MacLaine that made her different from other actresses – or indeed other stars of either sex – a peer at her passport would give a fairly broad hint.

Shirley was making it very clear to those who thought it worth noting – and, again, a great number were thinking just that – that life was too good to be wasted simply by sitting in the sun at Malibu or other parts of the Los Angeles area.

The world was to be seen and Shirley was making it her affair to see it. Not for her the places to which most wealthy Americans were migrating like birds in the summertime. She wasn't satisfied with driving up and down Park Lane or even strolling down the Champs Elysées. The notion of seeing the Carlton in Cannes was enough to get the freckled MacLaine cheeks creasing themselves into a yawn.

No, Shirley wanted to see where her friend Mr Khrushchev came from. And when she had done that, there was always Africa. No going on any conventional commercial safari for her – even if she had been attracted to the idea of shooting wild animals, which plainly offended every principle in her bulging book of truths – that was much too ordinary. She wanted to go to Kenya, yes – but to meet the Masai people. And not just to see the traditional war dances that were laid on for the benefit of tourists and, much more significantly, for that of the government coffers. If she were going to meet the Masai it had to be more than merely shaking hands. She wanted to know how they lived, how they gave birth and how they died. It meant a lot of questions, but then Shirley MacLaine had got where she had got partly by asking and by probing and offering advice even where it wasn't likely to be expected or, sometimes, considered totally polite to give.

Travel had become a virtual obsession with her in the early years of the 60s. 'I'm not looking for a place to settle down,' she insisted – and then illustrated her sense of priorities by pointing out that the Parker family didn't even have a decent set of table silver – to say nothing of a matching assemblage of towels. It didn't worry her, although clearly there were people who thought it should.

That would, of course, be ample reason to let fly with a typical MacLaine response of 'Up yours'. As she would explain: 'I'm never home long enough to worry about those things. I never want to be. Material possessions just hold you down.'

But she knew that it was unconventional and probably good enough reason to offer an explanation or two.

'I'm a terrible wanderer,' she said about this time. And that was only saying half of it. She wanted to go to Africa before the animals were all gone, but only, one imagines, because that was a place on this earth to which she had not yet been and in which she had not yet left a piece of her heart. As she was to say: 'When I go to a place, I don't feel then that that's it. I'm homesick for every place I've ever been. I'll be one of the first broads on a rocket.'

(Why she hasn't volunteered for a place in America's space programme in the subsequent years is a mystery: except that perhaps she would have been regarded as something of a rocket herself and one rocket inside another is not usually the most stable of propositions.)

There were those who thought they detected a sense of running away in Shirley's travel expeditions. Since Hollywood loved playing psychiatrist, this was hardly surprising. Shirley knew what they were suggesting. 'I'm running *to* places, not away from them,' she said.

Her first big overseas tour – ignoring the mainly private trips to Tokyo and points further east like Bangkok – took in the Soviet Union. If her previous encounter with the Soviet Establishment on the set at Twentieth Century-Fox had caused raised eyebrows, that was like a dance round the maypole compared with what happened when she herself went to Russia in 1962.

She was woken up by her Intourist guide in the middle of the night, asking her to change some American dollars for roubles. But that wasn't the crisis that really got her mad.

She was so upset by what happened that she was willing, she said, to accept any invitation that might be extended to dance the can-can naked in Red Square. There was, for instance, a little matter of a lost suitcase when she arrived at her Leningrad hotel. Then, through a bureaucratic mix-up, she was ejected from that same hotel at midnight, the time she was due to catch a train to Moscow. She had met a group of American exchange students at Leningrad University who persuaded her to come to talk to them and their Russian colleagues. As a result of getting carried away chatting with the students, she missed the train and ended up having a row with the government – who decided it would be a lot better for all concerned if nothing were said about either of these things.

Intourist, the government travel agency, had assumed that she was leaving that evening and had told the hotel to lock her door. At the same time, they ordered her luggage packed and taken down to the lobby – from where it was stolen.

The tourist people wouldn't allow her to move into a different room – such things were not easily arranged in Russia – and she spent the night walking up and down the hotel lobby, which they presumably didn't like either. But would she kindly not say anything?

To Shirley this was like a red flag to a czar. She immediately said that she was going to allow no such thing. In Moscow, she let word out to foreign correspondents that she had been badly treated – even made to pay twice for the trip – and her idea of free speech was something her hosts would have to get to understand.

Eight policemen came to talk to her, but did little more than listen.

'I guess,' she said some time after the affair, 'the Soviet government was punishing me for "deviation". By this I mean I missed my train.'

It is fair to say that she and Russia didn't get on very well. Once on this trip, she was thrown out of a restaurant – for laughing too much.

Following the previous episode in California, the Soviets were not unreasonably a little sorry that they had ever heard of Miss MacLaine.

They were so angry with her that they brought their influence to bear on the government of Czechoslovakia, who promptly refused her application for a visa to attend the Karlsbad film festival.

Her baggage had included traveller's cheques worth a total of $4,500, all her jewellery and furs and her tickets. Since, when she got to Moscow, Intourist did not believe she had had any tickets in the first place – after all, where were they? – she would have to pay for them all over again.

It couldn't have worked out more precisely if Mrs Khrushchev, still nursing a few bristling nerves from the indignity of seeing her husband enjoying Shirley's lace panties on the set of *Can-Can*, had arranged it all herself. (Which perhaps she did?)

'It was just like Kafka,' said the well-read Miss MacLaine. 'So far as they were concerned, I wasn't there any longer.'

Her eyes were red, her nose was running and her hair was matted when this all happened – and when because she didn't have any luggage or evidence of identity, she was refused the chance to cash the traveller's cheque she had on her. That was when she made her offer to provide some unscheduled entertainment for the pedestrians in Red Square.

And if that wouldn't do it, why, she was going to ring Mr Khrushchev personally. Since Mr K. was engaged in other matters like a few missiles on their way to Cuba, this might have been pressing it somewhat. On the other hand, he would have found Shirley MacLaine an even tougher adversary than John F. Kennedy.

Not that everything she did seemed totally contrary to the wishes of the Kremlin, however.

When she arrived back in the United States, she did have one suitcase – made for her by a friend. She had been so incensed with her treatment that she crammed the case with piles of anti-American leaflets which she had collected on her journeys around the two principal Soviet cities – the authorities were more than happy to oblige.

At Idlewild Airport in New York, she declaimed. Her treatment was disgraceful. The Soviets behaved ridiculously. The anti-Russian press was delighted with everything she told them. Just then a customs man approached her. While she was still on her feet, emoting, the man had opened her suitcase. . . .

She even saw a political aspect to the way Americans travelled. On the whole, she didn't terribly like it.

'Every year,' she wrote in *Carte Blanche* magazine, 'millions of Americans and, for that matter, millions of people around the world, decide to take a trip just for the purpose of going some place. They don't know where they are travelling, the kind of people they will meet, the cultures they will be expected to encounter and the conflicts of interests, both politically and sociologically, they must abide by and understand. Thus, they become that well-known marketable brand of cliché in red, white and blue known as the "American traveller".'

She spoke with 'particular disgust' of the American woman who wrapped herself in mink. And she hated the notion of diplomats' wives driving around the countries where their husbands were posted in Cadillacs and Thunderbirds while everybody else seemed to be walking or riding bicycles.

No, that wasn't the way she was going to travel – even if nothing was going to stop Shirley herself going round the world.

'I prefer to just go away between every picture,' she said in another interview. 'I might go to Tasmania, Istanbul or maybe just Fargo, North Dakota. My vista is not bound by a soundstage at Twentieth Century-Fox. Nothing pleases me so much as learning.'

Shirley's feet were decidedly itchy. She had decided to spend the much delayed absence she wanted to take from Hollywood and its studios in travelling.

She had a home now in Switzerland as well as the ones in Los Angeles and Tokyo. And when she and Steve went to Hong Kong, they bought themselves a little pad there, too.

'I want to go on living out of a suitcase for the rest of my life,' she was saying. 'I'd love it if I had a suitcase 50ft by 30ft.'

That certainly wasn't the conventional way of living. But it fitted very well into Shirley's idea of happiness. Audrey Hepburn wouldn't have approved of that – because Shirley wouldn't have included a mass of evening dresses and valuable shoes. Since she couldn't get a 50-by-30 suitcase, every dress she took had to be guaranteed non-creasable. She didn't take a lot of make-up – she still barely wore any at all off the film set.

In fact, she was saying that she was not cut out at all for the traditional life of a film star. When she went to a party dressed up to most people's definition of the nines, she left halfway through. She felt so embarrassed by the number of people telling her how beautiful she looked. If she wanted to look beautiful, she somehow hoped it would be a secret between herself and her mirror.

Fellow actress Edie Adams once told her she had to spoil herself more. Buy more dresses. Pamper her feminine ego. Shirley bought herself a yacht. It was yet another way of getting away from her usual environment. It didn't mean it would be any easier to travel to Tokyo to see Steve, but Steve wouldn't have expected this. He had his own life and she had hers, and the fact that they barely saw each other now wasn't to be allowed to give anyone the impression that they weren't deliriously happy. They weren't – at least not together – but nobody else was supposed to know that.

Shirley was much too busy getting to know more about the world into which she had been born.

Flying to Morocco seemed no more a problem than was driving to and from the studio. Seemingly on a sudden impulse, she landed at Tangier, rented a car and drove all the way to the capital, Rabat.

She stopped in the desert and once in the capital it wasn't the sights that intrigued her. She spent, she said, eight hours doing nothing but watch with fascination a boy who was just four years old. During those hours, he was weaving cloth, using both his hands and feet. To Shirley MacLaine that was what travelling was all about.

But why did she do it? Was it simply the answer of the mountaineer who climbed the highest peaks because they were 'there'? It seemed to be that way. Shirley was even a little embarrassed at what she imagined might be a potential question – so she pre-empted it. Travel was very expensive – and that's why she worked so hard as she did.

'The only reason I work in pictures is to pay for plane tickets to the places I want to visit. I don't have any money. It all goes for travelling.' Which one might think either meant she was having some very, very expensive plane tickets or that she wasn't being paid nearly enough.

In 1964, Shirley was giving the Himalayas her personal attention – at the invitation of the Prime Minister of the pocket-handkerchief kingdom of Bhutan. Later, when she wanted to leave, it was with the help of the King. Such was the authority conveyed by the name of Shirley MacLaine.

She had a love affair with the Himalayas as she did with almost every other part of the world which she visited, seemingly the way other women called on neighbours.

She had no personal guru – she would always say that Steve was that – and she kept insisting she was not after any kind of Beatles-like transcendental meditation. In fact, the people she knew from that region, she would say, usually laughed at Westerners who sought a crash course in peace and serenity. You may be sure that she discussed the matter in great detail; when Shirley went anywhere she posed questions like a one-woman United Nations delegation.

On this trip to Bhutan, Prime Minister Llendhup Dorji had heard of Shirley's wanderlust and invited her to visit his country, an offer roughly equivalent to being asked by Hal Wallis ten years earlier to take a screen test – with apparently none of the strings. At that moment, it seemed to be precisely and unarguably what she wanted to do more than anything else.

She went in the company of Mr and Mrs Denys Rhodes, cousins of Queen Elizabeth II, who seemed to present the opportunity to open all doors that might otherwise be shut.

It was what Shirley believed holidays were all about. She saw mountains and she climbed them – there were no attempts to get to the top of a mountain, but there were plenty of other challenges in the neighbourhood. Someone suggested she might like to try her hand at a bow and arrow. The girl who had been a sensation at left field wasn't going to be put off by that and, naturally, excelled.

102

When she heard there were monasteries nearby, there was only one thing to do – pay them a visit and ply the monks with some searching questions. Had it been possible, she would have as readily donned their robes and lived with them for a month or so. She had to be contented with a specially blessed strip of saffron cloth which had been presented to her by the senior lama.

The fascination was complete.

It wasn't to last, however. The peace, the tranquillity, but not the excitement came to an end with a message rushed to the party from the Prime Minister's office.

It seemed that at that precise minute Shirley – not surprisingly to anyone who knew the kind of fuse she always managed to be – was in the midst of a new revolution. She and the rest of the party were invited to make immediately for the Indian border.

Sound advice, which even Miss MacLaine was not averse to accepting. But as usual when she was involved in things, it was not as simple as that. The party had an Indian guide with them on the trip. His name was Bhalla and for reasons not readily apparent, Bhalla was either not very popular or too popular with the Bhutanese. The party was told it could proceed across to India. Mr Bhalla could not.

Now what would Shirley have done in one of her films? Undoubtedly, the script would have laid it down firmly and clearly that she would take whatever action she could to stall and then forestall her friend's arrest.

Bhalla, she insisted, wasn't the man the Bhutanese thought he was. He was simply her driver. Needless to say, it didn't work.

That was when Shirley's super-sized luggage came into use. She hid him in a suitcase – fortunately Bhalla wasn't very big – and at the border told the guards precisely what she thought of them and the waste of time caused by all this. It was enough to freeze one of the hot-fudge sundaes which were about the only American things she missed. At that moment, however, there might have been a few other things about the States she would have welcomed.

Bhalla escaped – but when the armed guards couldn't find him they decided to keep Shirley and her friends as hostages. They weren't imprisoned or badly treated, simply refused permission to leave the country till Bhalla was returned to them.

When she tried to ring the American consulate, the phone was unceremoniously removed from her hand. Later, a dishevelled and handcuffed Bhalla was brought into the same customs post; he had been discovered before he could make off into the Indian hinterland.

Somehow, even then, it seemed that Shirley had some sort of magic about her that scared the hell out of the armed guards who held her prisoner. They heard her gasp and fled. That was a perfect opportunity for Shirley to show that an American movie star had an influence which even they couldn't imagine.

She demanded a telephone and was granted one. Then she dialled the King. 'Free my friend, your Majesty,' she requested – and His Majesty said yes, Bhalla was free.

That, at least, was the story she told in a number of contemporary interviews. In *Don't Fall Off the Mountain* she embellished and varied it. She said she was denied access to a telephone and finally her party was free – because the Queen – not the King – ordered it.

What she may not have realised at the time was that King Wanchuk hadn't been sure whether or not he would be able to contain the revolution – a coup wrought by her friend the Prime Minister. The King had been in Switzerland, receiving medical treatment. But he returned to his kingdom in time to thwart the revolution and free Shirley's friend.

Shirley left the post wearing her strip of saffron cloth round her neck, flashing her camera in the eyes of the guards who were totally mystified by what was apparently a kind of American black magic. She said she would never remove the cloth from her neck. But she wasn't all that happy. Her holiday had been spoiled.

'I'm tearing mad,' she said. 'It broke into the marvellous time I was having.'

The fact that she did it without a husband in train didn't seem to make it any the less satisfactory.

She was telling everyone she admired the way Steve had made it on his own – it would have been even less easy now to avoid trading on Shirley's name had he stayed in Hollywood.

Steve was now producing about four pictures a year for what was termed the 'Oriental market', with the occasional foray into Hollywood movies. He had bought himself 11 acres of seafront in Japan and was planning to build a marina there, American style. Shirley said she approved of that.

As she said: 'When you marry and have a child, you become a unit. But each individual in that unit should be allowed to express himself, not always perform in concert. We give each other freedom. It's a fact . . . the more freedom you have, the less you want. The people who feel compelled to put a label on everything label my marriage "an experiment". Some of those very same people are finished with marriage number three and are working on number four.'

For much the same reason, she admired her brother Warren. Not only had he added a 't' to the family surname, but he had quite determinedly decided not to call himself MacLaine. He wasn't anything like ashamed of his sister, but he wanted to do his own thing in his own way and with his own name. Early press releases for his first film, *Splendour in the Grass*, hadn't even mentioned the relationship. Later, people became aware of it and then took it all for granted.

Warren was now a full-blown star in his own right. The fact that he had a sister who was equally big in the world of films was no more than coincidence. Both of them seemed to like it that way.

Shirley was also to admire what he did in *Bonnie and Clyde*. It wasn't the kind of violence she enjoyed. But any girl who had taken the law into her own open hands with the man from the *Hollywood Reporter* wasn't about to be fazed by a little physical response. When *she* had an altercation with a man quite 100 pounds heavier than herself, she simply picked him up by his shoulders and threw him into the hallway outside. That was all part of the legendary Shirley MacLaine willpower.

But her real interest was in showing the strength of her constitution – particularly when it came to travelling. It was a love which she hoped she would be able to transmit to her daughter. The world was about to become, thanks to jet travel, 'as small as a golf ball. She must know everybody in it.' Many of them, as we have already seen, were quite influential. Not just the King of Bhutan and Mr Khrushchev. She was on hobnobbing terms with Indira Gandhi and President Bourguiba of Tunisia, a country which she and Steve liked so much they had bought property there. But having roots in Tunisia still didn't compare with the

105

chance to hop on and off a plane with just a suitcase to be collected from the baggage carousel.

That was why she did finally go to Kenya and live among the Masai tribe, the best-known warrior people in Africa who live by a code that hasn't changed in the last thousand years. Today they are about 300,000 strong but as threatened with extinction as a herd of elephants or a nation of Ethiopians suffering from famine.

It wasn't famine she saw when she went to Kenya.

Being a tourist in that country gave the impression of khaki shorts and shirts, bush hats and the constant clicking of camera shutters – from a safe and comfortable eyrie somewhere in a tree-house, with the promise of drinks and canapés served by black waiters wearing crisp white tunics.

That wasn't what Shirley had in mind now any more than when she first planned her months of travelling. If people went into the heart of Masai country they were there to take photographs as tourists or as journalists, with the occasional academic thrown in. So she was going to be different, just by going there at all.

Shirley saw her visit more as some kind of fact-finding mission. A great deal had been said about the role of the Masai as a nation of warriors, men whose initiation came with an elaborate demonstration of bravery – in the course of which the young adolescents would rush a charging ox, trying desperately to touch its huge horns.

But these were the men and boys. What about the women? Shirley's idea of women's lib required her to examine the way they lived. It wasn't a happy experience. She saw and she wept. She watched hopelessly the effects of illness, the kinds of disease which could be eradicated by a simple injection of penicillin or any one of the other antibiotics Western doctors take for granted. But the Masai had neither antibiotics nor doctors – apart from the witch doctors and the women who dispensed 'cures' that were frequently worse than the original disease.

The worst disease of all was syphilis – which did not necessarily reflect the sexual dissipation of the population. It was rather, as the Bible would have put it, the visitation unto the second and third generation of the deviations of their ancestors.

She saw a newborn baby suffering from the disease – the very

106

illness which had made the child's mother demented at the time of her birth. More than that, Shirley had been there at that birth, inveigled into the mud hut where it was taking place by a group of women. In her first autobiography, she described how she saw the woman squatting on the floor to give birth. Afterwards, Shirley tried to clean up the spot on which the mother had been labouring. She then witnessed the other women of the tribe spitting into the mouth of the poor screaming infant – to whom a couple of years later, on a second trip, she was able to bring medical help to rid her of the illness which had driven her mother mad.

She became godmother to the child, named Shuri – which, as one might expect of any project involving Shirley MacLaine, she took very seriously indeed. The women declared her to be a 'blood sister', which immediately made her qualify in their eyes as a midwife – which was why she had been allowed the privilege of cleaning up after the birth. The Masai women regarded the 'office' as a privilege.

With the other tribespeople Shirley drank a concoction very definitely not on the menu of the nearest Hilton hotel, a mixture of warm milk and cow's blood.

She spent a lot of time with the village children – most of whom sat spellbound watching her peel off her nail polish. They had no idea that her nails were only painted. They perceived Shirley's ritual of removing the polish as an unknown white woman's art of removing her nails which, because she was white, were pink instead of brown like their own.

Obviously, she had scored as big a hit with the Masai as she had with the people who had seen her in *Irma La Douce*. They particularly enjoyed her freckles, she said.

The local Chief guaranteed her safety wherever she travelled. Later, when she crossed over into what is now Tanzania, she was greeted by more Masai warriors who promised to take care of her.

How did they know about her? That was one of the mysteries of Black Africa. It might also have been seen as one of the mysteries of the power of Shirley MacLaine who had found herself an entirely new public – not a new audience, but a people among whom this white, red-haired freckled American fitted in as though they were her neighbours in Los Angeles, and their rituals no more strange than those at the nearby country club.

107

(They possibly seemed a lot less strange.)

It was part of the exotic lifestyle that appeared to suit her a lot better than the geisha costume she wore in Japan or the sari she had had to don for *Around the World in Eighty Days*. This may have been the reason she did so much travelling. Could it be that there was some subconscious challenge represented by that film's title which she was determined, one day, to emulate?

Nobody did speculate about that, but it is a question worth asking. Any number of people have been influenced to do things that were to shape their lives from much less cause. She agreed that it was a powerful drug. 'It's like taking dope,' she admitted. 'The more I travel, the more I want to travel. . . . The more you learn, the more you realise how little you really know. That's why I have this wonderful wanderlust.'

Her European travels continued apace, too. With Jack Lemmon she travelled to Hungary, on a cultural exchange visit organised jointly with the Foreign Ministry in Budapest and the State Department in Washington.

She learned a great deal about the cultural divide between East and West, at a time when that was about as divisive as one could imagine. The abortive 1956 Revolution was still fresh in everyone's mind, even if there were an instinctive desire to break away – leading up to today when Hungary is the least restrictive of Communist countries, with a degree of private enterprise and signs of prosperity most Westerners believe is their province alone.

On this occasion, the difference between the two cultures seemed best expressed by the woman tour guide – who wore the severest of clothes and no make-up. Gradually, Shirley noticed that she was changing. One day, the guide wore a little lipstick. The next there was more make-up. The day after that a colourful, tasteful dress – and then, high-heeled shoes.

Seeing this transformation was symbolic for Shirley, the girl who enjoyed living out of a suitcase. By getting over the way Americans did things, she helped bridge the gulf between two different countries.

Of course, not everybody else would see things that way. But when Shirley MacLaine travelled there had to be a good reason for it. She found plenty of reasons – even if not that missing luggage in Leningrad.

108

Chapter Six

SHIRLEY BECAME EASY meat for writers who said they hoped girl stars would behave the way girl stars were expected to behave. The courtly Anne Scott James wrote in the London *Daily Mail*: 'I *can* see what men see in Miss MacLaine – and I don't like it.'

And she went on to elaborate: 'All the men are raving about a piece called Shirley MacLaine and as she's nothing much to look at, it must be her character which charms them. This (in her film persona) is predatory, mercenary, calculating, ruthless, social-climbing, cold-blooded, cynical and mean.'

Now Miss Scott James was not saying for one moment that that was the way she saw the real Shirley MacLaine, but it was the kind of cattiness that got people reading and it was only worth being catty about people who had really arrived.

She went on: ' "Sweet . . . fresh . . . enchanting," say the men of two continents about the toughest little character ever projected by Hollywood . . . .' (This was itself a sturdy declaration about Miss MacLaine.)

'She is, I suppose, the female answer to the new cad heroes like Joe Lampton of *Room at the Top* and Albert Finney. They ought to get together in a picture – the clashing of financial interests should make one of the epics of all time.'

It wasn't a notion picked up by any of the studios, but it certainly seemed tempting at the time.

She was an important woman, this Shirley MacLaine, important enough to be grabbed by whatever causes could persuade a top name to back their ideas. In the early 1960s, it was the Civil Rights movement. Whatever her Virginia parents may have thought about it, Shirley was taking on the campaign as though her own life was at stake. She passionately believed in equal rights – equal rights for women, equal rights for blacks, equal rights for anyone who didn't already have them.

Suddenly she became the first woman star to get involved in political movements, and to a degree practically unknown in show business for a generation. Now she was openly speaking up for political opinions which only ten years earlier might have got her hauled before the McCarthy hearings. It might have had a little to do with her membership of the 'Clan'; after all, Sinatra was a frequent figure on Democratic Party platforms – he later changed his affiliations – and the other members were ardent Kennedy supporters. But Shirley, even at this early stage, was taking on individual causes that went beyond anything either of the two parties was likely to put on its platform.

The word on her tongue was 'progressive' and the leaders she admired most were the 'progressive' ones, like Gandhi, Mother Theresa and the man who was about to be virtually canonised by the Civil Rights movement, Martin Luther King. Did it really matter what she believed? It seemed to, and the endorsement of a film star called Shirley MacLaine was worth millions of dollars in paid advertising.

The party machine was not above thinking hard about the value her glamorous image offered. The Democrats suggested running her as a candidate in the Senate primaries in California, but she couldn't take the notion seriously enough – when comparing it with what was on offer from Hollywood. It wasn't the money that limited her political activities merely to making statements or joining the occasional march. She was as keen to develop her career now as she had been while working under Hal Wallis's patronage, when she earned a great deal less.

There were those who still doubted she would really make it to the top. David Niven was one of them. He told a writer: 'She was a lovely, fresh, unspoiled young woman with a lively sense of humour and a strong sense of dignity. I really didn't think, with her kind of sensitivity, that she would ever survive Hollywood.'

But surviving Hollywood she still was. What she was not surviving was her marriage. No one ever imagined she would. But it suited her and it suited her employers, the studios, to pretend that all was well.

She feigned indignation whenever a writer suggested in

either a quality newspaper or a fan magazine that her marriage arrangement was so bizarre that it couldn't possibly work out.

One man went no further than to suggest that the whole idea was very strange. 'You should have it so strange,' she answered.

And she went on to say that she spoke to Steve almost every night. That was true, but the calls were made to Tokyo because Sachiko was there, living with her father, and she spoke to Steve as a sort of by-the-way as she was talking to her daughter.

'I may not have a conventional marriage,' she said on another occasion, 'but then a lot of people don't have conventional marriages. Marriage is a very hard state as practised today. I just have done the best I could with the situations I have been given to deal with.'

She worked hard and played the same way. She was an inveterate party-goer, who chose her own company. When there were no parties to which to go, she stayed home at night and read – consuming a book, someone said, the way she ate hot-chocolate sundaes, in gulps. A long novel would take her three hours to read. One had the feeling that if she wanted to, she would have been able to write a book in about the same time. (That was on her agenda, too, but the timetable was not quite ready for it just yet.)

'Nobody really knows me,' she told *Family Weekly*. It could be said that that was the reason the papers and magazines were so keen on finding the answers – except that journalists are always most interested in finding out more about the people who are best known (as all the articles about the British Royal Family and the residents of the White House so regularly show). The reason Shirley was such an interesting proposition was that she cut a notably imposing figure in Hollywood.

'Nobody is born an actor,' she said. 'It may start the first day you are alive, but you are not born with it. It is a quality of being alive and observant and understanding.'

Now that much about Shirley MacLaine was true: she seemed to jump over the hurdles that were placed in front of actors desperate to succeed in a business never noted for its ease of movement. She knew that for every greeting of 'darling' and every fond peck on the cheek, there were a dozen hidden metaphorical stilettos whose owners were waiting for an opportunity

111

to stab, or at least cheer when the stabbing was done by other people.

'All my life,' she said, 'I've simply refused to accept what anybody tells me. I want to find out for myself.'

That is sometimes a comfortable retreat for an actor or actress, trying to make excuses for a lack of talent or apparent opportunities to demonstrate that talent. Plainly this was not Shirley MacLaine's problem – although, like so many other performers, she couldn't depend on only playing roles that excited both herself and her audiences.

After all, Hal Wallis had said that the biggest problem was finding the right roles for her – in the right pictures.

The Yellow Rolls-Royce wasn't one of them. This was yet another one of those movies that satisfied the desires of studios who thought all they had to do to guarantee success was find a product that had more stars than story lines. There were three different stories here, about three different owners of the same car, a yellow . . . of course.

The others included Rex Harrison, Jeanne Moreau, George C. Scott, Ingrid Bergman, Alain Delon and Omar Sharif.

Shirley played a Mafia godfather's moll. George C. Scott was the man – and he didn't talk to her once while the film was being made. He just played chess with his make-up man, she said.

Whether it was one of those tongue-in-cheek statements or not, Shirley was to say that this was her favourite movie. Certainly, nobody could see her cheek protruding as she said it.

Mind you, she believed there was a need for more people to show a sense of humour. The United Nations, she was convinced, would be a lot more effective if more people took off their shoes and banged them on their desks.

That was her philosophy, anyway. Steve once broke his ankle skiing. So bad was the break, in fact, that she feared the foot might have to be amputated. She and Sachi went to the airport to see him off – both bandaged from head to foot.

After her last movie, one would have hoped that Shirley would wait for something really big. The only thing big about the film that followed was the title – *John Goldfarb Please Come Home*.

Leslie Halliwell, that mine of information about movies, the kind who makes every other cinema buff seem like an inarticulate sponge, says of this film: 'Would-be satire on the cold war, anti-feminism, American football, American-Arab relations, etc. None of it works for a minute and the actors' desperation can be plainly seen.'

Shirley's skill was in trying hard to hide that desperation when she played a newsgirl at the palace of an Arab sheikh. The most desperate feature of the film was the fact that she was here at all. Although it offered undeniable financial advantages, Mr Wallis wouldn't have said it satisfied his requirement of a suitable part for the star. The mysterious factor that this film showed up was simply that – Shirley was a star. Even in such unadulterated rubbish as this.

Why would she do it? It is not an easily answered question. One can only hope that she believed her own abilities would transcend the script, which ought never to have found its way out of one of the Twentieth Century-Fox typewriters. On the other hand – and there is nearly always another hand – there *were* plus signs and the kind that most actors and actresses value highly. What Shirley clearly was developing was a perfect rapport with other actors.

Wilfrid Hyde White, for years the English gentleman on film – he was the quintessential Colonel Pickering when he co-starred in *My Fair Lady* with Rex Harrison – seems to have fallen in love with Shirley while making the *Goldfarb* movie.

'She's a genuine eccentric,' he told me, confirming what most people already knew – after all, she was telling people that she had so many freckles that if they only spread a little she'd have a lovely tan.

But then there was this much more revealing statement: 'Beneath it there's a sweetness that she doesn't want to show.' She was simply very much more comfortable appearing to be more difficult, as if that would help her left-wing iconoclastic causes, which were becoming more and more important to her.

Shirley and Hyde White went to restaurants together – but sometimes didn't get further than the man on the door or the head waiter. 'We used to get so drunk,' he said, 'that they wouldn't let us in. She just got a bit too boisterous, and people started complaining.'

A lot of people complained about *Goldfarb*. It was anything but a good film, although Shirley said she couldn't see it. She liked the script. 'I even liked it when it was done,' she said later. 'But it was a time when people wanted something to rap. And you rap the comedy giant by not laughing.'

But Shirley also knew that could seem like an easy way out. 'You have to make mistakes and you might as well relax about it.' (Alfred Hitchcock would have approved.) 'The worst thing is to make mistakes but feel that other people have made them for you.'

Perhaps the best part of *Goldfarb* was making the film and the fun she was having off the set with people like Hyde White.

None of that was new. Nine years earlier, when she appeared in her first film, *This Week* magazine's movie editor Louis Berg was making the well-informed comment: 'The trouble with Shirley is that she is too darn lively.'

What she was was unconventional. Could it be true that sometimes she didn't comb her hair for a week? one writer asked. 'Well,' she answered, 'I'd rather be myself than anyone else. I've always had an absolute rebellion against worrying what other people think. Sure I forget to comb my hair for a week. What am I doin'? Just livin'.'

'Just livin' ' was sometimes difficult for the other actors – like Mr Hyde White whom she could approach with the most disarming of questions – for instance: 'Are those teeth real?'

What was certain was that Miss Shirley MacLaine was very real indeed, even if now after those nine years in the business she was taking herself and the job she did a lot more seriously. But her apparent gaucheness was attractive. It was also a very clever wile. She was much too intelligent not to realise the advantages of appearing silly.

But what *was* Shirley doing when she wasn't in Japan? *Confidential* magazine, which regarded going to court to fight libel actions as much a part of its regular routine as going to press, decided that Miss MacLaine was a chicken ripe for the plucking.

Word sped like news of a big studio firing.

'Shirley MacLaine's Roman Fling' proclaimed the scandal sheet above the legend: 'We Have The Photos!' It all happened in Rome, where Miss MacLaine spent some time in the company of film producer Kevin McClory. She had first met him on the set of *Around the World in Eighty Days*, on which he worked as an assistant director.

114

The photos showed Shirley in a fur hat and coat with McClory in the street, and sitting in a car looking to the floor as they fought off the attentions of passers-by – notably the *Confidential* paparazzi.

They also showed her at a restaurant with Italian heart-throb Rosanno Brazzi. Nothing more incriminating than that, but no doubt it got a few tongues wagging in an altogether much simpler age.

The other papers seemed to concentrate on Mr McClory – after all, he was an Irishman, and put two people of Irish descent together and you get chemistry. The newsmen were waiting anxiously and hopefully for a chemical explosion, since he and Shirley were both staying at the same Hotel Excelsior in the fashionable Via Veneto.

They were seen dining and dancing nightly at Brikstops, which was where everybody who was more than an anybody went in the wee small hours.

The photographers enjoyed it all much more than either of their subjects – even when the fiery Irishman and a photographer exchanged more than greetings with each other. What they exchanged were pieces of a chair from outside the nightclub, which they proceeded to rain on each other as if it were a scene from the kind of film made long before Shirley ever stood before a camera.

This was in the same category as the MacLaine games of baseball a few years earlier. It wouldn't have been ladylike even for a star who had, in her time, slammed into a columnist, to join in such an activity. She walked away, across the street, in an apparent gesture of nervous superiority and called on her companion to follow her, marching smartly and trying to ignore the opposition. It was one of the few occasions on record when Shirley MacLaine did her best to play ostrich.

The Italian newspaper *Il Giorno* decided it had discovered Shirley's secret. 'She thinks of divorce,' proclaimed the paper. Well, everyone else was thinking that, so why shouldn't she? If she was thinking of it, she wasn't doing anything about it.

Less controversially, people wanted to know why Shirley didn't appear on television more often. Her explanation was simple. She didn't want any 'deodorant manufacturers telling me what I can or can't do,' she answered. 'Besides, I consider most of the television shows like doing a rehearsal in front of sixty million people.'

Later experience would confirm the wisdom of that statement. Like much else she has said in the years since she became a Hollywood household name – if that isn't a contradiction in terms – it proved her to be a fairly prescient woman at a time when people thought of her as little more than that eccentric bundle of laughs covered with freckles.

Leonard Mosley, writing in the London *Daily Express*, described her as 'probably the most resilient female in films today'. As he said: 'One of the reasons why Shirley MacLaine is such a likeable person, aside from her looks and charm, is the fact that she manifestly doesn't mind the rough way she seems to get treated by her directors, by life or by herself.'

Shirley herself, on the other hand, saw things slightly differently and was delighted to do so. 'People no longer report when I sneeze, thank God. It never was that they just wrote that I sneezed; they judged how I did it. Was it loud, soft, amusing, defiant, as illusionary as possible? It became a terrible strain to live up to a good sneeze. But let's face it . . . a sneeze is a sneeze. The whole thing gets a little ridiculous.'

But the interest people had in her paid off. Despite fears about being box office poison, she was nothing of the kind. In March 1965, the United Theater Owners of the Heart of America named her International Star of the Year.

As she said in that interview with the *Los Angeles Times*'s highly respected correspondent Charles Champlin, it got quite ridiculous. But, to repeat, that was what being a film star was all about.

She said she was able to get a little privacy nowadays (nowadays being in 1966), possibly because she was spending so much time away from home and had no further intentions of slugging Hollywood columnists.

'I've fixed it so that I can be me and get away with it. Shirley MacLaine, the star, exists from nine to six. It's as if I'm walking down the street beside her.

'After that, self-analysis takes over. For 11 years I've been struggling to be myself. You do change. You're not the bug-eyed innocent any more, the flushed starlet. You know who you are

116

and why you are the way you are. And you wonder if the image on the screen will change: will THEY still buy you? It's a terrible responsibility you feel sometimes. You look at the screen and say: "She's carrying this one; the jury's out on this one; what will they decide?"'

It was a remarkably intelligent summation of the role of the star who knew she was a star, wasn't knocking the position that would have been craved by a million other women of her age but who also wanted some of the things that million took for granted. The grass may have looked greener from her section of Los Angeles, but she realised that her own lawn was nicely and perfectly manicured and watered.

Not that that meant that she wasn't bothering to look more seriously now at what she did. A contract she had signed with Twentieth Century-Fox landed both her and the studio in the kind of trouble that normally only benefits the lawyers in the film community. The reason was that the studio signed her for a film that never came off – and then tried to get her to make a picture that she had no intention of filming.

Shirley was going to make *Bloomer Girl*, which looked as if it would be a very attractive proposition for Miss MacLaine. But the studio couldn't get together the picture about the early years of the century and abandoned it. Instead, they announced that Miss MacLaine would make a film called *Big Country, Big Gun*. Miss MacLaine in turn announced that she would not.

For *Bloomer Girl*, Fox had promised to allow Shirley the right to approve not just the screenplay but the director, too. For *Big Country, Big Gun*, no such approval was in the offing.

There were the expected comments that it was all a ruse to remove Miss MacLaine from the studio's books – after all, her last movies hadn't exactly set the Hollywood Hills on fire. But for whatever reason, Shirley wasn't giving the front office at Fox the opportunity of doing anything of the kind.

She said that she had turned down $1 million to appear in *Casino Royale*, the James Bond spoof that starred instead Ursula Andress – and Peter Sellers and David Niven and Charles Boyer and Orson Welles et al – because of her commitment to *Bloomer Girl* and Twentieth Century-Fox, and if that was the case the studio was going to have to foot the bill. She sued – and then collected.

117

In the California Superior Court, Judge Ernest J. Zak agreed and ordered them to pay her $800,000 – the largest amount a studio had ever paid for a film that was never made.

The matter was then taken to the Supreme Court, where the lower court's view was upheld. Justice Louis H. Burke declared:

'The mere circumstances that *Bloomer Girl* was to be a musical review calling upon plaintiff's talents as a dancer as well as an actress and was to be produced in the city of Los Angeles, whereas *Big Country* was a straight dramatic role in a "western type story" taking place in an opal mine in Australia, demonstrate the difference in kind between the two employments.

'The female lead as a dramatic actress in a western style motion picture can by no stretch of imagination be considered the equivalent of or substantially similar to the lead in a song-and-dance production.'

All that impressed people mightily. If a girl still in her early 40s could take on the studio system so effectively, then how about seriously considering her political clout?

She had already turned down the chance of running for Congressman(woman) in California. Well, how about now trying for the next step on the ladder – the Senate? One of the two Senate seats for her home state was comfortably occupied by another Hollywood figure (although one from an earlier generation), the former dancer George Murphy.

She thought about it, over and over again – and so did the people who felt there was great political capital to be made by a kook in the Capitol. She decided that she was happier working before the cameras and doing the outrageous things that people thought charming for a star but might consider . . . well, outrageous . . . for a senator. Chances are, however, she would have done the job amazingly well. A generation later, there are still those who think she might do it just as well.

There were plenty of people employed in placing Miss MacLaine on some mythical psychiatrist's couch, trying to work out just what it was that was ticking beneath her.

Sachi went to an international school in Tokyo, which Shirley liked because it meant that she was surrounded by other children from many other environments, which very much suited her ideas about the brotherhood (or rather, giving credit to her views on what she considered of greatest importance, sister-

118

hood) of the world. 'Here,' she told *Carte Blanche* magazine, 'she is surrounded by children of all colours, all creeds, all religions and a myriad of complex and conflicting ethnic cultures and backgrounds. Here the world comes to her, preparing her for the day when she will emerge into this greater society to take her rightful place. She is learning appreciation of the customs of other people, as they are learning the mores of our way of life. This preparation, I feel, will enable her to communicate to peoples all over the world in a language they will understand.'

And perhaps as much to make things as easy for Sachi as anything else, Shirley was insisting that the house in which she and her father lived in Tokyo was *'our* house'. As she explained in the same interview: 'We wish to feel accepted. This, I feel, is very important. We don't want the Japanese to have a feeling that we think we're superior to them. We are living in their country. We want them to make us feel at home. . . . We abide by their customs, study their habits and live according to the social, moral and economic dictates of their society.'

Sachi had graduated from Japanese nursery rhymes to more detailed literary material and Steve spoke the language fluently. Shirley herself had picked up more than a phrase or two.

Because she still phoned Sachi practically daily and because she spoke about her every time she faced a newspaperman, it seemed there could be no doubt that she was a totally loving mother.

There were those who thought otherwise and an intelligent woman like Shirley MacLaine couldn't have been insensitive to this. She would say herself she was a lousy mother, but she didn't like to hear others saying so.

'For years,' she was to admit much later, 'I guess I was uneasy about how I dealt with my life in regard to her. But now I think that those feelings had a lot more to do with prevailing notions than with reality.'

No one doubts that she did what she at the time thought was best. Her career contributed towards keeping the child in a life of luxury, and fostering that career was helping Sachi as much as it was helping herself.

'I guess I wasn't an ideal mother. Maybe that is not one of my virtues. I had Sachi with me for most of the first six years of her life, but making movies took me away from home so much.'

After the further six years living with Steve, Sachi was sent to school in Switzerland. Shirley's house in the country ensured that they were together as much as possible.

But she could no more be confined to a home in which she cooked the family meals and did their washing than she could have gone back to live with her parents and started sharing their views on the niceties of life. There was always a country to visit or a Cause to embrace.

For two years she was Chairman of the Thomas A. Dooley Foundation, a charity that went about looking for ways of helping the sick and the underprivileged.

She got very little publicity for these activities. Shirley may not have pleased the Foundation in that, but she decided that any value she may have brought to that organisation would be dissipated if it looked like some elaborate publicity stunt for a top movie star.

When the Foundation provided funds to set up two 'floating hospitals' on the Mekong River, her presence behind the scenes wasn't overstressed. But Operation Showboat was just about the most successful achievement it had ever undertaken and it had about it the stamp of Shirley MacLaine's initiative. For months, she was in the Foundation's offices, or on the phone, cajoling and drawing money from people who she knew could help the work in hand.

She said: 'I think the American public – certainly the public of the rest of the world – accepts commitment in movie stars. In fact, it won't accept noncommitment. Remember, most of today's moviegoers are under 23, and they demand to know where we stand. They ask our Mary Poppinses, our hookers with hearts of gold, "What about Civil Rights, what about the men in the trenches in Vietnam?" '

She wasn't claiming any great achievements on her part for which she expected an extravagant pat on the back. No, her demands were more simple – mainly a recognition that everybody had a function to perform for the benefit of others. She, however, accepted that not everybody felt that way.

'If you're capable of sitting at home with your turquoise swimming pool and three Caddies in the garage, that's OK – if you want to be a vegetable in your own time.' No one was ever going to call Shirley MacLaine a vegetable. Or if they did, they were either out of their minds or with a totally different definition in view.

Her own feeling, however, was that her responsibilities lay elsewhere. With Sachi now more than ten years old, she was very proud of her and her achievements. She spoke five languages – Japanese, Cantonese, Thai, Burmese and pidgin English – and, according to Shirley, practised five religions. This might have confused some people, but not a daughter of Shirley MacLaine, who plainly regarded that sort of upbringing as an essential feature of civilised living.

'I am by nature a willowy creature,' Shirley told the London *Daily Express*'s correspondent John Ellison. 'I bend with the wind.' That wasn't the way many people saw Shirley. She had the undoubted gift of making the people she was with do the bending – principally to her own demands.

Her involvement in things apart from filming had tended to liberate her even more than she had expected. Now she was independent, free, unconstricted, she would work at doing the things people most knew her for *only* when she wanted to do so.

Nothing any more was going to make her feel – the way she had – like a commodity. There was every chance that the feeling of constantly being knocked down by a truck would be relegated to the past.

For more than two years, she stayed away from the film studios completely. Then she made *Gambit* with Michael Caine, a fluffy confection with mini-skirts that makes it look now a typical product of the decade.

Once more she played a lady from the East – this time defined as a Eurasian involved in a conspiracy with Cockney Caine to relieve a multi-multi-millionaire of a statue with a special meaning and a very special value. Herbert Lom played the owner of the statue and proved a very interesting foil.

Hiring Caine was Shirley's idea. She and the bosses of Universal had screened *The Ipcress File* because they were planning to hire its director Sidney J. Furie to direct *Gambit*. No deal was made with Furie and Ronald Neame was appointed director. But Shirley loved Caine's performance so much that he was brought into *Gambit* as her co-star. By all accounts they got on as famously as *The Ipcress File* – if not *Gambit* – became.

Fame was not, however, what Shirley herself was out for

121

when she made the film. Outside her dressing-room was a card inscribed in copperplate writing, 'Lizzie Glutz'. She figured that Shirley MacLaine might have trouble keeping the sightseers away from her doorstep. Lizzie Glutz would find it easier. She didn't. Most rubbernecking tourists realised that Lizzie Glutz was a pseudonym and they therefore wanted to know who she really was. So she found herself attracting even more attention. She probably thought it was worth it.

This time, her $850,000 fee was augmented by a percentage of the box office take. The movie was not one of the greatest in her career, nor one of the most successful of the year, but it was entertaining and at times exciting.

Her next film had a more pronounced English accent than even Mr Caine's tones could provide for *Gambit*. *The Bliss of Mrs Blossom* had very little bliss about it and failed to blossom at any box office. It was the story of a businessman's wife who had a secret lover – in the attic of her house. The businessman made bras, which provided a certain sexual content, but even the presence of Richard Attenborough couldn't help it along and it all needed a great deal more support than the manufacturer's bras could provide.

People were noting something about Shirley. The MacLaine clothes no longer looked as though they had just tumbled out of a dryer without ironing and her hair showed frequent evidence of not all her money going on travel: she clearly spent something at the hairdresser. One friend said at this time that she didn't seem to be drunk at parties any more. Wilfrid Hyde White may have told me that they both did this often, but that wasn't the usual reason she seemed to sway at parties like that willow tree. 'It was just that with her natural ebullience she can give the average social drinker a six-slug handicap and still come out ahead.' No, it wasn't drink that made her so intoxicating – to be with, if not in practice.

There were still those who thought Shirley's principal contribution to American life was as a political figure – and compared with most of the other political figures in the late 1960s now that Kennedy had gone and John Lindsay had given up being Mayor of New York, a potentially very attractive one, too.

She wasn't beyond admitting that. Just a short time later, she was to write: 'It is the actor's special task to emulate life with as much power and faithfulness as he or she can command. Our perceptions and knowledge of human motivation govern how good we are at what we do. Those same perceptions should help determine the quality of our politics. Politics that are void of the insight of art – its passion, humour and laughter – are doomed to sterility and abstractions.

'If for example, I play a housewife on welfare with six children and a husband who's disappeared so she can collect the welfare cheque, I am involved with life . . . I must understand her environment and her anxieties.'

She was obviously an attraction as much for articulation as for her personality and her appearance.

Much of her political activity was still devoted to the Civil Rights movement – which again was frequently seen as a reaction (which it probably was) to her Southern background. Some saw it as the pricking of a guilty conscience (if it was, it was subliminally so, about the attitude of ancestors and the people among whom they lived). And that was unfair.

She believed in the cause with a deep conviction and there was nothing anyone could do to take that away from her.

Just as she had with the Masai, she went to see the problems of the black people in America at source.

At Issaquena County, Mississippi, she moved into the heart of the ghetto community and suffered from the reactions of both the blacks and the whites, all of whom were united in deciding she would be better employed minding her own business. She worked with the Student Non-Violent Co-ordinating Committee in their efforts to get the state's schools desegregated.

Shirley knew what she was letting herself in for. She fully expected to be lynched, if not just raped, for participating in the blacks' campaign. She even expected trouble from the police. When a traffic policeman followed the car in which she was driving with two black men, caught up with them and then drove alongside, she felt her day had come. She wasn't doing anything illegal, but that in itself was never enough in the Deep South, particularly in those days when the old was desperately trying to fight the new. Sensitivities had probably never been as strong. The old separatists knew that their time was short and they were making the most of it. They still believed that Patriotism wore a white sheet and a pointed hood.

Now what would Shirley do in a situation where she was about to be pounced on by a bigoted policeman who didn't like what he saw?

It was not, she decided, a moment to get angry, to use the tactics she had adopted in Bhutan and in Leningrad. She played the coy little girl. As the puzzled and irritated cop peered into her window, she waved, smiling nicely, just as her mother had told her to behave at birthday parties.

Getting a motel room at Jackson was much harder. The motel owner wouldn't give her a single room and the men a double. Anybody practising mixing the races the way she did wasn't welcome, no matter how big a movie star she was – and everyone recognised her. They seemed to come by the bus-load to see Shirley MacLaine having this little local difficulty.

They hissed, they booed, they sneered, they laughed, they swore – and they all were calling her Nigger Lover.

She asked where she could have a room – still being very polite. The man at the motel desk suggested simply that she and the 'nigras' move off out of town. Her worry wasn't going to be his.

Eventually, some sharecroppers agreed to give her somewhere to sleep.

Word spread. The jeerers came in open cars to see – and to shout again. Some threw bottles.

The local sheriff turned up, too, and demanded that she move out. Shirley wasn't doing his campaign for keeping the 'nigras' in their place any good at all.

For a time she considered making a phone call to the Associated Press and letting them put the whole place and what was going on there on the map. She decided against that. She would keep quiet, she said. But she would stay. And she told the sheriff: 'I'm still asking for your protection.' It was a situation which was clearly 'scary' – but one from which she wasn't going to flinch. She would never have forgiven herself if she had done that.

So the Ku Klux Klan moved in. They burnt crosses outside the house where she was staying – and one of the men at least fired shots in her direction. That was when she decided that for the safety of the people she was with, as well as her own, it would be more sensible to drive back to Atlanta. Doubtless there weren't many people on either side who were sorry to see her go.

The sheriff had sent a message saying that she herself would get more abuse, might even find herself daubed with tar and feathers. Neither was anybody guaranteeing safety to her hosts.

While in the Deep South she slept in an uncarpeted, uncurtained room, sometimes one of four to a bed. In *Don't Fall Off the Mountain*, she recounts her father's reaction when she told him about her experiences and those of the people among whom she lived and worked for the cause. He told her the furniture had just been cleaned and asked if she would like to take a shower.

Like most people of her generation during the election year of 1968 and her political inclinations, Shirley believed that Robert Kennedy offered most hope for the future. She campaigned for him, spoke at rallies on his behalf, travelled for the cause. There was the promise of a new Camelot and she wanted to see it, to breathe its air. When he was assassinated, there didn't seem much else to fight for – particularly as the hope of many Kennedy supporters faded day after painful day that year.

Without Kennedy to support, Shirley was campaigning enthusiastically – some would say almost fanatically – for Senator Eugene McCarthy, who represented the principal hopes of the liberal Left. She was a member of the California delegation to the convention – which didn't make the occasion any happier for her.

It was a scene of virtually unprecedented mayhem.

Hubert Humphrey had upset the liberals who were considered his main power base by his support for President Lyndon B. Johnson's Vietnam War policies and his refusal to condemn the way the convention had been conducted.

Shirley had tried to speak at the convention, but the local machine stopped that. Party boss Mayor Daley had stepped in to prevent her being heard. Shirley was so angry at being censored in this way – not a usual or easy thing to happen to her – that she decided she had had enough of politics and would take no further part in political activity.

Chapter Seven

SHIRLEY WAS SO busy with her various activities that it might have seemed difficult to remember that she was above all a movie actress – except that like everything else she did, she was supremely efficient. Her holidays and her travelling were all between films. Her political activities were in the evenings or on the days when she wasn't actually facing the cameras or a director's instructions.

'I'm a person who needs to express herself,' she explained to Kevin Thomas of the *Los Angeles Times*.

And there was another reason: 'The money. There must be a better way to make $850,000 but I can't think of it. Really and truly I enjoy it. I don't express myself in art, but as a reflection of the people I see.'

She was a girl who some people said thought much too much for her own good. There wasn't a thing, for instance, which she said that did not arouse some sort of controversy.

Other people would slip in a comment about modern youth and merely have, as a result, a series of heads nodding in agreement. Most people said that youngsters were giving everybody else a lot of trouble. Shirley said that she 'dug' the youngsters of the late 1960s. Her words went round the world in a way most film studio publicists would have given anything to achieve – if only she'd been talking about her movies.

'I don't say they're always right,' she remarked about the kids she knew. 'But they're righter than I was. I'm sort of in-between,' she went on.

'The kids of America are doing a lot of hard searching outside themselves for new explanations. This country is getting an old-fashioned newness in the pioneer spirit just because of them.'

That was why she liked the flower people. She loved the way the kids of San Francisco were presenting blooms to everyone they met and was thrilled that it was being copied in other parts of America, too. 'I've gotten the flower concept,' she said – although she knew it would never be as simple as that.

It may well have been a subject for comment when Shirley and Steve answered an invitation to the White House in the declining days of Lyndon Johnson's Presidency. Shirley was never awed by surroundings, nothing ever prevented her offering people the benefit of her advice, least of all the presence of the President of the United States.

Shirley wore a 'simple black dress' for the occasion. No jewellery, because she really didn't own very much – as she said so often, material things didn't interest her particularly. Steve was in a dinner jacket.

They were staying at one of Washington's smarter hotels where things were just not allowed to go wrong. The night of the party, they stepped out of their room; Shirley with a bag in her hand, Steve carrying a newspaper. In the hotel corridor, he ceremoniously – and it seemed outrageously – slung the rolled-up paper to the floor. Shirley, being of a tidy nature, bent to pick it up – just as her husband knew that she would.

Inside was a diamond and pearl ring. 'Here,' he said, 'that's for you.' It was a wedding anniversary gift from the husband the gossips were saying was barely on the fringes of her life. It was his way of expressing himself to her. Hers was showing the President and the other guests that they still cared.

Shirley was also expressing herself in writing, with her first volume of autobiography, although at first she was having difficulty with the title. She originally planned to call it *It's Better With Your Shoes Off*. But friends persuaded her it sounded just a little risqué. Other ideas came up from time to time, such as *Me and the Bamboo*. That, too, was dropped. But it would be four years before the book she had written on thousands – literally – of sheets of scrap paper would be published – and with a different title completely.

It was an important decision for her: she couldn't understand why it was not taken by everyone else in her business.

'I'm amazed,' she told Charles Champlin in the *Los Angeles Times*, 'at people here, at their willingness to relax in their affluence and regard it all as the end, instead of using their careers as a springboard to other things or other selves. They dry up creatively and in their personal relationships. People spend their time comparing themselves with others instead of with their own potential. If you look at the world as if you're the centre of the universe, you get a crazy view.'

She said that she had no ambitions to be on top – although that was a highly subjective position to be in, and there were any number of people who would have said she was well and truly there already. No, she said, that was so high up, it would be all too easy to fall and that would hurt. 'It's too dizzy up there. I leave those last few steps to the others.'

Shirley preferred the view from the Himalayas – and she might not have been able to see it from there had she not been free and only halfway up that mountain she was to write about in her book.

One of the problems she was admitting before the manuscript went to the publishers was the reaction of Warren Beatty who, she insisted, had not yet read it. But, instinctively, she knew he wasn't going to like it. And, almost as if to pre-empt complaints which she foresaw coming, she was explaining both what he was going to say and her own reasons for barring him from reading the book.

'He would say I've been dishonest,' she said in an interview in *Look*. 'He wouldn't be right, but that's what he'd say.' Which might strike one as strange this early on, before Warren had uttered a word in public – except that he had plainly uttered several of those words in private, all of which were aimed at getting her to change her mind about baring everything in print.

Warren was anxious about his parents and he was well aware, even before he heard of Shirley picking up a ball-pen and her scrap paper, let alone a pad of lined stationery, of the somewhat delicate relationship that still existed between the two generations. Their father's suggestions for instant hygiene following her expeditions in the Deep South only heightened that tension.

That wasn't what Shirley was herself admitting, however. What she was suggesting was that she and her brother both had tinted mirrors and when they looked in those mirrors they each saw a different image before them. As she said: 'He can look back at all those Sunday school picnics we went on and think one thing and I can look back and think another' (although little was to be said in the book about Sunday school picnics or any other similar activity).

But she emphasised: 'You can get more straight answers out of me than out of Warren.'

And, true, if people managed to get into the Lizzie Glutz dressing-room, she would try not to string them along. She still wasn't claiming to be a great actress. In fact, what she was claiming more and more was that performing in the movies was her job, which she tended to enjoy more than any other. But above all, it paid for her plane tickets and her hotel bills.

Since that was her belief, it was reasonable perhaps to think big – in terms of numbers. In her next film in 1967, the year after *Gambit*, Shirley played seven different roles. There was no suggestion that for *Woman Times Seven* she got seven times the normal fee, and there were reviewers who suggested she played them all as though they were the same woman, but there was a certain amount of fun in what she did.

Among the parts she played in the film were those of a sedate widow, a young girl who liked walking around in the nude – not to be confused with the stripper, another role she played – and a woman trying to persuade her lover to commit suicide.

The movie was seen as a follow-up if not a sequel to *Yesterday, Today and Tomorrow*, in which Sophia Loren had played three different Italian roles. Shirley's were all set in Paris – which one is inclined to think owed more to her love of travel and the affection she had for the city after *Irma La Douce* than any real requirements of the script, which could have been adapted without too much trouble.

Like *Yesterday*, *Woman Times Seven* was directed by Vittorio De Sica and written by Cesare Zavattini. Which also prompted the question of why Sophia Loren didn't make it, too. The main reason was that she didn't want to. As *Time* magazine said: 'Shirley is no Sophia, although even Loren would have had trouble with these amateurish anecdotes.'

Not even the presence of Peter Sellers and Alan Arkin as co-stars in these seven vignettes could save it.

De Sica kept telling Shirley during the making of the film, 'Trust me, trust me, my dear.' There was plainly a little too much trust.

Shirley was the first to agree that it hadn't worked – even though she had gone through such a gruelling time modelling seven different characters.

'We were all convinced that it would be a good film – even that talented shmuck Arkin.'

Arkin had gone on record saying that he took the part simply because he needed the work.

Shirley added: 'I read the script and knew it had no substance. But De Sica is the most persuasive, seductive talker in the business. If I had read the scripts of *Bicycle Thieves* or *Umberto D* I wouldn't have thought they were very interesting, either. I know he doesn't pay much attention to the script.'

De Sica 'seduced us all into thinking it was a good picture, even while we were watching the daily rushes.' And everyone accepted those rushes were just about the worst since the ones from which Moses was lifted in his basket.

Time noted: 'All seven stories suffer from the same fault: they start promisingly but run down, like jokes with weak punch lines. Part of the fault is MacLaine's. Despite heavy help from the make-up and wardrobe departments, she seldom departs from her customary screen self, and all seven women suffer from an unflattering family resemblance. Most of the blame, however, must fall on De Sica . . . in a ponderously directed, flaccid work.'

It was hard on Shirley – whose previous roles had certainly not been all alike, even if she had seemed to specialise occasionally. If any director had a part on offer of a young lady who believed her moral character was like her laundry – ready to be washed in public – then Shirley was ideal casting.

Part of the trouble was simply that Hollywood and the film industry which spawned it was in a constant state of flux, not knowing whether even now it had found a way of beating the small screen and certainly not sure it had a formula for bringing people into the cinemas.

'The trouble with Hollywood has been they are in love with perfection,' said Shirley – although what she meant wasn't exactly what she said. The impression was that she was accusing the film-makers of only wanting to make perfect films, with superb acting, marvellous directing and the kind of writing and camera craft that guaranteed a sideboard full of awards. But that wasn't it, and nor was it what she meant.

'They want the women beautiful and the men handsome and chiselled. There's a rainstorm only during a murder. Now has come the crack-up of fantasy. Film-goers want reality.' Not that reality was *exactly* what she was offering herself, although she was about to portray a girl a few people might recognise.

Her next part was right up her red-light district. It would reintroduce the girl she had played before in *Some Came Running* and, of course, the sweet *Irma*. But this one would be much sweeter. Her name was *Sweet Charity*.

People were to get very hooked on this particular girl. Not because Charity Hope Valentine was any less immoral than the hookers she had played before. She wasn't a hooker at all – just a girl who sold dances. Her body she gave away – all too easily because that was the only way she thought she could land a man. If the man threw her into the lake at Central Park and then ran away with her purse, well . . . it was a mistake, wasn't it? It had to be? She was so dumb, you felt as you sat in the cinema, watching her over-rouged face and her dyed hair and her appalling taste in clothes that hardly covered her, like taking up a collection to send her to someone who would give her lessons in facing the big, bitter world. The fact that she made you feel such sympathy was a tremendous tribute to her talent as an actress.

The way you went out of the cinema whistling 'If They Could See Me Now' showed that she wasn't a bad singer either. And that dancing . . . !

She was playing the part initiated on Broadway by Gwen Verdon, no mean hoofer herself, who had done brilliantly in the screen as well as the stage version of *Damn Yankees*. But Universal wanted greater box office insurance than they believed Miss Verdon could provide. That was why they brought in Shirley MacLaine. A shame for Miss Verdon, but Shirley MacLaine was nice enough in the part, even if there were those who shook their heads.

The film would have been a triumph if only . . . so many things . . . if the colours had been more muted, if the screen had been a little narrower and if even the songs and the dance numbers had been arranged and choreographed differently.

Shirley didn't even need Sammy Davis Jnr in a marvellous cameo role as a flower people's preacher – with his one superb number, *The Rhythm of Life*. *Sweet Charity* could have been a one-woman show and as such a preview of the one-woman stage shows that would follow. No one – least of all the studio or its investors – regretted giving her the role: a part that brought her back to the public attention, away from politics, from travel, from race riots, from every other Cause that had threatened to dilute her reputation as one of Hollywood's most impressive stars.

If she had ever doubted that she was on top, *Sweet Charity* put her in that dizzy position from which it would have been very painful indeed to fall off. Not even her detractors – and there were enough of those – could deny that.

Gwen Verdon wasn't too put out by the choice of Shirley to play the Charity role – or if she were, she didn't let on. She was happily married to the show's creator, Bob Fosse, and Fosse was both director and choreographer of the movie.

The point worried Shirley herself. She made two journeys to New York to discuss the matter with Gwen, and then wasn't sure. Miss Verdon it was who finally persuaded her – perhaps knowing that in any case she wasn't going to be offered the role herself by Universal, who thought they needed a big, big name to carry off their multi-million-dollar investment. By backing Shirley at that stage of the proceedings, Gwen was also protecting her husband. Fosse and MacLaine looked as though they were going to get on, which is not always the case when a third person appears on the scene.

There was one mitigating feature in it all. Gwen told her she got some of the ideas for the Charity character from an exhibition she had seen in New York – caricatures by Philip Noyes of a 'kookie' girl like the one she was about to play on the Broadway stage. Noyes, she found out, was basing his pictures on the way-out Shirley MacLaine. When she found that out, Shirley figured that perhaps the part had been hers all along, without really knowing it.

In fact, Miss Verdon helped Shirley behind the scenes. She was on hand at the studio and in her home explained how she saw Charity and both how and why she had played some of the dance routines.

And Gwen did actually play in the movie – although there is no credit for her at the end of the picture. In the routines with Shirley's fellow 'taxi dancers', Chita Rivera and Paula Kelly, the taps and hand-claps on the soundtrack were recorded by Miss Verdon. It may have been a token sop to the original star. Whatever the reason, they worked and added to rather than subtracted from the final good.

It was Bob Fosse's first go at directing a movie. The fact that he did so well had a great deal to do with his cameraman, the Oscar-winning Robert Surtees, who helped the director put into the lens the ideas he had formulated both on stage and on the blackboard choreographers used for such purposes.

Not everyone liked the film. Leslie Halliwell didn't like it at all, and gave the film just one star in his famous *Film Guide*. I beg to differ, even with his suggestion that the New York locale fitted ill with the story. On the contrary, it fitted beautifully.

Never had Manhattan's Central Park looked so good in film sunshine. Even Wall Street looked good – if a little unreal, since the dance routines were plainly shot at dawn on a Sunday morning. But no worry on that score now or when it was all made. It was one of those pictures that ought to be included in any list of movie *standards*, if only the film industry adopted the terminology of Tin Pan Alley – and I have never been able to understand why it didn't.

Shirley herself said that she had been waiting for 13 years to play Miss Valentine. How, she never explained, but it didn't matter.

This was her first musical since *Can-Can* and in effect her very first musical, the first one in which she got to sing and to dance anything but a turn-of-the-century French routine.

Perhaps as much as anything else, Shirley took to *Sweet Charity* like one of the ducks in the Central Park lake into which she was pushed.

The picture seemed to be as made to her measure as the costumes she wore on screen, yet there was something about it all that was slightly worrying. Charity Hope Valentine was a door-mat. A pretty girl had she had the make-up scraped from her face and the dye washed out of her hair; attractive if only some-one had explained that purple stockings didn't go with the dress she had on – a kind of clothes sense which Shirley MacLaine even in her early period wouldn't have wanted to have had associated with her when she was carted off to the morgue.

But it was not the kind of part that would have pleased the women's libbers who still hoped that Shirley would officially become their standard-bearer. While these females were ceremoniously burning their bras, Shirley was letting an altogether different pose hang out – a woman who wanted a man desperately, extravagantly, who couldn't see anything wrong in anyone who seemed to show an interest in her, whether he was the cad who threw her overboard or the aristocrat who locked her in his closet (Ricardo Montalban). Even the man who was plainly being caught on the rebound when he promises to marry her (John McMartin) was allowed to use her dreadfully.

Shirley didn't see the movie as doing any harm to her cherished Cause. 'I'm a kind of militant lover,' she declared. 'I sort of believe in forcing people to love their neighbours. *Sweet Charity* allowed a kind of sense of liberation . . . I had to believe in love and believe in the film's tenets.' That she did.

She regarded herself now as that 'specialist', someone who knew all about the girls and how they felt once those hearts of gold had been exposed.

Now, as much as that, one might have expected. But equally predictably, Shirley was prepared to go further: 'It's not an accident I played all those hookers. I know just how to do it. Sure, in many ways, I was an emotional whore. I . . . was whoring my talent in so many ways. . . .'

And there was plenty of emotion left over for this film – no more so than when she is rescued from the Central Park lake and finds her way back to the dance-hall. When she takes off her blouse revealing a bra that no 'lady' would like to be seen wearing under any circumstances, it is a scene to be treasured as much for her acting as her body.

Playing that kind of doormat was in its way a much more positive demonstration than it seemed to most people. 'It is my way of identifying with the human race, which also doesn't win very often.'

What *Charity* represented more than anything else most of the time was hard work – particularly limbering up for the part before a single roll of film was turned in a camera.

Work began the day she finished *The Bliss of Mrs Blossom* –

which was released after both *Woman Times Seven* and *Charity*.

Dancing her feet off, it seemed she was either trying to prove to herself that she could still play Cinderella if asked or that her ankles were as strong as she was telling everybody. Nobody could doubt that. She came out very strong indeed. It was almost as though the hit number of the show, 'If They Could See Me Now', was going to be directed at the doubters and the scoffers in the business, who were always the most vocal elements in the bars and delicatessens of Hollywood and Beverly Hills.

She had no idea how out of practice she had been. Had anyone thought that dancing was like riding a bicycle, a private peep into Shirley's rehearsing routine would have rapidly convinced him otherwise.

This was a star who was considerably out of breath, as well as out of training. As a result of her training programme, dancing, tapping, jogging, her lung capacity expanded five times, although the Shirley MacLaine bosom had always seemed pretty enticing even heaving when it was out of practice.

When she went to a Harley Street doctor in London for an insurance medical – it wasn't only ships that were insured by Lloyd's in the City of London – he was anxious to find out how she had given up smoking so easily. Did she do it gradually? he asked, wheezing as he searched his desk for another fag. Was it a case of three an hour becoming just two and then one? No, she answered. She just decided to give up and that was that. Willpower, they called it. Others would know it was just simply part of the way Shirley was.

From the beginning, some were expressing doubts about the viability of the *Charity* project which had caused as much disappointment among some studio executives as excitement in others.

The 'excited' ones got their way. With the millions spent on the project, the publicity department were brought in to work almost as hard as Shirley herself had worked.

Jules Stein, head of the MCA conglomerate, decided to bring *Charity* firmly under his wing. He launched a three-day film feast which looked extravagant even by Hollywood standards. Stein gave a party at Los Angeles's Sheraton-Universal Hotel, which is also owned by his company, and told the guests to stay for 72 hours.

For those three days 600 people were entertained to a series of parties that they were told – although sometimes they may have forgotten the reason – were being held to give them a good time and make them think of *Sweet Charity*. It was plainly one charity that wasn't going to be allowed to begin or end at home.

Beverly Hills society joined gilt-edged names from outside to celebrate Shirley and her film. Gregory Peck and Bob Hope and their wives came along with the Duke and Duchess d'Uzes and Artur Rubenstein. Naturally, they all left saying nice things about *Sweet Charity* and Dr Stein (he was formerly an ophthalmologist).

Some of the guests liked it all so much that they gave up their free return tickets and stayed on in Beverly Hills to extend the parties. In the end, *Sweet Charity*'s publicity bash lasted for seven days and nights.

There were those who didn't think they ought to have bothered. *Time* magazine for one. It didn't like the film, didn't think much of Shirley's performance.

Declared its critic: 'Orson Welles said it best. "This is the biggest electric train any boy ever had to play with." Broadway choreographer-director Bob Fosse obviously felt the same exhilaration. But all he could do with the expensive equipment was play around. The result is a chuffing, tooting, O-gauge musical.'

The anonymous critic didn't think Shirley was up to Gwen Verdon's standard, which must have pleased Mrs Fosse no end. Her 'wide-screen pathos and galvanic energy does not quite match her predecessor's', he wrote. He said that too much emphasis was placed on Shirley's face – which was 'not film making; it is map making'.

If that wasn't bad enough, the sting came in the tail. 'The idea of a musical about a warbling hooker approaching 40 remains as attractive today as it was in 1966 when it opened on Broadway. They ought to make a movie of it some day.'

The New York Times was equally critical. 'Although,' said the paper, 'she often looks like Miss Verdon, she never succeeds in recreating the eccentric line that gave cohesion to the original.'

And the review went on: 'Miss MacLaine can sometimes be very comic, but she is a dull shapeless dancer, an ordinary singer and an actress incapable of registering – outwardly – contradictory, funny internal anxieties. When she is required to be

137

pathetic, she is like an out of control jet fighter, yawning wildly through the sound barrier that separates pathos from bathos. . . .'

Reading that, it sounded awfully like the early studio reports on Fred Astaire's film test: 'Can't act, can't sing, can dance a little.'

Words were about to be eaten, even if *Sweet Charity* was not everyone's glass of champagne, at one of Dr Stein's parties or anywhere else.

'Miss MacLaine,' the review added, 'occasionally assumes the cockeyed waif pose, but in a four-walled Hall of Records, it suggests someone with a bone problem, not an attitude towards life.

'It's no accident that the best numbers . . . exclude the star entirely or put her into a supporting role.'

The need to eat words seemed even more appropriate after the paper's second review the following Sunday: 'The show was largely successful because of its star, Gwen Verdon. Shirley MacLaine . . . can be a very good comedienne but she's a lumpy dancer. . . .'

Shirley MacLaine a lumpy dancer! It really was hardly a prophetic view of the way she would be earning her living within five years. Nor was it the least bit accurate an assessment of what Shirley was doing in *Sweet Charity*.

It was as unkind as it was untrue. *Sweet Charity* really was Shirley MacLaine at her best, and at her best she could be very good indeed. True proof of this is the sheer datelessness of the film, mini-skirts and flower people and all. It seems even better in the mid-1980s than it was in the late 60s.

Not that Shirley herself hasn't been critical of the movie or the 'acceptable' pretence of Charity Hope Valentine being nothing more than a dance-hall hostess who gave the impression of being available for bookings in a motel room.

'It was splashy and slick, one of the best visual musicals since *West Side Story*, but I should have fought harder to make Charity a straight-out hooker. Her hung-up vulnerability would have been much more devastating if you'd seen her tough side, seen her doing anything for money. A lot of authenticity was lost.'

That was Shirley's *Irma* training speaking. Like many women's libbers, she knew enough about hookers to be at times more a trade union leader on their behalf than a mere public relations adviser.

She wore a black silk hat and had a horrible tattoo on her upper arm, saying 'love'. But in this film she didn't need it. The love she said she saw cascading all around while making the movie jumped into the auditoria too.

Despite the carping, many a writer tipped Shirley for an Oscar or a nomination at least. It didn't happen; the only Academy Award nomination was for the musical director Cy Coleman.

The film was, in the popular terminology, a box office bomb, which exploded to the tune, it was originally suggested, of a multi-million loss. Shirley denied it could have been anything like as bad as that – and said she thought it would eventually break even. Later, television sales would work towards that aim. Despite the lack of financial success and her own criticism, she wasn't entering any periods of depression.

She had, of course, received a healthy fee, although there were critics of that. She wasn't having that sort of complaint. 'As long as they were making $25 million pictures, why shouldn't we get our million? Now that pictures will cost less we will adjust accordingly, but as long as they were throwing money to the wind, I wanted to be there to catch some of it.'

Besides, she had 'caught' enough of it to do her various good deeds.

'I think I've reached my goal,' she was saying now. 'I've found ME.' If this was HER, a very attractive woman she was. The abrasiveness which had struck Mr Connolly of the *Hollywood Reporter* so forcibly seemed to have gone. She was upsetting fewer people. There was no Hal Wallis on the scene now, but there was a lot to suggest that even if there had been, she might have been more understanding – and then again, she might not. But she was more tolerant. 'I have become aware of what I am and I can honestly say that I am a happy lady.'

She was no more a Method actress now than before. Parts were not to be 'lived', just played – that's why she was spending so much time still on her book. It was about a life she had truly lived as well as loved.

Neither was she going to go all out to play the great classical roles. Could you see Shirley MacLaine playing Desdemona? Shirley MacLaine couldn't. She had made up her mind to play only contemporary parts. In truth, there were no offers from studios for her to do anything else, even had she wanted them.

If it were true that – to use her own expression – she had only just found herself, only just discovered a respect for her work, then she was in for a stormy time ahead; and not just professionally.

Chapter Eight

IT WASN'T EVERYBODY who could understand Shirley MacLaine. Their confusion was not merely caused by her marital situation, which was continuing as before, and went on to mystify practically everyone.

How, for instance, could a woman who was so patently a product of the American affluent society be spending so much time on espousing ideas that would upset a great many people?

In 1969, she was declaring big political ambitions – not for herself but for her country. Richard Nixon was just getting into his stride when she called for a 'socialised society' in her own country on the British and Scandinavian patterns – Harold Wilson was nearing the end of his second government at the time – and then added: 'I don't think we have a democracy in America any more. The way we pick our candidates is a sham.'

It didn't cause a great political storm, but the fact that she said it was enough for it to be noticed and to fit very conveniently in news pieces that were ostensibly part of a campaign to plug her various show-biz activities. She didn't believe in what today would be called a 'hype' – she thought that would be counter-productive – but she only had to appear in a foreign country or in any city other than Los Angeles to be mobbed.

That in itself was strange. *Sweet Charity* apart, she hadn't done anything of note on the entertainment front for years, and yet there was nothing that was going to keep her out of the public eye. That was what being a star was all about, apparently.

In fact, she was saying that not only was she not interested in politics, she was hoping for 'social revolution'. She was also admitting that she smoked pot. But she wasn't addicted to it. How could she be? Shirley let it be known that she could get high on a sunset. Such were the beauties of the world before her.

Sachi was now at boarding-school in Sussex. That, like the stay in Switzerland, was part of Shirley's desire to keep the child 'internationalised', although the emphasis was on countering her hitherto 'predominant Asian psychology'.

The fact that a mere film actress could use phrases like that fascinated people who enjoyed going to the movies or watching television, but still seemed to think that a performer should never be expected to have a brain.

That was why when in 1970 she was called before a House of Representatives subcommittee, as many people turned up to see the film star as to hear her evidence. She didn't dress like a star any more on this occasion than she would normally, but there was as much magnetism about the unmade-up woman in the plain dress without jewellery as ever there had been.

She was called by the subcommittee as a witness in support of the National Endowment for the Arts and Humanities, and went in the company of George Stevens Jnr, President of the American Film Institute.

Stevens had said that the film industry was going to become much less centralised as the years went on. Good job, said Shirley. Hollywood was far too regional – which seemed to mean that Shirley MacLaine was now revealing officially what a lot of people had been saying for a long, long time; that the glory days of the old film capital had passed.

The matter had come before the subcommittee in the first place because President Richard Nixon had asked for $40 million to finance the endowment during the coming fiscal year. It became the first time on record that Shirley had gone all out to support anything that Nixon proposed.

She was on one of her culture-promoting missions. And the cinema, as she saw it, was instrumental in revealing America's many subcultures. It sounded impressive, especially when she referred to a 'device through which ordinary men and women reflect their identities'. She meant the movies.

'We have always judged the level of social orders of ancient cities according to their arts that survived. Today, film has become our art form.' It was perhaps as much an announcement that Shirley MacLaine, film actress, was back in business as anything else.

142

It also fitted in very well with her sincere belief that if a person was going to succeed in the movies, he or she had to know something about the business – and the only way to do that was to see movies as well as act in them.

Five times she tried to get in to see the Stanley Kubrick-Anthony Burgess film *A Clockwork Orange*. And five times she couldn't get a seat – she even 'stood in line' she claimed. In the end and in sheer desperation, she rang the cinema manager, announced to him she was the Queen of England and would he please find her a place. Naturally enough, he did.

That was no more than one would expect of the self-assured Miss MacLaine who was no longer claiming that she only worked to pay her travelling expenses. Films and filming were beginning to take on the importance of a crusade for her – or at least, a Cause.

She would repeat that, despite her statements about a change in the constitution of her home country, politics had ceased to interest her. At least not as much as her family – when had she seen Steve last? 'Four days ago. Surprise!' Sometimes, however, it did seem that she was protesting too much, and that she countered all the questions about her marital state with such a severity that one was entitled to ask why she was so upset. Were things again not so hunky-dory? Was she merely trying to deflect criticism? It was an anxiety that wasn't to be assuaged just yet.

The interesting part of it all was that at no time was Shirley claiming to be faithful to her husband. As she said, 'monogamy is not one of the inherent natural forces.'

Life, she continued to insist, was to be lived and she was enjoying every minute of it. It was true that she had experimented with many things – including drugs. But a woman strong enough to resist so many of the norms of conventional society wasn't going to worry too much about this, or about what people thought.

She hadn't tried anything much stronger than marijuana. But she always gave the impression that had it been cocaine or even heroin, it would have been her business, and she would have been able to give it up as easily as the cigarettes she puffed before starting on *Sweet Charity*. Shirley was no more promising never to smoke pot again than she was going to take up permanent residence in Tokyo with Steve.

'That's like saying, "Will you have another Martini tomorrow?" ' If the Martini seemed exciting, the answer was pretty obvious. Of course, she would do anything that appealed to her. On the other hand, she wasn't going to do it just to upset someone else.

One mustn't always take the things Shirley MacLaine says too literally. As with many another top star, there was considerable charm in a self-depreciation which should never be seen as false modesty. 'How do I look?' she would ask in her dressing-room, having completed a fairly thorough make-up operation. 'Pretty shitty, eh?'

In 1969, what appealed to her most was a film called *Two Mules for Sister Sara*, in which she appeared as a nun – although she was no more a member of a religious order in this than she had really been a geisha in that other movie. In fact, this was another one of Shirley's repertory of hookers. Even though this one was dressed as a nun, it was 'Sister Sara's' real job that seemed to be the habit, and one which she might have done herself a favour by thinking of kicking.

She played a woman whose virtue – such as it appeared – was saved by an itinerant mercenary who looked like Clint Eastwood.

Once more, her heart was bright and shiny in this story that even included a revolution. Shirley's only worry was being able to ride, with or without her habit. 'I'm the mule,' she said after falling off her mount twice in one week.

Time magazine put it nicely: 'Shirley MacLaine's screen career careers from pillow to lamp-post.' The fact that she was a whore and not a nun came as more of a surprise, said the magazine's reviewer Jay Cocks, to Clint Eastwood than it did to the audience. He got the idea about the kind of cloth she was wearing when they ended up in a bath together.

Cocks was impressed with Shirley if not with Sara. And what he said ought to have been taken close to that heart of gold: 'Shirley MacLaine . . . has considerable range and some charm, both of which have been pretty well blunted by the monotonous consistency of her roles. Things do not bode well for the future either. Next year, she will be making a television series for the 1971–72 season, which is like going from confinement to prison.'

Actually it was going to seem more like a concentration camp, but that is rushing the story somewhat.

'I love a lot,' she would say and it wasn't difficult to believe her. And yet when people heard her speak from public platforms, it didn't always seem that love was the emotion uppermost in her thoughts.

Shirley MacLaine fought with a deep conviction and a toughness that at times looked abrasive. When in 1969, the Theatre Community for Peace held a rally in Times Square, it was obvious that Shirley would be there among them. Leonard Bernstein and she shared the starring honours, although that wasn't how she saw it at all.

She was describing herself these days not as an actress, but as a communicator – which fitted in very well with the book that was about to be published.

That was how she was billed when she appeared before the National Democratic Club of America at New York's Madison Avenue, the first woman to speak there in 137 years – and you can imagine what she made of that.

She saw it as a great opportunity, not to plug the two films she had made virtually one after the other and which were about to be released simultaneously – *Desperate Characters* and *The Possession of Joel Delaney* – but to let American politicians know what she felt about over-population.

With a rallying call of 'Let's tax diapers' she was asking aid for people who limited their families, and penalties for those who didn't. She wasn't saying that limiting *her* family to Sachi was her contribution to saving the world from instant doom, but one got the message.

There was more than a hint, that day in August 1971, of what she would be doing come the summer and autumn of the following year. 'God!' she said, 'George McGovern is an extraordinary man.' To most people, the senator from South Dakota was no more than an 'also-ran' who, next election, was going to have a go at a couple of primaries in battle against Hubert Humphrey, Edward Muskie, the newly-converted John Lindsay and George Wallace. Shirley predicted he would be the Democrats' candidate to fight Nixon – and she was right.

The Democrats assembled in New York that day seemed to like the way she looked at their world, even though some of them regarded her presence among them as a kind indulgence

145

on their part, and Shirley herself as an eccentric who was helping to colour their lives. She told them to get themselves sterilised – or if she wasn't talking about them, she meant other men everywhere.

'The question of over-population should not be left to old ladies in sneakers or seminars in Ivy League schools,' she told them.

'The number of babies you have has nothing to do with how many times you make love. Men don't have to have children in order to be masculine, do they?'

She went on mounting her hobbyhorses – and a lot more successfully than she rode the mules in *Sister Sara*.

She was again hinting that Senator McGovern was the man she wanted to see one day in the White House. Senator Who? Even if people had heard of him, they were saying in the very early 1970s they weren't going to vote for him. So why bother? The man and his campaign had Loser stamped all over themselves.

Shirley had the answer to that. 'Are we in the business of winners or of Presidents?' she asked. 'If you want an actor, elect John Wayne.' (Funny how nobody was yet suggesting Ronald Reagan.)

'If you want a President, elect someone whose moral fortitude is commensurate with the office. Anyway, he's not exactly running against Mr Charisma in Nixon.' Shirley was still certain that McGovern would run when nobody else gave him a Harry Truman ghost of a chance.

That, as she saw it, was McGovern's principal weakness. Having seen the senator at work at the 1968 convention, she was convinced he was the only one for whom people needed to work. He stood closer to the ideals of Bobby Kennedy than anybody she knew. But how did the senator convey his message?

Shirley knew that publicity was vital. She was helping him in that regard in every way she knew – and her praise of him was getting plenty of coverage, simply because it came from Shirley MacLaine, not because it was about an unknown and seemingly unattractive politician. She also knew that McGovern had to be introduced to others with clout – so she gave a party for him at her home, to which she invited everyone in Hollywood who she thought would give some support. It seemed to work. The Big Names lined up to be with him – which Shirley took to be reason enough to suppose that the California delegation would support him too.

The speeches were the things that got her noticed by the politicians and the newspapers. But it was her films that were seen by the public – or were not seen, as the case might be. The box office was not recording any sensations.

But she wasn't to know that when she made her speeches. She had just done a great deal of work which guaranteed her, one way or another, a great deal of money and she wanted a change. She couldn't have known just how badly that change would be needed when her work projects first got under way.

In September 1970 she signed the contract for *Desperate Characters*, which she was going to co-produce with Frank D. Gilroy. *Joel Delaney* would come later. And so would TV.

The picture would be distributed by the then Sir Lew Grade's ATV company – which was doubtless a sufficiently international concept to please her – and he was putting up most of the money, which made it more pleasing still.

It was part of a unique deal in which both were exchanging ideas at the speed of a Wimbledon championship match.

Grade wanted Shirley for a TV series, something she had not begun to contemplate before. Shirley said she would do the series on condition that he agreed to make the films – *with* her; she was only interested in going into movie-making as a partner now.

'I'm not going into television for you unless you go into feature films for me,' she told him.

She laid down her own law, which Lew accepted like Moses about to descend from Mount Sinai. He was totally mesmerised by the whole scheme.

'Lew and I are going to have some ceremony to acknowledge we're married,' she laughed soon after the agreement had been made. Since both she and the tycoon were already committed elsewhere, Sir Lew contented himself with sending her a present of a huge colour television set – still quite rare in the London of 1970 – but it was as much a token of their splicing the knot as any ring.

They had an agreement that the second film would follow and

then she would make the television series. This would be the biggest departure of all for Shirley. It had also already been sold for $5 million to an American network, before a camera was turned or even a script typed.

'He's an extraordinary man,' Shirley said of her new partner (which summed up their relationship much better than describing him as her boss). 'He says yes to everything if he wants to get you. That's how he ends up running the store.' The store *was* mostly in his hands, although his principal manager was going to have some problems from her side of the counter.

If the conclusion of the agreement was a marriage, then the meeting they had with each other setting up the whole scheme was a courtship dance.

Shirley reported 'a wonderful sense of rapport between us'.

Grade invited her into his swish office – expensively plain with a squeakily clean desk – ordered coffee, told his secretary he did not wish to be disturbed (which meant that his number-one business aid, his telephone, was out of action), locked his door and then proceeded to spend three hours lecturing Shirley on television as he saw it.

What he saw was a mammoth series that involved filming all over the world, which while costing a great deal of money would be worth it because the stories would match the quality of acting and personality that Shirley MacLaine would contribute. He made it sound irresistible and his star was ready to take one of the gold pens from his desk and sign then and there, providing her lawyers would agree the details, which they soon would.

In fact, the only contract they had was a letter which Grade dictated on an aircraft over the Atlantic and then signed 'Lew'. As Shirley said afterwards, it could have been Lew anybody. But that was of no matter.

'Sir Lew saw me in a way to make more dents in the American as well as the worldwide television market with what he calls heavyweight stars,' she said, obviously flattered.

The whole deal was attractive to Grade, who had a reputation for making grown men quake like infants on their first day at school. He smoked cigars which Winston Churchill would have regarded as too extravagant. He arrived in his office at the crack of dawn and left late in the evening. It was a lifestyle he couldn't understand anyone else not adopting just as easily. Shirley

MacLaine was his type of girl – not because, like most Grade favourites she was pliable, but for precisely the opposite reason.

The first of the movies, *Desperate Characters*, was still the number-one priority. It was going to be cheap – very cheap with a budget of no more than $350,000. It was completed, in the event, for $50,000 *less* than that. One of the reasons was the economy of the set. The picture was shot entirely in and around a house in Brooklyn Heights and Shirley even wore her own clothes – which wouldn't have pleased a wardrobe designer any more now than when Edith Head first took her to task. She took the subway to the 'studio' each day from her Beekman Place apartment – one of eight homes she now kept in various parts of the known (to Shirley) world.

Frank Gilroy wrote and directed the film as well as co-producing it with her, although Shirley was to do her bit in sharing the direction, too. As she declared in a statement which she didn't consider in the least pretentious, but perfectly apt: 'When artists' minds come together to make a thing called a movie, their sense of absolute feeling about it should be allowed. When Pope Julius wanted a work of art he didn't ask what the youth market wanted, he hired Michelangelo and went ahead.'

The film was about the loveless marriage of a middle-aged New York couple, with Shirley throwing away all her kookie conventions and getting very serious – as well as, much to her father's disgust, exposing her breasts along with her reluctance to change her state of affairs.

The fact that she was a partner helped her considerably and for all sorts of reasons – not least because originally Frank Gilroy said he had seen 'a Joanne Woodward type' in the lead role. But he didn't have that amount of say in the matter and as a result Shirley managed to escape from her hooker image. She wasn't going to make a lot of money from it, but what money there was came in a cheque through the mail and not in a bundle of grubby dollar bills left on the dressing-table.

Shirley said she was trying to fill a void in the American Cinema with a movie which she herself described as about 48 hours 'in the lives of two people who have the best that life in New York can offer – in other words, it is a horror story.'

The film was well received. At the July 1971 Berlin Film Festival, Shirley shared the Silver Bear Award for Best Actress with

Simone Signoret, who won it for her part in *Le Chat*, a tribute indeed both to her acting and the film.

Her experiences in Berlin proved almost as exciting as her trip to Russia. She, of course, went on a tour of East Berlin. At Checkpoint Charlie, where every other American visitor was flagged through in a rather perfunctory way, she was detained for three hours before the guards allowed her to proceed to the West. Then they made her pay ten marks and ordered her to have two new passport pictures taken before crossing the border.

They searched her bags and took everything to pieces – including a bar of chocolate which they carefully, very carefully, unwrapped before handing back to her. They didn't think that was as funny as she did. The trouble was that Shirley had now allowed her hair to grow long, almost to her shoulders, and the passport snaps showed the *Pajama Game* gamin most people knew. Clearly, the East Germans hadn't been to the movies of late.

Desperate Characters was seen as a reasonable example to other potential film-makers.

Reviewing it in *The New Yorker*, the eminent British writer Penelope Gilliatt said:

'If this picture makes its money back and goes on to do as well as it should, something will have been proved about the kind of film that can be made as long as people aren't greedy. Novelists and poets and painters are ready to work on spec – why not people involved in film?'

By that time, Shirley's interests were elsewhere. Her book was published, with a new title. *Don't Fall Off the Mountain* had confirmed her new role as a communicator who could reach people as effectively in print as through her voice.

The New York Times lumped its treatment of the book in a composite review of several others on feminism, although the reviewer John Leonard acknowledged that the autobiography was not so much a slogan as a poem, which was praise indeed.

Plainly her collection of odd bits of paper had worked.

'Miss MacLaine has not employed, and does not need, a ghost. She writes with grace and wit. . . .'

The paper was flooded with letters – some from people who thought it wrong to waste space on a book written by a

Hollywood star. Other letters claimed that it was an impertinence for a male reviewer to do the piece, since only a woman could get into another woman's psyche.

'Is she not allowed to have a brain?' asked Mr Leonard. 'And am I not allowed to notice it?'

The book became an instant best-seller. Suddenly, her value as an author was even bigger than as an actress. She was immediately persuaded to write another book. It was an offer she could not refuse. The next one, Shirley said, would be more of a novel, although she couldn't really be sure at this stage exactly how she would do it.

There was less doubt about her political stand. As if limbering up for the next presidential election, she was no longer saying that she wasn't interested in politics, or in the various fringe activities that made up the political spectrum.

Just as with the earlier theatrical rally, there had to be no doubt that when women protested against the expansion of the Vietnam War Shirley would be there among them, leading the crowd in what was seen as a sacred campaign. In the company of Shelley Winters and ten other 'well-known mothers', she called on the Women of America to mark Mothers' Day 1970 by protesting at the spread of the conflict into Cambodia.

They demanded that women all over the country should immediately lobby their Congressmen to make their view known. It wouldn't have made any difference, but people who thought like Shirley felt that it was part of the continuous drip-drip-drip of politics which eventually got a point through.

Later that year, she joined Bella Abzug, the most notable women's libber in Congress – as famous for her big hats as for her big body – and comedienne Joan Rivers in lobbying the Mayor of New York to support the idea of free abortions and child-care centres.

Even more effective, however, was the work she was doing for those Causes of hers in the Far East, which changed in detail as the years went on, but not in substance.

Shirley was responsible, she said, for about 114 Japanese orphans, helping to provide them with the necessities of life.

After all, she explained, 'I'm very rich.' And apart from her homes and two or three diamonds – earrings and the pearl and diamond ring given to her by Steve – she didn't have or want

151

much in the way of material things.

On her last trip to India, she had been terribly moved by the plight of 80 children rescued by a priest from living, literally, like dogs. The children had been sleeping in dustbins. They walked on all fours and barked – because that was how they saw the dogs among whom they had lived behaving. The 80 youngsters became her adopted children. She sent them money, she enquired about their conditions, got to know each of their names and what they needed.

Somehow this all seemed to be more important than the things for which the public still thought of her first, her film work and the TV shows to come. What excited Shirley professionally was contemplating the time when she would direct her own film. That would happen soon, she assured people. But it wasn't as important to her as helping the poor and the homeless.

Meanwhile, Shirley continued to live in her big house in California and in her seven other abodes. Was there anything incongruous in that? Not really, but people thought there was. 'I'm very rich,' she said again – no more statements about needing the money for travel. 'But I don't feel I have to live in a block with them to help. I still want a nice house and I've earned the right to live in it. You've got to keep some balance.' She thought she best showed that balance in the work from which she became 'very rich'.

The Possession of Joel Delaney might have been seen as being as unbalanced in its appeal as *Desperate Characters* undoubtedly was. Neither was aimed at the mass market which caught up with *Sweet Charity* (but which didn't help it make any great fortune yet).

It was about another crazy, mixed-up woman living in New York – this time on the East Side – who, though wealthy, never seemed to have enough money for the clothes she bought compulsively. Not exactly type-casting. Shirley worried about that, couldn't see herself wearing a mink cape, as the script said that she should. (Her days of wanting to show off at the airport were long over.) But she liked this mink so much, she felt as if she were living in it – and decided to wear it all winter. It looked quite classic, she concluded.

That was only part of the story, however. In the film, she gets mixed up with a strange group of Puerto Ricans who are involved in the occult, ritual murder and the sort of things that Shirley MacLaine was not known to encourage.

Shirley played the elder sister of the said 'possessed' Joel Delaney, which accounted for the profusion of diabolical items left casually lying around his apartment, like a severed head and the required amount of blood to go with it.

This picture, too, was shot on location in Manhattan, some of it in the New York Public Library, where she browsed through books, looked up newspapers and pondered her new hat, surrounded by people who really were at the library simply to browse through books and look up newspapers.

There were those who would disparage Shirley's conversion to the world of semi haute couture. Not at all: she saw it as all part of the actress's craft, and since she never tried to get too deeply under the skin of her characters – at least not to take their characteristics home with her – it didn't bother her. And yet there did seem to be something peculiarly infectious about her proximity to the products of the American rag trade.

'Whatever you put on your skin is a sign of what you are,' she told *The New York Times*'s Bernadine Morris. 'All of us who say we don't care what we wear are not being honest.'

More than that, she believed she could tell a woman's personality from the clothes she wore – the way some people can from looking at strangers' bookshelves. When she went to London, she took off for Carnaby Street and the King's Road. The Swinging Sixties were over and clothes had settled down to what La MacLaine took to be the normal state of affairs. Colours were drab. The dresses covered every inch of visible flesh below the neck and Shirley said she just knew everyone was going to vote Conservative at the next election – which they did. Nobody, it must be said, thought of employing Shirley as a one-woman opinion poll, using women's dresses as her sample, but it might have been a good idea.

The *Joel Delaney* film was based on a book which Shirley had read and thought would make an ideal vehicle for herself. She saw it, she said, as 'an elegant mixture of the psychological and the occult'.

Writing in the *Illustrated London News*, Michael Billington commented: 'Some see the film as a political allegory; I see it as a piece of political tosh.'

But Shirley also saw it as a business proposition – again working from a private home, this time the luxury apartment of one Carol Haussman on Central Park South. She found it no more difficult to read a balance sheet or a projected film's budget than she did to study a script. When she was given a book, she automatically sized it up for its movie possibilities, and once having decided she did want to turn it into a film, was able to work out to a close dollar how much it would cost to put in the camera.

Even so, she was confessing that she wasn't likely to make much money from films any more. No more cheques for $800,000 were likely to come her way. But she didn't need the money now and there would still be enough from *Delaney*, no doubt, to pay for the next lot of tickets she was intending to buy and at least a few nights in a luxury hotel somewhere far away.

That didn't mean that she had reconciled herself to no longer being a star. The amount of press interest in her was indicating that her role was very well established.

'If the word "star" means anything at all, it means an image of identification. People go to movies to see people. The star has to have something in his or her personality the audiences will respond to. If I have it fine, but I always thought of myself as somebody in this business.'

As an independent star-producer in the early 1970s, Shirley MacLaine was showing that she had come right up to date with the way films were being made. The studio system had gone and even the biggest stars could no longer just sit back and wait for work to find them.

What was perhaps more significant about the making of this film, however, was the way she worked. To younger, less experienced players Shirley took on the mantle of earth mother and teacher – an elder stateswoman's role which was comparatively new to her.

Now, though, she recognised that there were responsibilities in being a top star, not least to those working with her: those who looked up to her. Shirley MacLaine, star, became Shirley MacLaine, teacher. One of those she taught was the picture's juvenile lead, Perry King, who in more recent years has become known as a TV star.

Perry played the title role and as such was Shirley's brother. In the movie he calls most of the shots, some of which were pretty deadly. On the studio floor, it was Miss MacLaine who ran everything – much to King's eternal gratitude.

'She taught me a very great deal,' King told me, recalling the 1970 shooting of *Delaney*.

'Shirley's powerful, dynamic. But you can't go and play games with her. You have to know what you're doing.'

Therefore, despite her willingness to teach, there was also an unreadiness to accept fools or the uninitiated gladly. Whoever came into contact with her soon found out that there had to be a two-way contribution – and that went as much for discussing politics as how the movie was going to be shot. You talked Republicans v Democrats or Americans against the South Vietnamese at your peril.

'If you *did* discuss politics with her, you'd have to have a very strong argument to offer,' said King.

It was the time Shirley was planning her first TV series, 'and she had a million things going on. She was deeply involved in the production of the film at the same time. All I could do was concentrate on my films.

'She was a tremendous person to have around one at a time like that,' he told me.

'The thing that was important in my mind was that this was my first experience of film.' Real film, that is. He had taken part in a student movie while at Yale. This was very different. And very difficult.

'No one knew what the hell was happening,' he said. 'Everybody was frantic. I was trying to do my work, but it wasn't going very well.'

It was in one of those 'not going very well' moments that he felt a light, feminine hand on his shoulder. 'Perry,' said a seemingly dismembered voice, 'you missed your cue.'

As he says, he 'didn't know what the hell was happening'. Shirley, probably remembering her troubles with Hal Wallis, her frustrations with Hitchcock and Wyler, decided to come to his aid. She knew he was in trouble, she understood he was flummoxed by the crowds of technicians and extras around, by the people who seemed to treat any film set like Grand Central Station. So she ordered the set closed.

Someone complained that there wasn't enough time for all the inconvenience a closed set could bring. He was a senior executive. 'Screw you!' said Shirley and the set was closed according to her instructions.

'She gave me a detailed film course in half an hour,' Perry King remembered. 'She ran through the whole litany of film techniques. If you worked on a film set for a week, you might at the end of that week find out what a mark was. Shirley explained why the mark was there – and a whole lot more detailed matters. She saved me from having to learn stuff for years to come. It was one of the nicest things that ever happened to me.'

A number of actors have been able to recall the contribution to their careers made by the stars of the films on which they worked in their early days. A larger number can tell a very different tale – about how they were considered something less than the hard-working, hard-learning beginners that they were trying to be. As King says, it made such a deep impression on him that he vowed one day to return the compliment. 'Now I try to behave that way to beginners working with me – thanks to Shirley MacLaine.

'I may not be able to close the set down the way she could, but she was right to do it. She knew that if someone didn't take me outside at that very moment, we'd be wasting a lot more time explaining what was going on while we were supposed to be shooting.'

That was one side of Shirley MacLaine that Perry saw. The helpful Shirley, the considerate Shirley, the Shirley who respected the efforts of one who was desperately trying to make his way in a very tough business.

He also saw the other side of her. 'When she felt someone was not doing their best, there was less than respect from her,' he remembered. 'Respect? There was even contempt.'

That was something other people were to notice, like the assistant director working on the movie who she felt could have put a deal more enthusiasm into the task, a dogsbody job at the best of times – he's the fellow who at the peak of his day is allowed to call out 'Quiet please'. Shirley told him what she thought.

'She fairly slammed into him,' King said.

'But to me the kindness continued. I remember once I was in her key light. She just moved out of my way. There was an incredible patience.'

When she discovered that someone else on the set was giving King a hard time, she let him know that was not something she was very happy about. Teasing a younger, less confident actor was considered very cowardly, and this man was laying into the most junior member of the cast. Shirley flattened him like Muhammad Ali in the ring with a junior school flyweight. Her words were more cutting than any blow from a gloved hand. The man was a bully who looked like a sheep for most of the rest of the filming.

She took Perry aside and gave him the advice of a mother sending her child off to school on his first day away from home. 'Never pick a fight unless you have to – and if you need to, figure out the way to destroy him straight away. If you have to fight, fight to win.'

There were other lessons for less experienced players. The ever busy Shirley MacLaine, then 36 years old, had discovered the art of conserving her energies. Between takes, she took naps. She felt refreshed by them and was always ready when the director and cameraman were in a position to go.

King was impressed as much by the film as he was by working with Shirley. He saw it as the chance to play a young man who is 'basically a very good person trying to make his life work. His element of society – that of the wealthy East Coast WASP – is vile. It's dead. He goes to live with Puerto Ricans because they're alive. No matter how horrifying the living conditions of minorities are, the people still have a kind of pride, an intense realisation of what they are. What pride can you have at being a WASP?'

In that description he was telling everyone he hoped would see the movie why Shirley MacLaine was being identified with it.

At the very end of the film, Perry and Shirley were supposed to fight. Again, his inexperience showed. Shirley's hairpiece fell off and the fight was cut before any more damage could be done. Before long, it would be.

When Perry hit her, he really hit her. He moved badly, as a result of which she slipped, banged her head and twisted her ankle. She was sufficiently badly hurt to require medical help. The studio was in ferment, as though the place had just been struck by an earthquake registering two on the Richter scale.

157

'I just can't understand why we're not using doubles,' mumbled a man from Lew Grade's office, as concerned about the effect on the budget as on Shirley's rapidly swelling ankle and her laddered stocking.

'I'm sorry, Shirl,' said Perry. 'It's OK,' she replied and the way she said it sounded like a line from a film in which the heroine has just come through major surgery and been told she has six months to live.

'I hurt her very badly, but she said nothing, unlike other people who would have blamed me. I've rarely had an experience like that before – and from a woman, a real woman, very, very sensual.'

He had reason to think that. At the end of the fight scene, young Delaney has to plant a long, lingering but, of course, incestuous kiss on his sister's lips. Poor Shirley, after the fight she felt too bashed about to enjoy it. But it proved to be nothing compared with the battering she was about to receive professionally.

And now that real woman was going to require what Queen Elizabeth I almost said were the guts of a pretty strong man. She was about to take on Lew Grade and television.

Chapter Nine

SHE DIDN'T ADMIT it at the time, but Shirley knew right from the start this was a gamble she ought not to have taken. Her first steps into television – the odd appearance apart – were more of a leap, which perhaps she ought not to have made without looking.

In the years since, she has pulled few punches about saying she regretted making *Shirley's World*, as the series became. She seems to place most blame on Lew Grade – then still awaiting the preferment to the House of Lords which was to come later – and on Sheldon Leonard, the American producer.

In her second book *You Can Get There From Here* – which didn't turn into a novel after all and was to be yet another best-seller when it appeared in 1975 – she seems particularly upset about them both. More than giving the impression that they talked her into doing something she didn't want to do, she seems to indicate that both had some kind of mystical power.

Grade only had to walk into a room, she wrote, to revive flagging enthusiasm. He told her he wanted her simply because she was so well known, anything she did would be an instant hit – which was why he was going to pay her more than had been paid to any other star in television history.

Shirley herself said in those halcyon days when the deal was about to be sealed that the great thing about the tycoon was that he taught her to respect a medium she had previously despised as 'mediocre'.

The impression Mr Leonard left on her was of a man constantly at war with the amount of sweat he manufactured, who kept saying that things would be better, a promise she felt he was unable to keep.

The idea of the series was that Shirley would play a news-paper girl on a string of assignments that took her to various parts of the world – England one week, Japan the next, Hong Kong the week after that. Knowing that Miss MacLaine was not exactly antipathetic to the notion of getting on and off aircraft, it seemed that she now had a ready-made slogan of Have Camera Will Travel. It was, indeed, a very sensible way of getting round the world, but Shirley knew right from the very beginning that this was going to be no holiday, and the way she enjoyed seeing places was with the reassurance of knowing her time was entirely her own. Now she had Sir Lew and Mr Leonard compet-ing for that time.

None of that should indicate that she was a mere employee.

When there were shots needing to be called, she was the one who called them – and, according to some of the people who worked with her on the series, they weren't always the same ones being called by the director. But, as she had said before, the best films were often the result of collaboration between director and star. The only trouble was that these weren't under any circumstances the best films.

Mr Leonard might not necessarily have been after quality. What he was much more likely to be seeking was a clutch of money-makers under his company's belt. If he could do only a fraction of the turnover he had notched up with *The Dick Van Dyke Show* and others he was in for a new fortune – which wouldn't have been bad for the man who played Harry the Horse in *Guys and Dolls*. He played craps with Big Julie, who was doing so badly at the crap game that he insisted on using his own dice, which had no spots on them, although as he assured every-one, he remembered where the spots used to be.

Shirley's World looked much less of a gamble. After all, how could it go wrong? Shirley MacLaine was a Name. Everyone knew it and they'd watch it just to see her every week in a movie beamed into their own living-rooms.

What was more, even those TV stations and networks around the world who had hesitated to buy the series would see one programme and then positively line up to sign for rights to show the rest.

All that was very bad television business psychology. For all manner of reasons, *Shirley's World* was going to earn very little

Previous Page: With Steve at
the time she made *Spinster* –
or *Two Loves*, as it was
known in Britain.

Opposite: Even the beautiful
Shirley could look like an old
maid, or at least a *Spinster*.
With Laurence Harvey.

Above: With Tony Franciosa
and Dean Martin in a serious
role in *Career* – which didn't
do all that much for her own.

Right: With Jack Lemmon
in *The Apartment*, a
career milestone for them
both.

Above: Yves Montand wasn't alone in liking her Japanese touch – in *My Geisha*.

Right: She made a profession out of playing the sort of girl she portrayed in *Irma La Douce*. It was a role she researched in great detail. As did Jack Lemmon.

Left: Gene Kelly really should have played opposite her more. They looked good together in *What A Way To Go.*

Below: 'Hey Big Spender' – the girls from *Sweet Charity* – Shirley is in the middle.

Opposite: With Anne Bancroft. The two ladies spat as much as they smiled in *The Turning Point.*

Overleaf: She was looking much, much older – and that won her an Oscar in *Terms of Endearment.*

beyond the money paid up front to the various people engaged in making it. It would also prove to be one of the nails in the coffin Sir Lew Grade – whom everyone hitherto had regarded as the Midas of the entertainment world – was making for himself as head of Associated Television in Britain.

The series was originally going to be called *The Shirley MacLaine Show*, but was changed before too long to *Shirley's World*. Such a change of title in public doesn't usually augur well for success.

Shirley wasn't sure she liked the idea of playing Shirley Logan, the photographer. She was even less sure that she liked the first outline scripts. Above all, she didn't like Sheldon Leonard's sweat or the cigars he smoked – ever since that day she had emptied her stomach after sampling one of her father's Havanas, she and cigar-smoke weren't friends.

But Leonard was determined to keep her. Without Shirley MacLaine fronting his deal he had nothing to offer to all those customers. As for Grade, he walked into her room and thereby persuaded her.

The show was being plugged like a new recipe for Coca-Cola. As *Daily Variety* noted: 'Few film stars entered television this season with all the attendant ballyhoo of Shirley MacLaine.'

Before very long Shirley was promoting the programmes as though it was the most important commitment into which she had ever entered.

She saw it as a kind of *Perils of Pauline* adventure series, spiced by more comedy than Pearl White had ever been subjected to in her entire life.

'If I'm going to be in people's homes, at least I want to take a crack at bringing the world to them.'

She was readily caught up in all the hype that was being used to sell the films – which at times looked a little desperate. 'If I can communicate with 20 million people through a movie, then I can reach 150 million on TV. Through television I can do so much more.' The will was there if not the way – and whichever way Shirley turned, it seemed to be blocked.

When she realised that the series was not looking too promising she admitted in public that things weren't working out. She was apologising in advance – and explaining that even such luminaries as James Garner and Tony Curtis had caught the TV bug. Like them, she said she took it because it *was* work and who knew when she might be able to work again? That didn't sound like the Shirley MacLaine who had radiated nothing but confidence ever since the time she took on Hal Wallis single-handed – to say nothing of Mr Connolly.

Then she explained: 'We must do everything we can to get audiences back into motion picture theatres to see their favourite stars – and in stories tailored for today's demands in film entertainment.' So she saw it as a publicity campaign to keep her large-screen image alive. If people liked her in their homes, they would pay to see her in the cinemas.

But she wasn't publicly blaming anyone – yet. She said that her own biggest problem was figuring out her character. Like Pearl White, generations before, she would appear in a new film every week. It was hard work, but in a way the hardest part was working in something that patently was not giving her the slightest feeling of excitement.

Another indication of the way things were was given by the contradictory statements Shirley was making. One moment, it was the frank admission that she was merely interested in keeping her career going, the next she was saying: 'I went into television for idealistic reasons. OK, so I charged them an arm and a leg. But I didn't have to do the series financially. I don't *have* to work any more.'

She wanted the series to do some good. 'But it's very difficult to raise the quality of TV. There's the time element. But more than that, people running TV have a lack of respect for the audience. I'm sure the viewers are smarter than they think they are. I'm speaking now as a viewer.'

The plans were ambitious. After trips to the Far East, they would take off for the Mediterranean.

The series was going to be worth some $15 million to her.

She was being paid $47,500 an episode, which was believed to be more than any Hollywood star had ever received on television – Rock Hudson's $50,000 for *McMillan and Wife* was for a show almost twice as long as Shirley's.

In addition, because she was Lew Grade's partner, Shirley was in for a share of the profits. The forecast of her $15 million didn't seem necessarily over-optimistic. There were going to be 26 episodes and already Sir Lew's office was revealing it had earned £2 million in export orders.

But Shirley and her partner were as anxious about the other implications to the deal as they were about the TV series itself.

'What is important about this deal,' said Sir Lew, 'is the films we are to make for the cinemas. We are handling our own distribution, which means that when we offer stars a share in the profits they will get a real share. It will make Shirley a great deal of money. More than she can normally earn for a film and that is about a million dollars plus 10 per cent of the profits.'

The series would be run from Pinewood Studios, where all the interiors would be shot – which was convenient for the way it was being planned, and also for the luxury house Grade had rented on Shirley's behalf at Windsor.

The character she played would be based in London, where she also happened to run a kind of orphanage. It wasn't long before it seemed a good idea to find an orphanage willing to take a party of television executives, looking all too seriously for a place to hide their faces.

The first three episodes were shot in Hong Kong, which to Shirley seemed almost desecrated by the presence of the television teams. When these were shown to the heads of the ABC network, Shirley reported hearing one of the men mutter that they were only grateful the films were in focus. There wasn't much else that was right about them.

Before long, those first shows were dumped.

A new first episode was shot in London. In this, 'Shirley Logan' had the bright idea of blackmailing a member of a gentlemen's club – by having him photographed with a party of strippers, all in the course of securing an interview. Would anything stop our girl getting her man? Not Shirley. Not this new TV Shirley.

Imagine a photographic cliché and, you are right, it was used. The Guards were seen changing. Of course. The pigeons in Trafalgar Square were seen flying and landing on Shirley's shoulder. Of course. She was filmed at the Tower of London. Of course.

In between, she hosted a launching party at the Savoy Hotel for *Don't Fall Off the Mountain*. It was such a popular event that there just wasn't room to contain all the journalists who wanted to come. She managed to talk to one star Fleet Street man in

163

between the autographs she was signing. Shirley was so carried away by it all that she dipped her fountain pen in the newsman's champagne.

Britain followed America in awarding the book a place on the best-sellers list. PEN International, the world association of 'writers of standing' instantly elected her a member, which one would suppose was worth as much to her feelings of self-satisfaction as an Oscar.

Graham Lord, writing in the *Sunday Express*, said of the book: 'Not the sort of story many Hollywood stars would tell about their nearest and dearest.' As Mr Lord went on: 'Miss MacLaine's humility makes you forget she is a star. Her book is readable, honest and humane.' Most people who came across her at the time seemed to discover that, although not everybody knew all the details. There were things about her life that even Shirley contrived to keep to herself. Her freckled face still managed to smile more engagingly than anyone since the Cheshire cat puzzled the Queen in *Alice in Wonderland*, but about certain details she was keeping a very poker look indeed.

On the surface, there wasn't much to make her happy in London. She was even robbed there – twice. She still wasn't enjoying making *Shirley's World*, although there were times when she tried to turn it into part of her bowl of cherries.

Her co-star in the first episode, playing a down-at-heel, long-haired artist to whom she was offering her encouragement was the British character actor Ron Moody. Ron, who had enticed audiences back to the cinema with his magnetic portrayal of Fagin in *Oliver*, said at the time he was terribly impressed to have her as the lead in a programme in which he appeared.

He told me: 'I couldn't understand it then any more than I can understand it now. I kept asking myself, "What's Shirley MacLaine doing in a TV series?"' It was typical Moody candour, the Cockney sounds expressing a degree of incredulity few Americans would allow themselves to muster.

'I think she's one of the greatest clowns in the world and she's doing a TV series!' On the surface, that seemed to sum up a lot of people's doubts. Why was Shirley MacLaine wasting her time and her talents in such an unforgiving medium that ate alive other performers of note and standing?

Said Ron: 'But I did think then it was a great compliment to television.'

With the perspective of the passing of 14 years, Ron was less sure of both the show and the honour that Shirley was paying it.

As he told me: 'We could tell from the day we started to work, it was all going to be a terrible flop.'

What Ron couldn't tell was the kind of person Shirley was – not just an actress with whom he worked, that marvellous clown he was honoured to be with, but the woman who liked to say she saw everything from a human perspective. He says he just couldn't get to know her.

'And there just was no way I *could* get to know her. She was a different woman every time we met. I just couldn't be sure about her. I used to say "Cheerio" at night and she wouldn't even look at me, let alone acknowledge it or return the goodnight. Other times, she was all over me.

'One moment, she was like an old mate, and it almost got embarrassing. The next, you'd realise she had stopped being friendly and indeed had stopped trying.

'It was somewhat disconcerting. At times, she was great, warm, charming and quite intimate. The next, you knew she just didn't want to talk to you. She kept saying, though, that she was very happy to be working with us.

'I prefer to know where I am with someone. I like consistency because that indicates a degree of sincerity. How can you judge someone who changes so frequently?'

Ron Moody saw it wasn't going to work long before Shirley started hinting at her own doubts. 'Oh,' he recalled for me, 'despite all the money they were spending on it – a bloody fortune – it had the stamp of cheapness about it. This was like *The Saint* or *The Pretenders*. Despite the fact that it starred Shirley MacLaine and was produced by Sheldon Leonard, the man I'd admired so much from all those gangster roles he played, it had the stamp of an English serial about it – which meant that it lacked the polish and the excitement of what the Americans were doing with their television series.'

That was a point which might or might not have struck Mr Leonard or even Sir Lew. In any event, neither was saying very much about it. What they did know, even better than both Shirley MacLaine and Ron Moody, was that the series, which

Leonard had announced was the most expensive ever made (it was guaranteed an income of $20 million by that time, a figure many people were taking with a pinch of expensively-packaged genuine sea salt), was in big trouble.

Four times Shirley asked Sir Lew to forget about scripts that had been placed before her. She didn't like them and she didn't think they could be made to work. Four times, he said he thought she was taking it too much to heart, was being too critical.

But she didn't like the character she was meant to play – whom she was to describe as a 'banana head'. Being a 'kook' all those years was one thing, playing a crazy woman with a camera in her hand in her first ever television series was another.

Then there was the matter of the girl's morals. She was supposed to have a boyfriend in London. Shirley thought that was all right as far as it went. But what about when she was in Hong Kong? Or sailing the Mediterranean? Shirley thought she should have a lover in every port. Leonard, according to *You Can Get There From Here*, felt that would turn her into a slut. Which either indicated just how wide their generation gap was or how advanced the public's taste now is. As for Shirley herself, she was only telling things the way she saw them.

She would always claim that she and Steve had had an arrangement since they first began to live separate lives, that they would be free to have whatever affairs took their fancies. Shirley herself was in the midst of a Sexual Freedom that some thought was unbecoming in a woman of her age – except that she didn't look her age and she didn't feel her age. And that was the kind of girl she wanted to play on the small screen.

She said that it was her 'promiscuous' time. 'I thought it would be liberating for a woman.' She has never admitted that she was wrong. And, as far as she was concerned, she probably wasn't. There was usually a man with her when she wanted one. When she wanted solitude she got that, too.

When the first show was aired on American television, the doubts were confirmed. All of them. It was a total failure.

The New York Times's A.D. Coleman wrote:

'While my respect for her acting abilities remains undiminished, I can't help but wonder if the field of photo-journalism will be aided (or abetted) by its public image tailored to fit Shirley

MacLaine bouncing around London in the role of a photo-journalist.'

Commenting on the strategy Shirley Logan used to blackmail the club member, Mr Coleman added: 'If Miss MacLaine doesn't want to do the profession and the medium any more harm than David Hemmings did with *Blow-Up*, I hope she'll tone down the more arrant nonsense to which such series are prone. She could start by scrapping all those Mark Cross accessories. . . .'

Alas, it was too late.

Lew Grade wasn't interested in scrapping accessories. He wanted to scrap six planned episodes in their entirety. They were just going to be too expensive – no matter how cheap Ron Moody thought the series looked.

On November 16, 1971, *Shirley's World* was killed off by ABC, along with *The Nanny and the Professor* and Anthony Quinn's *Man and the City*, which had opened on the same night as the MacLaine show and earned the same kind of desultory ratings. It was a bare two months since the first episode and only eight months since the then *Shirley MacLaine Show* had been first announced.

The Neilsen organisation was being quoted as saying – unofficially – that the ratings were the lowest for any major series since they had started in the TV business.

How did it happen? It is easy to hold post-mortems. The difficult thing is finding a pathologist who will have the confidence of all the interested parties (although one of the problems with *Shirley's World* was that too many people had lost interest before any good could come of it all).

Sheldon Leonard tried to dissipate the damage – which he may have decided would be seen as an unpleasant reflection on his own golden touch with TV series. In typical American double-speak he said:

'Grade, faced with the prospect of continuing large deficits that couldn't be recouped, asked the network to abbreviate his commitment.'

Mr Leonard, a regular feature in scores of gangster movies in which he was never expected to be more articulate than was necessary to string together a collection of 'dese', 'dem' and 'dose', in his present incarnation never believed in using words of one syllable when he could find one with three or four. But what he said was right.

Sir Lew put it like this: 'Some 16 or 17 of the series were made and all of them were shown here (in Britain). To be frank, the reason I stopped them was because they were costing too much money, sending all those people out to Hong Kong, Japan and heaven knows where else.'

Not everyone was friendly or sympathetic to Shirley's case. There were stories of her laying down the law when nobody thought it was her place to do so, with the result that it took up to a fortnight to shoot films that should only have taken four days. Those were the schedules Charlie Chaplin had once had to work to – to say nothing of Pearl White.

To Shirley MacLaine, the actress who in her last couple of pictures had been delighted to swap huge budgets for quality and commitment, such attitudes were offensive.

But Sheldon Leonard was pre-empting what he knew Shirley was going to say about him in the not too distant future.

'ABC realistically decided with the rating the show had that for the price they were paying, it did not yield the expected results.

'If the show had had more promise, there would have been a desire to move it to another slot in midseason, but with extremely high costs, an amorphous format that didn't settle down to a comedy or straight drama, it wasn't particularly attractive to seek another slot.'

The show went out on Wednesdays – which was proving a difficult time for all programmes and not just *Shirley's World*.

Shirley, meanwhile, didn't blame Wednesdays or even ABC.

She told students at Yale's Senior Class dinner in December 1971, while the wounds were still open, raw and festering: 'Hollywood and television, with very few exceptions, are totally out of touch with the culture.' She said she was referring to her directors and writers.

Joyce Haber, the *Los Angeles Times*-based columnist who had taken over the mantle of Hedda Hopper, Louella Parsons et al, wrote stingingly: 'She'd better stop blaming Hollywood for her fizzles and devote more attention to her own career. She's a talented lady whose talent has gone awry too often – and talent doesn't excuse knocking the industry that nurtured it. Particularly when that industry is down.'

As soon as news of the series' cancellation leaked out, there was tension between Shirley and her partner, Sir Lew. She said that he almost had a coronary when it became plain that it had flopped.

The state of Sir Lew's health was as important to him as an insurance risk as it was for any actor. With Grade heading a show business enterprise, there were no problems with raising the finance or keeping a scheme going. But if he appeared to be in anything but the rudest of health, the mogul's bankability suddenly became a matter of conjecture. Probably, however, he managed to sway any doubting merchant bankers simply by walking into a room.

The tycoon didn't like Shirley's remark and denied it instantly. 'I don't care what she says,' he maintained. 'My relationship with Shirley MacLaine is excellent, the same as it is with everyone in the business. . . . We are good friends. As for having a coronary, that is a joke. I am the fittest man you will find in the whole of England.'

When the dust had settled somewhat, Shirley seemed to be a little more charitable – although her book didn't have charity as its main raison d'être. 'Listen,' she said, 'I love Sir Lew Grade. But people take advantage of the freedom and money he hands out and some of that happened with our show.'

Chapter Ten

No one was surprised that Shirley MacLaine took it upon herself to be a one-woman standard-bearer for Senator George McGovern – and then to be part of the huge party machine that was needed to put a man into the White House.

'McGovern,' she declared forcibly, 'is the only man who's telling the truth. He is the only man who is displaying any moral courage in the face of a possible loss of votes.'

In the meantime, she was analysing why she was in the election at all. Earlier she had declared her boredom with it, and now her campaign required a certain amount of justification, to herself as much as to anyone else.

She said the reason she finally allowed herself to be swayed was the prospect of President Nixon appointing three new judges to the Supreme Court who would reflect his politics.

Later, she would see McGovern in different colours, not all of them strong enough. But before the election got fully into its stride, she commented: 'I think that the only way we can survive is to do what we think is right, whether or not it will make us lose votes or hurt us at the box office. I know that whatever work I do for him is probably lost but at least I will be able to face myself in the mirror. I'll do anything he wants. I'll even give him talent lessons if he wants them.'

McGovern didn't – but it might have been a good idea had he taken the hint. Early on, however, things looked promising – until, that is, he had to face the Republicans instead of members of his own party.

One by one, McGovern started routing his rivals for the Democratic nomination, and one by one they fell by the wayside. John Lindsay; Hubert Humphrey, the nominee from 1968;

Humphrey's former running mate, Ed Muskie, who had made such a big impression last time and was seen by some as the conscience of the party, was defeated after one of those emotional moments that seem part and parcel of an American election campaign. Eugene McCarthy, such a powerful left-wing force in the early part of the 1968 battle, was out of the running and so was Ted Kennedy.

Shirley had told America that McGovern was their man, and now they were prepared to believe her.

For years, show business had played its part in running election battles. Irving Berlin had written campaign songs for Eisenhower and before that for both Roosevelt and Wendell Willkie. In 1924, Al Jolson had sung the praises of Warren G. Harding.

So Shirley was walking along a well-trodden path. Except that her footsteps were straying into additional territory – she was taking roads that no mere actor (let alone actress) had ever walked before.

Here was an actress best known for playing the role of the happy hooker, not just rousing support among her friends for the man she wanted to lead America, but actively making speeches on his behalf. Shirley was a member of the California delegation supporting McGovern at the party convention – but one who didn't merely wear a straw hat, raise banners and throw streamers around the convention centre.

It wasn't that Shirley had shown any great prescience about Nixon or the events at Watergate. She was, like many others, unhappy about his style of government, about the way that seven o'clock shadow of his seemed to hide much more sinister intent. Nixon had had four highly successful years, particularly in the field of foreign policy, he had established relations with China, and yet there was still the lingering feeling that he wasn't a man she would have wanted to buy a second-hand car from – if one could imagine the super-rich Shirley MacLaine even contemplating buying a second-hand car from anyone.

She didn't like Nixon. She did like and admire the hitherto underplayed, unsung McGovern and she was going to work for him. There were those who saw a place in the McGovern cabinet for Shirley (perhaps responsible for culture, the way that Melina Mercouri would eventually find herself responsible in Greece), but that wasn't on her shopping-list. She supported the idea of a country that had a man like the senator from South Dakota as its leader.

Not that she succeeded all the way. The first primaries were, as always, at New Hampshire. Shirley was on the stump speaking for him – although *for* him wasn't the immediate reaction of her audiences, whom she tended to confuse with statements such as 'McGovern has a lot of space between his thoughts'. Anyone who made a statement like that without explanation could be accused of having a lot of space between her ears. But Shirley knew what she was saying – McGovern spoke slowly and deliberately and, unlike Richard Milhous Nixon, didn't rush in to make statements for which he might afterwards be sorry.

Some of the other things she spoke about in that early speech didn't help much either. She said that, unlike other politicians, McGovern understood the 'bamboo theory' and about the 'inherent flexibility of Asians', neither of which statements, although sounding impressive, was ever properly explained.

Shirley was unflustered by the criticism. She said that she never knew what she was going to say when she got up on a platform or stood before a microphone. It had also never occurred to any of the McGovern staff members to present her with a written text before she started. But these were mere teething troubles.

McGovern was the man who was going to help her in her campaign to change the world. And did the world need changing! 'When man accidentally dropped a seed on the ground and four months later corn came up – son of a gun! he thought. I'd better own that ground. The property concept was born and from then on, we plotzed.'

She was sounding a lot more left-wing than ever McGovern himself had sounded and that, too, could be thought dangerous in the midst of an American presidential election campaign, but it was of no matter.

Within a day of McGovern's candidacy being considered a serious option, she became one of his principal public relations weapons. She was at once the acceptable – very acceptable – face both of the Democratic Party and of Hollywood.

So acceptable was she that there were occasional dangers that she might overshadow the candidate himself. She was everywhere, talking about everything – attacking Nixon and policies

173

on Vietnam, on civil rights, on women's rights. Shirley still wasn't burning her bra – although the idea, as another PR hype, had certain attractions – but she was, to coin a phrase, out front in the fight for women to be given the say they wanted on matters like abortion and equal opportunities. Abortion, she decided, was not a matter for legislation.

Her main worry was that Nixon would turn it into a big issue, with his right-wingers and their Bible Belt supporters taking up cudgels over the matter. Just as bad, she feared that McGovern would get into battles about abortion from which he couldn't extricate himself. 'He just didn't understand it at all,' she was to comment.

'My feeling about McGovern,' she said after the election was over, 'is that he was a conservative South Dakota farmer with a broad streak of missionary in him. He really wasn't and isn't a radical. His problem is that he wasn't radical enough. He believed in abortion, but he wouldn't tamper with states' rights. He wanted to see the penalties for marijuana decreased, but he didn't believe in its legislation.' Which, of course, Shirley did. But these were afterthoughts, or if they were before or present thoughts, she was not then in the business of voicing them.

She was saying so much about women's rights that at times there was a risk that she was overdoing it from the party's point of view – almost it seemed there was nothing else to say, and there were those who wanted women's rights at the expense of men's, which did tend to give the word 'equal' a completely different meaning.

Her brother Warren was in the forefront of the McGovern fight alongside her, which was something of a balancing influence – although those who wouldn't complain about the preponderance of women's activities would now suggest that the Beatty-MacLaine family were getting too close to the man they wanted to be their candidate. Not being able to please all the people all the time had some relevance here.

Together with Warren and with Jack Nicholson and Dustin Hoffman, Shirley was one of the celebrity ushers at a $100-a-seat rally at Madison Square Garden – dubbed by one spectator as a 'rock 'n' rhetoric' gathering.

When McGovern, in June 1972, visited a war veterans' hospital at Newport, Long Island, Shirley went along too. One aged patient asked her in a whisper: 'What do you hear of June Haver?'

Another for months afterwards was telling anyone who would listen: 'I slept with Shirley MacLaine.' Was that how far she was going to get votes for the senator from South Dakota? Not quite, even in aid of the Cause. But she had sat down on his bed and put her feet up. It was also one hell of a line about the girl who was paid with money folded up on her dressing-table.

'Give 'em hell, Shirley,' called another new-found fan.

'I'd rather give 'em George.' That's what the mob wanted to hear, it seemed. Certainly it was what George wanted to hear. Shirley MacLaine was his number-one asset. She could also have been his number-one issue – there was always the danger of people alleging the candidate had more time for film stars than he did for the important matters confronting America, but that showed no sign of happening.

But always it was the place of women that occupied most of her attention. Shirley told applauding delegates at the platform discussion readying for the Miami Beach Convention that a woman's reproductive system was the responsibility of that woman 'and her doctor and anyone else she may wish to consult, but is not an issue suitable to a presidential campaign.'

It was a hard decision to take on her part. She regarded the right of any woman to have an abortion, if she needed it, as the most important issue that female Americans could be asked to vote on. But, more than ever, she knew now, it was not likely to be a vote-winner.

The words of the resolution were hers, drawn up after an all-night session, with just a break for hamburgers to ease the tempo. They were then presented to the convention. Despite the applause, the form of words was rejected – carried first on a show of hands but then turned down on a roll-call.

In fact, women's rights became one of the big battles of the convention and one of the issues over which Shirley herself was to have a series of fights with other delegates, not least of whom was the formidable Ms Bella Abzug who would not tolerate any opposition. Shirley considered that the important issue now was simply to get McGovern nominated and then, against all the odds, elected.

To help achieve that, she was spreading the McGovern gospel

among everyone she met. She was giving just one message to her powerful friends in Hollywood and the other contacts she had made in the years before: McGovern is the man who's best for America.

But these contacts were simply peripheral. More important were the ordinary men and women in the American streets to whom she spoke. Now that may not seem an easy thing for a star to do. Everywhere Shirley MacLaine went, she was mobbed. But this time it wasn't Shirley MacLaine going anywhere. It was Shirley Parker, secretary from Arlington, Virginia, who did the talking. For all the publicity machine working on her behalf when she was performing, it was remarkable that she could indeed escape when she needed to do so. It is a strange phenomenon of our times that often people fail to recognise the most familiar faces when they meet. Somehow, they just don't believe their companion could possibly be anyone famous or important. They may feel a person is familiar, but they are either too shy to say so or genuinely can't place where they may have 'met' before.

And Shirley Parker really didn't look like Shirley MacLaine. She didn't wear any make-up – and who had ever heard of a big movie star without make-up?

For three months, Shirley went from place to place, talking to people and asking them what they wanted from a new administration. She said they all gave her the same answer: 'I am worried about getting my own piece of the pie.'

So that was now her mission – to help divide the pie. And to bake it the way she wanted it.

The 1972 campaign was notable for one aspect of electioneering that didn't immediately strike the nation's attention. It was the year that the 'Clan' divided – on strictly political lines.

For once, Shirley MacLaine and the 'Chairman of the Board' were firmly on opposite sides. With Dean Martin and Sammy Davis Jnr, Frank Sinatra came out hard and fast for Richard Nixon.

Shirley wouldn't allow even her loyalty to Sinatra et al to come between the obligation and almost fanatical devotion she felt for George McGovern.

She was in apparently very good company. Supporting McGovern with her were names like Woody Allen, Billy Eckstein, Jack Lemmon – hardly surprisingly – Burt Lancaster,

Richard Widmark and Ryan O'Neal. Even Frank Sinatra's daughter Tina declared herself for McGovern.

But with the 'Chairman' and ranged against Shirley's own gang were Fred Astaire, Hoagy Carmichael, Glenn Ford, Zsa Zsa Gabor, James Stewart, Charlton Heston, Fred MacMurray and, of course and inevitably, John Wayne.

But, of them all, Shirley MacLaine was seen as the leading show business participant in the 1972 election. Had anyone thought of running a poll on such matters, there would have been no contest.

It is interesting to note that when she was introduced Shirley was now described as 'actress and author'. The soubriquet didn't hurt the political activities at all. It seemed to add a degree of respectability to a practitioner of a craft which, Ronald Reagan apart, never seemed quite decent.

Once having introduced show-biz friends to her candidate, Shirley was more and more involved in getting the campaign on to a proper footing. She gave more fund-raising parties on his behalf at her home.

She fought off complaints that he was less than sparkling on the platform – one man, she reported, said that he was better than Secanol – by emphasising his plus points, stating that he had the ideas to make America great again. It was an uphill fight, with Shirley providing the glamour the candidate himself didn't engender.

Whatever one said about Richard Nixon, it wasn't glamour that he projected.

But what he did have was a mesmerising power – and that worried her. He was getting to the young people and that concerned her even more. 'No wonder Nixon wanted the 18-year-old vote to go through,' she said at the time. 'The young are just as frightened as the older folks. The majority of the young are still hung up with the old values system. In Kansas I saw them give a standing ovation for Nixon. I saw them do the same for Bobby Kennedy. They seem to go for Presidents.'

Now she wanted them to go for *her* President, but it didn't look as if it were going to be easy.

Then in the late summer of 1972, she saw her dream come partially true. George McGovern was nominated with 1,715.35 votes, comfortably over the 1,509 required for the nomination, although right from the beginning, shadows appeared on the scene that were never thrown during the pre-convention period.

First Edward Kennedy, now heir to his brothers, turned down an opportunity to be McGovern's running mate. Then Thomas Eagleton was nominated and had to withdraw, after it was revealed he had had psychiatric treatment. By the time Sargent Shriver took over as vice-presidential candidate, there wasn't a great deal to be done to keep the Democratic ship afloat.

In her second book *You Can Get There From Here*, Shirley says that McGovern was publicly offering Eagleton his full support while privately trying desperately to get him off the ticket. (This is one of the irritating features of her own writings; an analysis after the event which frequently attacks the people with whom she had been seen to be so close.)

At the convention itself, Miami Beach had never looked so exciting – and, it must be added, Shirley had never looked more pretty. She might now be 37-years-old, but in a simple black dress and with her hair down to her waist she was stunning.

And she was forthright to a degree even Shirley had never been known to be before.

Al Capp, creator of the L'il Abner cartoon character, didn't like at all the way some women were behaving at the convention.

He didn't like Bella Abzug's statements about Gary Hart – who was to surface much more effectively in the 1984 elections. The Congresswoman had come out with the seemingly innocuous statement: 'Who needs Gary Hart? He's a 34-year-old kid. I don't give a goddam about Gary Hart.'

Shirley's words might have been considered more offensive. She had answered one critic who suggested her candidate had not gone nearly far enough by saying:

'You mean you want McGovern to run on a platform that makes it OK to fuck a goat on the street?'

Demanded Capp: 'What women do these women speak for? Our Mothers? Our wives? Our daughters? Our granddaughters?' Now Mr Capp had never been noted as a leading liberal in American politics, but he *was* voicing words that other people had been known to mumble to themselves.

(It wasn't Capp's first swipe at Shirley. In 1969 he had brought her into his comic strip – calling her Shirley MacNympho.)

Shirley seemed to be saying that she was taking it on the chin.

With her friend Ms Abzug, she became Chairwoman of the McGovern-Shriver National Advisory Council.

Yet again, the question was asked: why don't you run for office yourself? The answer, which she gave to *Playgirl* magazine some time after the subject had become a matter for the history books, was that it would be like using sex to sell the party line, and she couldn't bring herself to do that.

'I'd probably be a pretty good vote-getter, I guess. They need a woman, a pretty one, so that would absolve them of the responsibility of not having any women. I can't compromise, though.'

Shirley MacLaine was up there defending one of the great tenets of the American constitution. 'If there ever was a colonised race on this planet, it's the female race. There's no question about that.'

She was and remained part of the women's movement.

'One of the chief aims of the movement should be not to cry for the right to have as much of the pie as the men do, but they should endeavour to make a whole new pie.' Now, she was behaving as though the pie was already sitting on a plate and she was about to start cutting into it.

Anything to avoid the current situation: 'All that spiralling and spiralling to acquire more (money) and bringing it home and getting a good roll in the hay because you've brought home more. It makes the women prostitutes and the men their keepers. So when the value system begins to shift away from the property concept . . . I think you will have a natural move towards equality.'

Governor Preston Smith of Texas gave a speech in Austin in which he said he wanted to make Shirley an honorary citizen of his state.

An honour? Not the way Miss MacLaine saw it. 'Next time I'm in Texas,' she said, 'I hope I'm awarded this by Cissy Farenthold.' Congresswoman Farenthold had been an unsuccessful candidate for the gubernatorial nomination. The Governor, sensing the value of having Shirley MacLaine on his side at a time like this, replied: 'Miss MacLaine and I are both Democrats. That doesn't mean I agree with what all other Democrats stand for.'

The worst thing you could say to Shirley was that she was trying politically or professionally to enter a man's world.

'The only man's world I know,' she declared, 'is the man's prison.'

All this she said she was going to put into her next book, which would be 'much more challenging' than the first which, she now confessed, she had grown out of before it was finished.

About her next book, Shirley said, 'It isn't going to be about politics, because that isn't what this is.' Other people had noted the same thing.

If it weren't such hard, hard work, the whole election business might perhaps have been seen as just another means of gratifying that insatiable desire of hers to travel.

She was speaking at meetings, working on those speeches now until the middle of the night or what used to be known as the early hours of the morning. Such apparent minutiae as the extent of the black vote or the sway of the Jewish voters was now of almost intimate concern.

She was interviewed on small-town TV stations, the kind she wouldn't have had the slightest inclination to appear on merely talking about herself or her own work – which shows the degree of dedication which she was now applying to her political activities in the autumn of 1972. And she was saying all the right things – like 'I smell brownies' as she was being conducted to a women's luncheon.

That smell and that reaction to it probably earned Mr McGovern a thousand votes. There's nothing women party members like to hear more than that their cooking smells great. Faced with that, all other matters are as nought and Shirley, seasoned campaigner that she was now, knew it as well as she might have known how to hype a film – an occupation in which she rarely indulged.

She had so got the politics game into her system that she was now saying she wasn't at all sure she was even going to think about returning to entertaining. Somehow the gilt had gone from show business. The election campaign was one way of 'performing' in public, which was supposedly in her blood for good, and achieving something at the very same time. It seemed worthwhile and she was getting some of the best notices of her life.

Newsweek magazine was praising her for being 'fiercely eloquent. She was eloquent, articulate – and elegant now. She looked marvellous on the stump, she sounded wonderful turning phrases around that exquisitely expressive mouth. The freckles reflected the sunlight and the sunlight seemed trained on her like a giant spot.'

There were no four-letter words for these audiences; no sentences that had no middles and ends, no obscure statements which may have sounded good to her, but which meant absolutely nothing to anyone else. Shirley was a politician's politician and the rest of the campaign could have done with someone like her.

No one was suggesting that she herself run for President, but had the Democrats' campaign had someone half as attractive at its head, the result might have been very different.

Shirley liked McGovern, but to most Americans – and the polls were more than indicating this long before the November election day arrived – he was still lacklustre, with little of the charm voters liked to see in candidates who had a chance of winning.

She knew that herself. 'I'd rather have a candidate who mumbles than a candidate who murders,' she said at the time – which might have been seen as a reflection on Richard Milhous Nixon but which fortunately for her and for the then candidate was not taken as such by him.

But she did say that the President was a 'crook'. Considering that, again, Watergate wasn't even beginning to be a real issue – aside from the burglary itself – that remark could be seen now as being as intuitive as her initial backing of McGovern's candidacy.

But she was getting more and more unhappy with the way things were going. She complained that McGovern wasn't well organised, that he told her one thing, his aides another. In her book, she said she was mostly concerned that he felt so uncomfortable with women, which, of course, gave her even more reason to work for him, another gulf for her to help him cross.

Sometimes, Shirley seemed like the old gal a few observers wanted to see and the one others were afraid would surface.

'You're a very precise young man,' she told one party official who seemed so pleased he fairly blushed. His face all but burned to a cinder when she added: 'How are you in the hay? Do you rumple the sheets?'

'We squirmed and we wanted to die,' one leading party man subsequently elected to the United States Senate told me, remembering that occasion. 'Any one of us would have given a fortune to get between those sheets with Shirley – she was so sensuous even when she was asking for votes – but to come out in the open and say so! Ladies didn't do that sort of thing. But this was a different kind of lady and she must have won five votes for every one that she lost.'

She also raked in the money. 'I'll go to Acapulco with anyone who'll give $5,000 to the campaign,' she said on more than one occasion – and on more than one occasion her offer was taken up. She didn't accept. Sometimes, she recognised that there was more at stake than the mere election of a President of the United States.

Her notions were clever and well thought-out. An offer like hers, on the whole, did no harm at all. She was at once assuring the women's vote that she was supporting it with all her might – showing she was master if not mistress of the sex game – and pleasing men, gratified to know that she was not above a tickle as well as a slap; this woman was a woman for a' that.

Other people did doubt that McGovern was the right man to wave the Democrats' banner. Could he really be wearing the shoes of the Kennedys?

Like Bobby Kennedy, Shirley talked of a gentle society. 'I don't think that's idealistic,' she said. 'I don't think that's naive. I don't think that's impractical. But I do believe it takes George McGovern to accomplish it.'

Once more, she had earned herself points that were in turn earning George McGovern's gratitude.

'As an artist, I care for the feelings of people,' she had said in New Jersey. 'As an artist, I have to study the feelings of the people I portray in my films. As an artist, I think I am privileged to obtain a special insight into the way people live and respond to the issues of our time.'

Another plus for being an artist, another reason for George McGovern to plant a huge kiss on the MacLaine cheek next time they met. That, too, did him more good than a dozen hours of talk about budget deficits and nuclear proliferation. Certainly, people cared about such things, but the votes came from those whose politics lay in deciding whether to buy a big or small tub of popcorn when they went to the movies.

'My reading of America,' she said (adding that this was based on her travels from one end of the country to the other) was that people were 'confused, that they are anxious, that they are angry at the way some of their political leaders are governing.'

And then came the answer the Democratic machine had been waiting to hear, spelled out firmly and finely: 'What Shirley MacLaine is doing is not performing but responding viscerally to the anguish of America and responding in a positive, activist manner.'

There were plenty who didn't think film stars knew the word 'visceral', so it was good to have one who didn't just know the word, but actually used it.

That was not to say that Shirley didn't perform in the course of the campaign. With Chita Rivera, Gwen Verdon and 'Mama' Cass Elliott, she went on stage at yet another women's rally at Madison Square Garden and danced and sang. The occasion was called a 'Star-Spangled Women for McGovern' affair. It was that.

Mrs Rose Kennedy, matriarch of the clan and – as some saw it – of the party, headed the list of distinguished guests and George McGovern's wife Eleanor made her first appearance of the campaign after an illness. But it was Shirley and her fellow troopers performing a parody of the *Damn Yankees* number 'You Gotta Have Heart' that brought this huge house down:

'When the polls say you'll never win, that's when the grin should start.'

'Voting for George McGovern,' the people at Madison Square Garden were told, 'is never having to say you're sorry.'

She wasn't always sure, however, of what to say to which audience – and sometimes it *had* to be sorry. Sometimes, too, her explanation was even harder to take than the initial mild offence.

She told a meeting of black women: 'What George McGovern is asking us is to evaluate our reverence for money.'

It didn't work out at all. Afterwards, she was told by one of the

183

women organisers that blacks didn't want to be left out of a share in all the goodies of the world.

Shirley hadn't 'evaluated the reverence for money' of an important voting group. To make things worse, she explained that she couldn't understand what had gone wrong. She simply found herself flanked by 'a sea of hats with fruit on them'. The women she was speaking to considered themselves middle-class wives of successful middle-class husbands. They didn't want white folks to think of them as having been part of a revival prayer meeting.

'That was very unusual of Shirley,' said the senator who now looks back on the 1972 election as demonstrating a kind of long-lost campaign art.

'She had a political antenna that all too few professional politicians have ever had. She got you to go to a meeting because you were going to see some glamour. You stayed because you were hearing a political argument you hadn't even considered before. That was an artist's art I hadn't experienced until then.'

Her right to 'perform' on the election platform as much as on the entertainment stage became the topic for conversations she had with party leaders, for her own speeches and even the subjects of articles she was writing. *The New York Times* invited her to write for the paper on this very subject, which would have been no mean compliment in itself, had she not already more than proved her capabilities as a writer and, more significantly, as a reporter.

'If I use celebrity status and the platform of the campaign trail to influence people, it is because I am seeking to affect human decisions. In a way, artists are historians of human feeling because people are our teachers and their lives are our classrooms.'

People liked to read that sort of thing apparently, particularly because Shirley was able so articulately to relate what she was doing now on behalf of George McGovern to what she had done on the screen.

This was not the moment to remember the 'kook' parts she had played or the women who worked looking to the ceiling.

It didn't mean that there were no crowds who wanted to know when she was next making a film. They asked about Warren and, of course, her views on sexual morality. 'I advocate sexual freedom in everything,' she said – which might or might not have been worth a few votes for Mr McGovern. (It tended to confirm his view that with such help he was on a hiding to nothing.)

There was quite a lot Shirley was prepared to do on behalf of this Cause. At a party she sang a version of the Alan J. Lerner-Fritz Loewe song from *My Fair Lady*, 'I've Grown Accustomed To Her Face'. That song, too, was parodied with subtle political overtones. Afterwards, she auctioned the manuscript of the new piece – for $1,000 which went, of course, to McGovern funds. It would have been a very hard-hearted group of party-goers who refused to co-operate in a scheme like that.

There were those who were convinced it was now only a matter of time before she took the step many had been forecasting for years. She was about to run for office herself, they said, maybe for the Senate, possibly for the next governor's seat that became vacant at the 1974 elections, perhaps even just feeling her way with an attempt at the House of Representatives.

No, she said, she was still not even considering such a thing. For the moment at least, she was George's girl and that was how things were going to stay.

Shirley MacLaine wasn't a Jane Fonda, who lobbied and fought. 'I've worked *inside* the Establishment,' she was to admit when the election was just a memory – a deep, sometimes bitter memory, but from her past just the same – 'and I always will. I don't see myself on the outside, saying: "Now I'm gonna tell you what's wrong with you." '

She turned down three picture offers to stay in the McGovern race. Shirley MacLaine was not going to have it said that she welched on promises, apart from those to go to Acapulco, that is.

She kept in touch with what seemingly had *been* her business. On a plane to New Mexico, she met Marlon Brando. It took some courage, she was to admit, but she went up to him and said she thought his performance in *Last Tango in Paris* was the finest thing she had ever seen. He was so shy, he blushed.

Her schedule now resembled that of an American tourist hauled out of bed one moment, shunted on to a bus the next, given a plastic lunch set in the middle of the day. It usually seemed funny to the tourists – after all, they even made a movie about them, called *If it's Tuesday, it Must be Belgium*. Shirley's schedule was now so gruelling, so unmitigatingly tough, with no tours of Roman ruins thrown in, that at times she not only didn't know which town or city she was in, but what day of the week it was to tie in with her timetable.

When McGovern himself couldn't attend a steelworkers' meeting at Atlantic City in New Jersey, Shirley deputised for him. The relief and the excitement were audible. It was the best bit of understudying she had done since *The Pajama Game*. She told them that McGovern was her man, he was going to look after their next wage agreement – and added, of course, that he was very concerned about the pressures of their work on their wives.

Blue-collar workers were to desert the Democrats in droves in the 1972 elections, but there's no telling how much worse the situation might have been for them had Shirley not been there to speak to groups like the steelworkers at Atlantic City.

They gave her a standing ovation and a guarantee of votes that made the pile of McGovern ballots a little higher at least.

In the end, the votes weren't anything like enough. George McGovern was trounced by Richard Nixon who before two years were up would be trounced by Watergate and forced to become the first US President ever to resign. He earned his place in American history for evermore because of that, and all the tapes that helped contribute to the scandal.

Others will choose to remember Nixon's Enemies List – a group of people, including numerous Hollywood luminaries such as Gregory Peck, whom he would not have liked to have around him. Shirley was on the list too.

Four times the CIA ransacked her New York apartment but four times concluded they could find nothing incriminating. It was not to lead to a great deal of affection for the intelligence agency in Shirley's mind.

Yet in January 1973, Shirley went to Washington and sat with the Republicans' strongest supporters at the Nixon inaugural ceremonies. When her father heard about it, he said he was pleased she had at last got smart. But for Shirley, it was something she couldn't avoid. She went because she wanted to watch the enemy camp, and to find out how that enemy had scored such an enormous victory. The answers weren't forthcoming.

Perhaps that was the most worrying part of it all. Shirley had worked hard – harder than she could possibly have imagined in advance – on the campaign and come out of it with more questions than when it first began. What happened – not so much in the voting booths but in the psychology of the campaign? Why had McGovern not known more answers himself? Why had she been so enthusiastic for a candidate who so patently was unfitted for the task of trying to beat Richard Nixon?

Perhaps when the history of American politics in the 20th century is evaluated from the perspective of future decades, the freckle-faced girl who joined in the campaign of 1972 may still find a place for herself.

Chapter Eleven

It wasn't easy to get over the 1972 election. Certainly the start of 1973 didn't draw the events of the campaign and the stain it had left on her psyche away from her.

She went on fighting 'Tricky Dicky' Nixon. When he came to Hollywood to attend the gala dinner given for John Ford by the American Film Institute in February 1973, Shirley was one of the movie personalities who said he shouldn't be welcomed.

The President was at the time campaigning for a federal censorship scheme to be adopted by Congress. Shirley said that the movie industry should fight such an idea with all its might.

There was a row between the right and left wings of the film capital, with AFI President George Stevens Jnr begging to be allowed to get on with the show and not upset Nixon, who deserved respect.

As a result, half of the Hollywood community boycotted the event, including Katharine Hepburn and Barbra Streisand, while Shirley was placed on the whipping-stool for being a spoilsport.

Charlton Heston, the AFI's Board Chairman, was biting: 'The AFI has better things to do than get involved in politics – John Ford will be remembered after Shirley MacLaine is forgotten.'

Shirley took it in her stride. She couldn't even, she was to say, bring herself to hate Nixon. That gave her a few problems, but she had to cope with them.

Now she had to think of ways of getting it all out of her system. She wrote about it. She talked about it. She decided to go to China – and before she went, she lived the crazy, madcap life that people had come to expect of her.

Shirley herself didn't think her life was madcap or even a little crazy. She was just carrying on doing a lot of normal things, like in the course of an hour or so rushing into a flower shop to buy tulips for a friend, then to another store to buy a briefcase for a press agent who bought her some theatre tickets, and at the same time send an identical case to the man's secretary.

When that job was done, she did some shopping for herself. The girl who had never gone overboard on jewellery was attracted to some sparklers she saw in a window. She went in to enquire about them. They were priced at $9,100. 'Overpriced,' she said. 'I could have them copied in Hong Kong for $1,000.'

The fact is, she could. Shirley MacLaine knew most things like that. If she'd wanted to, she could have started a consultancy specialising in business operations. Shirley MacLaine, actress and author, was not to be trifled with.

When she went into a dress shop, she cast an eye over the stock that set the staff buzzing. 'Are you in the fashion business?' one saleslady asked her.

'Fabrics,' Shirley answered as though reciting a one-word speech in a new film. The woman asked her name. 'Mrs Sam Parker of Beverly Hills,' she replied. 'Oh,' said the woman, half convinced she recognised her from somewhere.

Mrs *Sam* Parker? What about Mrs *Steve* Parker? As that Mrs Parker, there was little pretence these days. She and Steve were in regular touch with each other and with Sachi in Europe, but both were their own people.

It was because Shirley's life was so much her own that she jumped at the opportunity of going to China, not because it was yet another trip, not even because she had dreamed of seeing the Great Wall and listening to Chinese music in its proper setting since she was a girl at school in Arlington. This time, she was going officially.

The girl who had made *Irma La Douce* and *Sweet Charity* had been invited by the Foreign Minister of the Chinese People's Republic, Chiao Kuan Hua, because he thought it would be a way of showing the people of America what the Real China was about. The apostle of Communism – pure Communism, the way they saw it – had discovered the capitalist weapon of public relations and communication and wanted Shirley to help get his country's message across.

Shirley, for her part, was more than willing to co-operate. A year before the election, she had looked with her practised political eye at the situation in China and pronounced herself both fascinated and puzzled by it all.

Even then, she couldn't understand why President Nixon was going to Peking, why Chou En-lai wanted to invite him in the first place and why the President accepted. Now she was giving herself an opportunity to find out, although with the benefit of a certain amount of hindsight.

The form of her trip was developed over a series of conversations. Shirley wasn't simply being invited on her own. The Foreign Minister's idea was that she would lead a delegation of other women, all of them American, who would then go back home talking about what they had seen. More than talk. Shirley would make a film about the trip – not the type of film in which she played one of her usual scatty characters or even a dour spinster or money-mad wife, but a documentary which she would write and produce.

None of these things was even the slightest bit resistible. If she had turned down three conventional film offers to help McGovern wage his election campaign, there wasn't anything that could keep her away from this idea. Hollywood would have to wait.

Before long, it was decided that this would be regarded as the first ever official delegation of American women to China since the overthrow of Chiang Kai-shek in 1949. There would be 12 of them altogether: eight delegates and four members of the film crew.

Despite Shirley's love of men, of their company and of the sexual comfort they brought and she needed, she enjoyed feminine society and this was an opportunity she had craved for a very long time – not merely to see that great, huge land over the ocean, but perhaps above all to work for the feminist cause.

None of this should indicate that Shirley was unaware of what she could be letting herself in for, that she could be used quite as much as the liberal commentator Lincoln Steffens had been used by the then new Soviet government.

Steffens, the political philosopher once known as the 'American Socrates' lost most of his following after a trip to Russia, which it was alleged converted him to Communism. He had gone to what was then Petrograd in 1919 and expressed great delight in all he had noted. 'I have seen the future and it works,' said the writer. But Shirley was determined not to fall into that trap. 'Russia doesn't work,' she said, and if she didn't see evidence of China working, she would say so. At least, she wouldn't claim that it was a big success story if patently she thought it wasn't.

She would come back to America full of the work done by the women of China. First-hand, she could report in a series of meetings and a collection of writings how women in that country were on equal terms with the men.

Like most other people, she had read of the women doctors, the women engineers, the women farm-labourers in China. Now she would be able to return home and offer examples of how equal rights could be put into perspective.

At the same time, she could find out more about those Chinese women for herself – how did they do those things? Did they lose their own femininity in the course of their work? How did they run their families? Were there not insurmountable difficulties simply because they were still women? How had they managed to throw off the superstitious practices that had been part of Chinese life for as long as the people had been eating with chopsticks?

They were the obvious questions. The problems she and the other 11 women on the trip – Republicans and near-Socialists, a housewife, a 12-year-old girl whom she had met during the campaign, a clerk, a black activist, a sociologist and a Navajo Indian – met were not always the anticipated ones: among them was a marked resistance on the part of some members to the basics of Chinese culinary fare.

One of the earliest problems was simply of identification. It was important to list the people she was bringing with her in the kind of terms the Chinese would understand.

'They asked for some peasants and some working-class women. I'm bringing them housewives, an anthropologist, a psychologist, a civil rights worker and an engineer,' she declared.

When asked why she thought she had been invited to lead the delegation, she replied in the kind of enigmatic way that the Chinese would be certain to appreciate: 'Who knows which way the Chinese winds blow? Maybe I'll be good propaganda.'

That, of course, was precisely what the Chinese hoped and was the sort of answer she ought not to have given, although there was surprisingly little complaint about it at the time. But even before arriving in what used to be called the Forbidden City she was saying things that made the collective hair of the right-wing Hollywood Establishment stand on end. 'In China, the equality of women is an official fact, an academic fact. In America we have not achieved it. I'm just anxious to see how it all compares.'

If all the other things Shirley had done, her marriage to Steve, her commuting on vacation, her work for George McGovern, were unconventional for a woman film star, none of them was anything compared to this new role she had taken on herself.

What started out in American eyes as something rather suspect was before long to become a matter provoking considerable admiration. If she and her party had gone to China – the way Mr Chiao anticipated things – to bring back news of the way the People's Republic functioned, it was immediately obvious that they were also American ambassadors.

Such a trip a mere 15 years before would have got her thrown out of Hollywood. But, even with Richard Nixon sitting precariously on his chair in the Oval Office, times had changed. The President himself had been one of the first to preach the gospel of détente on his own various trips to China, in his discussions with Chairman Mao, or toasting Prime Minister Chou En-lai at a state banquet.

As predicted, the delegation saw the women working cranes in the docks, saw them doing hard labour in the factories.

In a hospital they watched operations – including a woman having a Caesarean section with acupuncture as the sole anaesthetic.

At the Great Wall of China, Shirley delighted in parodying President Nixon – taking no note of the diplomatic nicety which stated that one did not attack one's own government when abroad. She said: 'This is a Great Wall. The American people is a great people.' Whether her Chinese hosts knew what she meant or not, they clapped politely.

They went to trade fairs, saw nursery schools in operation (for that was what women were supposed to be interested in, a judgment that may or may not have irritated the participants).

There were difficult disagreements between the women – were the children being programmed, did they really take in the love of work in which they were being drilled, or were they simply enjoying themselves?

With 12 women on a single trip such disagreements were bound to arise and they did, several times.

They met Mrs Chou En-lai, who told them they needed to look at themselves in order to appreciate the other people they were seeing. The Prime Minister's wife ordered the cameras to be focused, for once, on Shirley and her party. They were.

Shirley was impressed. She wrote in *You Can Get There From Here* that an 'exaggerated sense of competition' was apparently absent from much that the children learned.

In Shanghai, they attended a meeting of the Revolutionary Committee of the People's Commune. Shirley took to heart the fact that intellectuals were expected to work alongside the farm labourers. She said that the only complaint she had was being unable to photograph the Chinese spirit.

She and her colleagues saw women at home, in the sort of crowded conditions none of them had ever experienced themselves at first hand. Neither had any of them known prices that were so low and streets that were so easy to walk at night, free of dope-peddlers, prostitutes and above all muggers.

Chinese culture was not neglected. They were shown the art treasures and went to the opera – *The Red Detachment of Women*, naturally.

As if to redress the balance, a choir of Chinese children sang 'Home on the Range' for them.

Shirley felt elated by what she had seen and confused, too. Was China a success? Or was it simply one vast propaganda machine? And was it just the way the state superseded anything done by private individuals that allowed it to achieve so much in the 20-odd years since the revolution? There were no easy answers, but an old-fashioned, American conservative (like her father perhaps) wouldn't have been happy about the things that Shirley said when she came back home to America – things which resulted in her film, *The Other Half of the Sky*.

Shirley's film turned out to be a huge, artistic success. It didn't make anything at the box office, but then nobody thought it would, and Paramount were thrilled about showing it as their contribution towards international understanding.

In May 1974, it was one of the studio's prize exhibits at the Cannes Film Festival. Shirley went to Cannes, told the world's press about the marvellous experience she had had in China and paid tribute to her co-director Claudia Weill and Aviva Slesin who had edited the movie with her.

'I'm still trying to figure out why I felt so happy in China,' she told *Playgirl* magazine in September 1974.

'Communism,' she added – and here one could feel the bones of Senator McCarthy turning over and over and over in his grave – 'isn't negative, repressive, rigid.' When she spoke to Chinese women it was with laughter.

She was struck by the differences, not least of all as far as sex was concerned. There was no pre-marital sex in China. Nobody had affairs – all very different from the way things were before the revolution when in Shanghai the world's most expensive prostitutes plied their trade, with no Shirley MacLaine to play them on the screen.

'Sexual freedom in old China, moreover, meant sexual freedom for the male alone – and therefore sexual exploitation of women.'

Another time, she said that what struck her most about China was that everybody there seemed to have a potential and was content to be able to live up to it, indeed worked to do just that.

But she wasn't afraid of adding: 'Of course, it's a cultural desert, with no freedom of expression, no controversy in the arts or philosophy or thought. And for an individual like me, who disagrees half the time just for the sake of disagreeing, that's tough.'

As she said: 'Freedom as we understand it has never existed in China and that's why I keep questioning the notion of freedom, asking what it really means.'

All these were sensible, responsible points to make. After all, Shirley MacLaine had not only been part of a sensible, responsible mission to China – she had also just celebrated her 40th birthday, which she was regarding as a milestone not to be taken lightly.

She didn't think she was getting old, but she thought she was approaching the menopause, which had many attractions to it. She looked forward to doing without 'that crap every month'. At least that was what she told *Playgirl* magazine.

'You can't forget that you're 40 in this society,' she said in an interview with *Ladies Home Journal*. 'They won't let you. But it didn't really bother me. The numbers have never bothered me. I've always had the opposite problem, bein' taken seriously because I look so young and I have a youthful nature. I've got to say, "Here, wait a minute, mister, I'm 40-years-old. Take me seriously".'

She need not have worried. People had actually taken her seriously for a very long time – which, despite what she said, was much more difficult. *Everything* she did was virtually public property, and that was truly surprising for an actress who was now spending so little time acting or performing in anything like a conventional sense.

Having made the journey to China, filmed it, talked about it, she was now writing about it, too. The visit and the McGovern campaign were the main topics in *You Can Get There From Here*, which *The New York Times*, among others, reviewed enthusiastically.

'She is an articulate, sophisticated woman of the world, who can write as well as she can talk,' wrote Mel Gussow. 'One knows that this "guerilla traveller" will soon be back on the road, exploring another *Shirley's World* and writing another book in her brisk, unmannered style.'

On the other hand, in another article in the paper, Jean Zorn, a law professor at the University of Papua New Guinea, thought the book was a 'let-down'. She said it was 'rather like one of those with-it Elliott Gould-type movies that begins with all sorts of controversial issues and ends with boy gets girl.'

Shirley's work in *The Other Half of the Sky* wasn't universally approved of. But that is not difficult to appreciate.

The *Times* was at first angry about the documentary. Walter Goodman said it was 'propaganda' and that wasn't what he expected.

Shirley didn't merely complain, ring up the editor – which as everyone should by now have realised, she was quite capable of doing – she wrote an article of her own.

Propaganda, she declared, was something you didn't agree with – which many another protagonist, not to say propagandist, would recognise.

'Not only,' she wrote, 'does our Government engage in the exercise of propaganda but our non-Governmental means of communications are dripping with it too. . . .'

And she went on to lay right into the paper itself. '. . . While the *Times* can hire an out-and-out conservative like William Safire to defend establishment views, it has not yet hired an out-and-out socialist or communist.'

It was the same with Hollywood, she acknowledged, perhaps more painfully. 'It would be hard to name a single American film with a socialist as a hero. There have been thousands of cops, cowboys and Mafiosi – all of whom pay obeisance to notions of property and competition – but never a film about Eugene V. Debs, never an American film about Sacco and Vanzetti. . . . On television, how many episodes of *The FBI* have shown J. Edgar Hoover persuing his private files on American Congressmen, or wiretapping Martin Luther King . . . ?'

In writing that, Shirley MacLaine was doing the media and the film industry a great favour. She was pricking its conscience and making a note for history. Things were soon to change very radically. Before long, Hollywood would film the story of Watergate for the big screen and the small; the McCarthy era would be vividly recalled in a number of mini-series and semi-documentaries; Hoover would be sucked into a vacuum cleaner from which his various activities would be very closely scrutinised; the viciousness of corruption on both sides of American industry would be fully gone into. The results were not always artistically pleasing, but nobody could again claim that these were matters, issues or people that were being ignored.

If Shirley's comments had anything to do with the change, then her contribution was considerable.

Goodman had attacked the concept of smiling children in the picture.

'In my film it was absolutely important to show children,' she said. 'We were, after all, an all-women's delegation. Among other things we hoped to find out how the Chinese were raising children, to see if we could learn anything new about raising children in the United States. Some of the women were disturbed by what they saw, others were terribly moved. But the children seemed happy. I saw no children growing up with the rats and rubble I've seen in Brownsville, the South Bronx or

Newark. I saw no kids being carried off to hospitals at age 13, dying from overdoses of heroin.'

It is not necessary to point out that these things would, if they existed, have been kept away from Shirley's party –just as American hosts would have deprived Chinese visitors of seeing the rats in Brownsville, the South Bronx or Newark.

But it was reasonable enough to accept that these problems were not endemic to China and that a great deal the group did see was highly impressive to them. More significantly, it looked equally impressive on film.

She said that she and her group had seen a country 'where everybody I came in contact with was doing the best they could at whatever they believed they had the capacity for. We all came back feeling like *we* could do anything.'

Even though the collectivisation of everything did tend to take away the freedom of the individual, she believed that China had a message for everyone in America.

Most important, and most convincing of Shirley's arguments in her *New York Times* piece, was that, like Mark Antony, she had not gone to China to praise any more than she had gone to attack. 'I went to China to experience it. In the Soviet Union and the Communist police states of Eastern Europe, I was appalled by the paranoia, the unspoken brutality, the sense of all-pervading fear and repression.' It was not the impression she got in China, although there were no guarantees it would not go that way in future – or, for that matter, that the United States might not go that way one day, too.

'You come back from China realising that maybe Sartre was right in saying there is no such thing as human nature. You ask yourself, "Are the Chinese people really feeling the hope and love and kindness and serenity you saw there, or are they just conditioned to feel it?" And then you've got to ask, "Do we really feel we are free, or are we just conditioned to believe in the myth of freedom?"'

The 'myth of freedom'? That could seem like a kind of conditioning too – although it was fair to believe that Shirley's philosophising was nothing more than just that. She was far too wily a bird to be caught in a brainwashing trap.

Her film became a subject for considerable public attention. *The New York Times* was full of detailed correspondence about it.

Peter Rupert Lighter wrote from that bastion of culture and learning, Princeton, New Jersey:

'I feel compelled to express my views after enduring the Channel 13 airings of Shirley MacLaine's Chinese fantasy. Though I hardly expected a scholarly presentation of the current scene, I frankly was shocked by the group's astounding ignorance of China and, as a result, its members' gross distortion of the situation they find in China.' And he went on: 'Miss MacLaine's disgraceful film and frightening non-critical opinions will gain wide exposure.'

But there was no doubt that her views were respected even by the so-called Establishment – which wanted to hear her. Kingman Brewster, President of Yale, asked her to speak to the graduation class. The subject was of her own choosing. She decided it should be Personal Freedom.

And what about Hollywood? she was asked. Shirley replied that it was out of touch with contemporary culture. Some people suggested that she was biting the hand that had fed her so generously. Not at all, she replied. 'I'm a Hollywood product. That place enabled me to work, to find out what I am in my profession. All I want is to contribute to it.'

Everyone who worked in a profession had a right to express a view about it. Her views were all part of her own recognition that she was still part of that world and its culture. But – and here her fans would agree – she had been away far too long.

For the moment, China out of the way, the writing and the filming done, she was going back to being the Shirley MacLaine the show-biz community and its audiences might recognise.

The welcome awaiting her was extraordinarily warm.

Chapter Twelve

IT WAS GOING to be a different Shirley MacLaine, Performer. And the emphasis was on her being a Performer with a capital 'P' to add to the titles of 'Actress' and 'Author' which had been appended to her of late.

She was convinced that show business represented the society from which it sprang. That was why *No, No, Nanette* had done so well. America was in the midst of another depression and Ruby Keeler's dancing proved people wanted the same sort of escape now as they had when Wall Street laid its famous egg, even if businessmen were no longer throwing themselves out of skyscraper windows.

The film *Love Story* depressed her. It was a symbol of the sick society which had spawned the country's troubles. 'Warm treacle down my back' was how she described it. Well, that wasn't the business she was about to go into herself. She had no intention of making *Love Story*, Shirley MacLaine style.

But that wasn't entirely a strike on behalf of feminism. As she said, one of the ironies of the greater strides women had made politically was that the number of good women's parts was declining.

In fact, there wouldn't be a film from her at all just yet. But she *was* going back to work, and with a vengeance; in a medium she hadn't appeared in for a very long time. She was going back to the stage for the first time since *The Pajama Game* (election spoofs apart).

She was promising to be the most talked-about star in Las Vegas, the town that her former 'Clan' partners Frank Sinatra and Dean Martin had more or less taken as their own.

Two questions were prompted by the announcement that the

MGM Grand Hotel's showroom would be echoing to the sounds of 'If They Could See Me Now': why was she doing it? And . . . more simply, *what* would she do?

She was doing it because she had been asked for years to appear on one of the Vegas stages. And what she was going to do was dance . . . and sing . . . and gag about the films she had made and the people she had met.

But she wasn't going into it lightly.

The hotels on the famous 'Strip' had been asking, almost begging, her to appear for years. She always said No. The reason was simple – she was scared. But in July 1974, the answer was yes.

It was her legs, she was to say, that persuaded her to take this step at the age of 40. She had worn slacks for five years and forgotten what those legs looked like. One day, she happened to see them in the mirror and decided they ought not to be wasted.

And now the longest legs in show business were going to be seen at their best – cantering up and down the stage, allowing no one else to compete for the eyes of the audience.

And not just any audience. The people who paid the top prices charged by the Vegas casinos – to some, the entertainment was a mere adjunct to a day's gambling, to others the climax to an evening's wining and dining – demanded to be put under a spell. A very good performer, even one who was universally accepted as a star, still had to show that he or she had something special. Shirley showed it – and then professed to be more surprised than anyone.

Surprise was indeed the reaction of most of the audiences who saw her at the MGM Grand. After all, she had danced and sung in *Sweet Charity*, and a few remembered her can-can, but to almost everyone else, Shirley MacLaine was the actress who. . . .

Because of that, the rest of show business, it seemed, came to demonstrate solidarity. Sinatra was there and so was Sammy Davis Jnr. Warren Beatty turned up on the third night and said he was so worried for his sister, he was prepared to dive out of embarrassment, under his table, hiding his face with the crisp white cloth. He didn't need to. The cloth stayed on the table and he stayed to cheer.

It was these celebrity visitors who worried her, not the people for whom the whole show had been set up, the ones paying the money. She knew she could cope – and even if she couldn't, she wanted desperately to appear in this show. The girl who had lost the role of Cinderella could barely do otherwise. It was dancing she had done first and it was dancing she always thought she would continue to do. The new show would be both a vindication of her ambitions and a return to what she believed were her roots.

But if she did no more than cope, and was able to con the paying customers, what would she do to her friends? They knew better.

As she sat in her dressing-room, quaking so much that she wouldn't have known a broken ankle even if she had one, it was as though she had never done anything else in her professional life. The films, the electioneering, the trip to China and everywhere else were distant things that had happened to another person.

Steve wasn't around, but then she no longer had any reason to think that he would be. She wasn't saying anything, but that was finished.

Shirley had been thinking of that night for weeks – and of past nights, too.

She had suddenly become obsessed with reincarnation. Had everyone been here before? Did people really die?

If reincarnation did have something going for it, then the dancer at Las Vegas had been prima ballerina in a dozen of the world's great companies in her previous lives and perhaps a 20s jazz queen and a Ziegfeld showgirl to boot.

Whatever her past lives had been, she wasn't depending on them to see her through. She was practising for her new role quite as hard as she had for *Sweet Charity* and dedicating herself to it almost as she had in the election campaign and in China.

China had taught her the need for people to live up to their potentials. She was going to work as hard as her body and mind would take it – to live up to her own potential. And that was every bit as big as she knew it was.

Not a day went by when she didn't run on the beach until by the time the show opened, she was averaging a run of five miles each morning. She also had sessions in a gym.

Above all, Shirley was hiring the best people to work with and for her – at her own expense, which was why she agreed to the MGM Grand offer. It was the best that had come her way. She may not have needed the cash to eat or even to travel, but there was no reason why she should lose money on employing people like Cy Coleman, her *Sweet Charity* buddy, producer Bud Welles and Alan Johnson who was brought in for the highly responsible role of her choreographer – in a way the most important of all the important back-room boys and girls. She was going to be seen and then remembered for her dancing. She had 'borrowed' Johnson from Anne Bancroft. It was a good move. If those legs of hers were going to have any impact at all, they had to be more than just two very pretty appendages. As she said: 'I think people will appreciate something good if that's what you give them. Junk doesn't take as much effort or money or love.'

It was love she was promising and it was love the audience were expecting. But the money was important, too. She employed a lawyer full-time to run her business affairs – although, because she was Shirley MacLaine, that was not enough. She was her own manager, knew where every asset was and how it could be improved.

Rightly, she concluded that the best asset of all in July 1974 – those legs apart – was her audience.

When she chatted with the people, it was by way of a break between dance and song. She told them about her favourite characters – the hookers. She sang 'Irma La Douce', which she wasn't able to do in the film, wearing a tight corset and a big wig, which she *had* done in the movie. It was only in that moment of reprise that she looked any older. She might have confessed to herself that she wouldn't have got the *Irma* role now at the age of 40 plus.

It was her one stand for women's lib, telling the tragic-while-funny stories of women who have so often pretended to love that they can't do it for real.

She sang just one other number, 'If They Could See Me Now'. Then she walked off – it was a lovely tease. She told the audience that she knew they wondered what she was going to do on stage, this film actress who had also had a production in China. Well, now they knew, and she was going home. They loved that.

All great entertainers focus on one person in their audience. It makes the chemistry between entertainer and public work. Shirley had the same one every night. He was a writer named Pete Hamill and they were in the midst of an affair, a very deep, very warm, very fiery affair.

Pete was watching every move and, like Steve in *The Pajama Game* days, was free with advice. He sent her regular notes. 'The second dancer on the left needs bucking up. . . .'

The show was just how she would have wished it to be. And how Pete wished it to be. For different reasons, Warren was pleased too.

For the second time in his life, he was incredibly proud of his sister, seeing her perform on a stage. The last time they had been together, he had thought she had let herself go physically. Now, she was in superb form. The exercises and the work she was doing there at the MGM had done marvels for what was still a marvellous figure.

'I've never had more fun,' said Shirley. 'I'm in it up to my waist and I might go in it all the way to my neck.' Just as Sophie Tucker had said, life was beginning for her at 40 – which was perhaps the best kind of reincarnation of all.

The only problem was that she had to be so careful. 'How I get out of a cab, how I walk across the street, how I might turn an ankle.'

Cecil Smith wrote in the *Los Angeles Times*: 'After the horrendous flop of her television series . . . and a succession of movies that attracted few customers, Shirley MacLaine picked herself up and went back to her original trade. . . .

'Shirley dances beautifully, sings better than I remembered, sits on a stool and talks to the audience about herself and her career and the movies she made and the life she led.'

The show had everyone talking and was so successful it went on tour and was the basis for a TV spectacular put out by CBS that November.

Cy Coleman said the work was easy – for him. Shirley simply had to be herself. He was drawing for her, but not creating for her. He couldn't do that. 'There hasn't been anything close to it before,' he said. And he was right. It was one of those magnetic occasions, the kind that Danny Kaye had had in London and Al Jolson had experienced half a century or more earlier at the Winter Garden on Broadway.

There were six men and four girls on stage with her, but as she and the hotel hoped, you wouldn't have noticed.

In fact, Shirley was now saying that she liked appearing on the stage more than anything else she did professionally.

The stage, whether in Vegas or in the collection of theatres in the round where she played afterwards, offered her a sense of fulfilment she had never experienced before. 'I like films but it's technological,' said this most technological of artists (because everything she did was conceived, practised, gone over with the precision of an Olympics coach determined to be responsible for a new world record).

But there was always that pinch of salt to be given due consideration. Not long before taking up the Las Vegas option, she had said: 'The proscenium stage no longer interests me at all.' Yet now that was where she saw everything about to happen to her professionally – although there was a film in her mind, too. But, she said, 'to be a brilliant actress on the Magnani level, assuming I could, doesn't interest me either.' Was she being totally honest there? Probably not. She enjoyed the plaudits handed out to her for her writing, because she was given the courtesy of being regarded as a writer of talent. She loved people's reactions to her show because she was showing herself to be a fairly superior kind of dancer – all of which was only right. She would have been no less happy to be called a great actress.

If nothing else, Shirley MacLaine had a marvellous way with words. The words weren't necessarily all her own, or at least had not necessarily started out all her own, but she knew which words to use and how to adapt them to proper circumstances.

Jewish literature is replete with references to the fact that you could take the Jew out of the ghetto, but you couldn't take the ghetto out of the Jew. Well, Shirley happily adapted it: 'You can,' she said, 'take the girl out of the chorus, but you can't take the chorus out of the girl.' This was her demonstration of the fact. Or rather, it was how she chose to demonstrate the fact. Shirley MacLaine was no chorus girl. She was very much on her own.

There were other thoughts at the back of her mind. Since she met so many important people and since she did so much travelling why not talk to these people for television interviews? The idea never got off the ground, but if fitted her programme of doing as many things as she knew how. It also suited her current philosophy: 'If I could only do one thing at a time, it would exhaust me. The way I am happiest is to do preferably four things, but certainly no less than two and a half.'

It was as someone once said, Shirley MacLaine isn't quite a corporation, but she's pretty diversified. One had the feeling that she would have been very happy as a corporation. But it would have had to be a corporation in which the chairman was allowed to sit in her office, meditate the way she had been taught in the Himalayas and contemplate what she might have been in a previous life – an actress, a dancer, a singer, a writer, a politician, or perhaps a businesswoman.

Enough people were content with her the way she was.

She earned the unquestioned admiration of others in the business, which has always been the biggest compliment of all. Band leader Ray Anthony told me: 'She is one of those people others want to copy. They greatly admire her energy and her artistry. She has tackled more new ideas than anyone I know. Quite a girl!'

Sometimes her ambition and her demands were too much. More than 1,500 people showed up at the Chrysler Hall at Norfolk, Virginia – almost her home town – to see a MacLaine show and were turned away. 'If they could see me now' was how the show was billed, but nobody could see her at all. She said she thought the sound system at the theatre was bad. So she refused to perform there.

If she had worries, Pete was there – consoling, loving and working on the script of a new film for her, about Amelia Earhart, the woman who had been the first to fly around the world in the days when that was known as being an aviatrix.

They were to be together for three years.

'I've been with a lot of men,' Shirley confided. 'But Pete . . . well, the relationship is very special. He is constantly growing. And we don't waste our time talking about marriage and the future and any of that stuff. Anyway, who knows? It could all be over next week.'

She admitted that the way she lived was scandalous. 'I've lived so scandalously for so long that nobody really gets too upset. A lot of young people live together these days. But not too many at my age, I guess.'

As she said, 'the Taylor-Burton combustion bit isn't for me.'

But while she was saying that Pete *was* for her, nothing was going to make her consider marrying him, even if she divorced Steve, which she still wasn't planning to do.

'A divorce for me would be as obsolete as another marriage,' she said – which meant that she and Hamill would continue to live together, he clacking away at his typewriter while she telephoned studio executives or stage show impresarios discussing future projects.

Amelia remained one of her ideas for years. It was obvious why Shirley was so enthusiastic about her – a strong-willed woman who went out and did her own thing and all that. More than that, she was a woman who entered into a contract with her husband on their wedding day, decreeing that neither would ask the other to be quite so ridiculous as to expect fidelity. Shirley approved of that.

(So much so that she decided to take flying lessons. It was only when she started taking an aeroplane wing apart – to see how it managed to fly – that she showed any signs of anxiety about taking the step.)

Another notion was based on the novel she was beginning to write. It was going to be hot and sexy – with a central character she would herself play when it was made into a film. Suddenly, the 'technological' medium of film was looking very attractive again.

Maybe not as attractive as Hamill, for whom she felt more than a mere sex urge – although, as she said, sometimes it was difficult to believe that anyone could find romance after 35. But sex wasn't as important to her as it was to Warren. Her brother, who remained unmarried, needed it as much as he talked about it, which was every time he met a journalist.

Shirley enjoyed going to bed with a man, but she did not believe that any men really wanted to get married.

'They ask you out of a sense of chivalry but they're usually delighted if you say no.'

That was why she was glad she felt independent. When she and Pete went out for an evening, she would take her own car. When she did that, she knew she was free to leave early if she wanted to and he could stay on.

When she thought about it again, she didn't consider herself a good mother, either. She liked to think she still got on well with Sachi, now an attractive teenager who looked extraordinarily like Shirley – which was why magazines so enjoyed trying to get the two of them to pose together, wearing similar outfits and hair-styles – but she wouldn't want any more children.

The National Association of Non Parents understood this. The association had decided that if a couple didn't want children, there was no reason in the world why they should feel guilty about it.

Shirley was fulfilled enough in that regard whenever she visited or heard about the various orphanages that still gloried in their adoption by her.

Undoubtedly, the scandalous MacLaine woman felt as liberated as ever. When she gave an interview to *Playgirl* she called a spade a spade and men's private parts. . . . As she said: 'It's time that a lot of . . . things hung out. I think it's good, I mean the more all of it can be exposed, it's not so threatening.'

A writer on the magazine had been talking to her about McGovern and had drawn the suggestion that the former candidate might get rid of some of his hang-ups – if the phrase can be forgiven – by posing in the nude. Shirley explained: 'Once men begin to look at each other's cocks hanging out, they won't compare. They'll think everybody does what they do with it, everyone has their own way of doing their own thing and so what?' A verbatim interview always did look somewhat strange in print!

On the other hand, she wasn't sure she wanted the exposure anymore.

In March 1975, she was telling *Ladies Home Journal*: 'I am basically a person who would like to be anonymous. I'm basically shy. I would have been a reporter, a person who goes around lookin' and then writes it all down. There's a whole part of me that would like to give up being focused on so that I could focus *out*.'

If she had been a reporter, she confessed, she would have got too involved in the things she would have reported and once again been the subject of a piece rather than just the one writing about it.

Chapter Thirteen

SHIRLEY WAS NOTHING if not international – professionally as well as personally and politically. It was now only a matter of time before she took her stage show abroad, too.

As 1975 turned to 1976, she was on her way to London to open at the place which was generally regarded as the temple of variety – the London Palladium. 'Temple' was not taking words too far. To those in show business, there was something almost sacred about the boards which singers and dancers, conjurers and jugglers had trod for almost 70 years.

Neither was it just the home of English variety: stars and lesser performers had come to the Palladium and seen it as a symbol of their success.

But its glory days had been in the post-war era. Then, the Palladium had taken on the mantle of Hollywood Transplanted.

In war-torn Britain, American stars like Bob Hope and Bing Crosby had come into people's homes via radio shows that were principally intended for the US troops stationed in the country before being shipped across the Channel for D-Day. Many of these celebrities had topped the Palladium bills and given British audiences the chance to see in the flesh performers they knew from the screen. The war had seen a huge renaissance for the cinema – it was the one escape route most people could afford to take. For sixpence they could queue on a Saturday afternoon to see the American stars who somehow told them that life was still romantic and exciting and, above all, that America was the land where everything was almost gold.

Hope, Jimmy Durante, Sinatra, Laurel and Hardy, Judy Garland all came for a series of shows that literally took the town by storm. Week after week, they filled every available seat in a season that went on and on, eclipsing the famous British music-hall artists and even the annual pantomimes that were as much a tradition of London as the Tower and the changing of the guard at Buckingham Palace.

And then there was Danny Kaye. . . . Nobody had taken London to himself and himself to London like the red-headed kid from Brooklyn. For years, it virtually became his territory.

But, like all things, the Palladium, too, was to have its day. The Beatles had their time on the Palladium stage. So did Tommy Steele. So, somewhat belatedly in both his life and his career, did Bing Crosby. But somehow it wasn't quite like those great Palladium days. Until, that is, Shirley MacLaine played there.

Not that the early indications were at all propitious. Right up to opening night in February 1976, it looked as though a lead-weighted balloon would be locked on to the launching-pad. Palladium officials were so desperate that day that they were handing out free tickets to passers-by. There was nothing that they weren't going to do to try to make it *look* as though the Palladium were a sell-out on Shirley MacLaine's opening night at the world's most famous theatre.

Yet even that wasn't easy. The show business expression 'you couldn't even give them away' had never seemed more true. People were looking at the tickets and saying, 'No thank you'.

The reason wasn't difficult to find. 'The trouble,' Louis Benjamin, the head of Stoll-Moss Theaters, the owners of the Palladium, told me, 'was simply that people knew Shirley MacLaine but yet had no idea what she could do. They knew her as an actress. They had seen her dance a little bit in films, but they thought of her playing opposite Jack Lemmon in *The Apartment* and *Irma La Douce*.'

He was being charitable in not referring to *Shirley's World*. The TV series had been seen in Sir Lew Grade's home territory and Shirley, like everyone else, might have wished that it hadn't. *Joel Delaney* and *Desperate Characters* had made no impression whatsoever.

What did save that first night was that the theatre was packed with British show-biz; all the stars that the British film industry could muster were there, all the leading names from the local television world came along, too. If nothing else, they would

212

guarantee pictures in the newspapers the following morning which would inevitably refer to Shirley MacLaine and her Palladium opening.

As things turned out, she got her mentions in the papers and would have got them without any extensive ballyhoo. 'It was quite one of the most remarkable evenings at the Palladium I have ever experienced,' Benjamin added, 'and I've seen a few. Suddenly, the vast crowd we did finally get into the theatre that night were transfixed by what they saw. The woman whose power as a draw at the theatre was completely and utterly unknown to us all at once became one of the legendary Palladium stars.'

The pandemonium she caused, echoing precisely what Danny Kaye had achieved, was indeed uncanny – once more proving either how little the *Sweet Charity* critics had really known about dancing and Shirley MacLaine's talents performing in it, or just how much she had learned since engaging her choreographer and the other staff for her Las Vegas opening less than two years earlier.

This time, the British press were unequivocally ecstatic.

Reported the *Daily Telegraph*: 'It's a long time since I saw a theatre so filled with joy.'

In the *Daily Mail*, Roderick Gilchrist commented: 'For one of America's most vocal political activists, a successful author and campaigner for female equality, Miss Shirley MacLaine really does have a nice line in song and dance.'

Irving Wardle in *The Times* wrote: 'She comes on in a sequined black suit, like a one-girl light show and leads off shyly with "If They Could See Me Now" and by the time she and her five-strong company have built it up to the top, the place is ringing with exultant shouts.'

He was particularly taken with Shirley's mock walk-out after the first number, now well honed and seen by people all over America. 'If They Could See Me Now' out of the way, she told her audience, 'You wondered what I was going to do. Well that's it.' Mr Wardle imagined there would be more. He was right.

'I've seen none of Miss MacLaine's films,' he was not ashamed to write, 'and from last night's performance it's hard to imagine her working anywhere but in a theatre.' There could be no finer compliment.

'She has the gift of honest contact with strangers, and the technical equipment to reach an audience twice the size of the Palladium's. What her show offers is the sight of a whale of a star bursting the confines of dramatic character to address the public directly.'

If the people who reacted so, shall we say, uncharitably to *Sweet Charity* could see her now!

The *Herald Tribune* reported from London: 'Shirley MacLaine opened last night at the Palladium and knocked 'em dead, which is to say the house became alive with cheers, tears, foot stamping and a standing ovation.'

It all seemed a throwback not so much to Danny Kaye at the Palladium, and the reviews were exceedingly reminiscent of those days, but to the opening nights of shows like *My Fair Lady* and *Guys and Dolls* which didn't so much take the town by storm as require the fire brigade to cool people off.

'The lack of interest in the box office changed overnight,' Louis Benjamin told me. 'There was a stampede once the reviews came out.'

Shirley played at the Palladium for two weeks and then was immediately booked for a second season later that year. Then she came back to the Apollo, Victoria for another run in 1982. But it was that first exposure to the Palladium audiences that opened up not just Britain, but Europe for her.

The papers lined up to interview her. Before the show, she had given a press conference. After opening night, writers who had only shown routine interest in an eccentric kook who had been known to have political leanings, now wanted to talk to her.

She told them that she became socially aware when she was three. She talked about Edward Kennedy being the man she would like to see in the White House, but was convinced he wouldn't do it because he would be shot.

That immediately led round to John F. Kennedy. Had she been one of his women?

Now, the answers published in the papers the following morning showed a degree of discretion nobody would dream of practising a decade later.

The papers reported her as saying that she wore Kennedy out just talking, he didn't have the energy to take her to bed even if he had wanted to. Or saying: 'I'd rather have a President who screwed women than screwed the world.'

Tony Wells, the Palladium's PR man who organised the gathering of 'privileged journalists' after the original press conference, recalls the meeting well. 'The papers weren't quite honest,' he told me.

What she actually said was: 'I'd rather have a President who had an occasional affair than played with himself in the War Room.'

Other writers still wanted her judgment on women's rights. Now she was thinking about men's rights, too. 'This question of women not having any good parts which bugs us: we have to face the fact that the reason is that we, women like me, have intimidated the Hollywood writer. I'm talking about intelligent, sensitive, radical men who see themselves as being on the side of women's liberation. They are terrified that if they sit down to their typewriter to write a good women's part, their male chauvinism will be exposed.'

She thought the way journalists worked needed looking into. Why should all the big investigative stories be left to the men? Why shouldn't women write them – and give writers like Malcolm Muggeridge the chance to do a six-part series on the menopause?

When she appeared on the Parkinson Show, Michael Parkinson's top TV talk programme, she flirted, joked and talked seriously about politics. That was different, she conceded, from the way either Jane Fonda or Vanessa Redgrave – two other highly politicised left-wing ladies with whom she was constantly being compared – would do it. 'People wouldn't keep listening to them,' she said somewhat immodestly. 'I'm not one of those who believes in leaving laughter till after the revolution.'

Pete Hamill was with her in London, which was remarkable for one other fact. She was admitting publicly that the famous marriage with Steve was over. 'We are separated,' she said – which itself wasn't news. They had been separated by those miles of Pacific Ocean practically all the time since they first said 'I do'.

But she added: 'This is separated with a capital "S".'

But there was no point in a divorce. She didn't intend to marry

215

again, which Pete and a few hundred thousand newspaper readers had already gathered.

Hamill himself wasn't saying very much – in fact, to get him to smile for the same picture in which Shirley was smiling was something of an achievement for any photographer. Their relationship was as 'combustible' as anything Taylor and Burton had, although she wasn't willing to admit it. It was the kind of combustion, however, that propelled both of them forward.

For the public she said that they talked about whether cats or dogs had souls and all that stuff about reincarnation. In private their fights were as active as their love-making. He used to tell her that going on stage was like a fighter going into the ring, which many a psychologist would say was a subconscious allusion to the way they lived together. For the moment, however, it seemed that both liked their lives somewhat fiery.

Nobody knew that another man had entered her life. Or at least, that is the story she tells. It was while at the Palladium that she met Gerry.

Gerry? Well, no one else knew about him until his name cropped up in her third book *Out on a Limb* seven years later. He is one of her well-kept secrets – the most secret thing of all about him is that he almost assuredly doesn't exist, but more of that later.

Gerry, she says, was a Labour MP to whom she was introduced, an exceedingly disarming attractive man whose hair used to flop over his forehead, who had a missing finger joint and whose birthday was in July. Who was he? She was to say that Gerry was a 'compilation' – of several men? Of several Labour MPs? Once, she denied that she even said he was an Englishman. Oh, but she did. A member of the English Parliament. She also says that her affair with Pete was over by then. No it wasn't. She and he were making London their love-nest at the time. But then Shirley knows her own life better than anyone and how she remembers it.

For the moment, according to her, Gerry flipped in and out of her life during the 1976 London tour. They would get very much closer before long.

But early 1976 was most notable for London as a show-biz

success story – and the tour that followed it.

The show made a fast but elegant progress through Europe. In Vienna, she went on stage with a temperature knocking 104 and found herself hallucinating – but there's no business like show business. . . .

In April 1976, Shirley was really benefiting from her London experience. She was playing Broadway – for the first time since *The Pajama Game*. The stage show had taken hold of her, and in a way the cinema never had. Unaware of it at first, she had literally found a Turning Point.

The audience loved her at the world-renowned Palace – American vaudevillians would like to claim it as the most important theatre in the world and Judy Garland sang 'If you haven't played the Palace, you haven't lived.' They are chauvinistically wrong. The Palladium is the greatest and most Hollywood stars would agree. In any case, the Palladium run and the shows that followed were just right to get her limbered up for her Palace show.

She gave them a potted musical autobiography, obviously but extremely appropriately called 'Remember Me?'

On someone else's broken leg I rode to fame. Remember me?

Everything wasn't exactly perfect, however. On opening night, she dropped the biggest clanger heard in America since someone dropped the liberty bell.

She said that she was glad to be back in the Karen Ann Quinlan of American cities. The joke thudded. Karen Ann Quinlan was the young girl lying attached to a life-support machine after falling into a deep coma following a too-heavy drink intake at a party.

The next morning, Shirley was on the phone apologising to Karen's distressed parents – who for the next decade and until she eventually died, paid daily visits to their daughter.

'The remark was off the top of my head,' she told them, 'and I wish it had stayed there.'

Later she explained: 'When I was talking about how great it was to be back in New York and what the city had been through, I remembered that line was going around Washington.'

That still needed some sort of explanation. So she gave it: 'Someone other than the person or the city involved is making life and death decisions. I was trying to say New York should have the power to make its own decisions.'

New York at the time was on the verge of bankruptcy. No one could promise the city's teachers that they would get their next pay cheque, the householders that they would have their garbage taken away or readers that they would be able to get into their public libraries the following week.

It may have sounded clever in Washington and Shirley recognised that it didn't sound at all like that to the Quinlans, but some people might have wished for a little warmer apology. It, however, did no lasting damage.

Remember her?

They remembered, and so did the people who paid to see her return to Las Vegas, this time playing Caesar's Palace and conquering it like a one-woman Roman legion.

In July, she was back at the Palace again – with no comments at all about cities or people who were on life-support machines.

'Dancing,' she declared, 'is like yoga, or driving a car. Once you learn it you never forget it. . . . Dancing is an honest art. You can't cheat the way you can in singing or acting.'

The show was basically as before – except that she added 'Steam Heat' to the routines. She said that, although she hadn't done it for years, people seemed to expect a reprise from *The Pajama Game*. The ironical thing was that it was the show in which she never got a proper notice that was constantly being referred to now.

That December, she was listed as a runner-up in the list of people who best epitomised 'class'. The winners were Betty Ford, then First Lady of the nation, Fred Astaire – seemingly for ever in his case – Princess Grace, Cary Grant, and Katharine Hepburn.

The runners-up were, in addition to Shirley, Queen Elizabeth II, Jackie Kennedy Onassis, David Niven, Representative Barbara Jordan of Texas, Alistair Cooke, Prince Philip and a designer named Bill Blass.

Shirley's one-woman shows were so sensational that she did a succession of them on television. They showed class, too. One of the best was the 1976 production *Gypsy in my Soul*. The gypsy she was referring to was the kind who travelled from one theatre to the next – the girls in the chorus, the sort of girl she was before Carol Haney broke that ankle.

It was election year again and everyone expected Shirley MacLaine to take as big a part in Democratic politics as last time. But this wasn't 1972 and she had no desire to. Jimmy Carter didn't inspire her the way McGovern did, although she sang at his inaugural celebrations and she was to display proudly in her living-room a picture of the President kissing her; they would become good friends before long.

She still made her opinions clear. She and Elizabeth Taylor jointly hosted a party for Bella Abzug's election campaign. But there wasn't a lot else she was doing, except finding a way of combining her show-business work with her political activities.

So many local Democrat supporters turned up for an evening of her show at the Palace in July that, noted *The New York Times*, they could have nominated Jimmy Carter there and then.

'Hello Democrats and closet Republicans,' she said at the beginning of the show. When she sang 'Hey Big Spender' she said she was dedicating it to a politician who was currently doing a little too much spending.

She went back on television and this time the success wasn't nearly so great.

John J. O'Connor commented in *The New York Times*: 'Miss MacLaine is a performer seemingly incapable of dull consistency. She tends to be very good or very bad.'

Gypsy in my Soul had, he said, been very good. This show, *Where Do We Go From Here?*, was almost the opposite. 'The special never really delivers its promise which is, in Miss MacLaine's words, "to sneak a peek into the future in a really unusual show".'

She was rude about Queen Elizabeth and Elton John which seemed to sum up the standard of the performance.

Could Pete have anything to do with all this? In 1977 her affair was over. As if part of the plot of a TV mini-series, he went off with another woman – in this case, Jackie Kennedy Onassis.

They had been together for seven years. Reflecting on it all afterwards, Shirley said it had been the biggest love of her life.

But then she hadn't yet started talking about 'Gerry'. According to her book – and there are no witnesses to the affair, which is quite remarkable – he met her in America; she joined up with him again in London.

Together, they swam in the Pacific and made love in countries from one end of the globe to the other. She thought of him constantly. He was a married man with children. She felt pangs of conscience about that – until he told her his wife ruled the family with an iron hand.

After three years of torrid love, constant frustration, they parted. But why were they never seen together? Not by a single newspaperman, or a freelance photographer ready to earn a quick buck?

Shirley's work was less secret. She had a new film now – which she didn't find technological at all, except that there *was* a great deal of technology in it.

In *The Turning Point* she teamed up with Anne Bancroft, almost as though it were a gesture of thanks for Anne lending her choreographer – although on screen, they were spattering at each other like two cats on the same patch, fighting over a fishbone and the local tom.

Arthur Laurents wrote the story about two former members of a New York ballet company meeting up again. Neither really liked each other before. Now, on the visit of the company to Oklahoma City, where one of the two women (MacLaine) is living as a too conventional housewife, they indulge in the luxury of unadulterated hate.

Miss Bancroft is the same age, but she is the star. It plainly rankles, even more so when Shirley's daughter gets the chance of the stardom she herself never had. The resulting jealousy bites like Jaws on a quiet day at the beach. In one scene, they actually fight, claws out, handbags flying. It was wonderful cinema, even if it seemed a bit pantomimic. As Shirley said, she had hit a man before but never another woman.

Anne Bancroft had had a fight with a woman and gave her some tips. Shirley said she was afraid of hurting her too much – after all, Bancroft was small and fragile; MacLaine thought that she herself was big and powerful. As things turned out, Shirley needn't have worried. Both showed they could look after themselves.

The only thing she couldn't understand about the plot was the confession that she and her husband, another dancer (played by Tom Skerritt), only had a child because he wanted to prove he was not a homosexual. The writer and director said it was necessary. She thought it was totally irrelevant, but that was free

220

Shirley showing she was more liberated than the others.

In this film, she was neither a sexy dancer nor a hooker. She saw it as the great woman's part she had been after for a long time.

It was frequently described as a soap opera. But as the *New Yorker* magazine put it, there were compensations in the dancing, particularly from Mikhail Baryshnikov.

'We get a glimpse of something great in the movie – Mikhail Baryshnikov dancing – and these two harpies out of the soaps block the view.'

Richard Schickel in *Time* magazine was somewhat kinder: 'You yield to *The Turning Point* reluctantly,' he wrote when the film was released in November 1977. The reluctance was overcome by 'knowing well that it is conning you with sentiment, with flamboyance, with sheer slickness.'

He added: 'It is hard to imagine anyone, with the possible exception of pre-adolescent males, who will not in the end turn on to *The Turning Point*.'

Shirley carried on as if there had never been any criticism or, more likely, as if she needed that criticism as a kind of fuel. In May 1977, she played for the first time in what was almost her home town, Washington DC at the Kennedy Center.

The White House staff was fully represented; Mrs Rosalynn Carter and her son and daughter-in-law Chipp and Caron sat in the presidential box; the other Carters didn't come, which was perhaps fortunate for Shirley, as there were no distractions in the form of little Amy declaiming politics or brother Billy running out of cans of beer.

Dorothy Padgett, the Assistant Chief of Protocol, later gave a party for Shirley at her Georgetown home.

She was as big with VIPs as ever. And not just in America. She flew to Havana for a special showing of *The Turning Point*.

Shirley was glad that Fidel Castro had the same feelings about women's rights that she had. As she said at the time: 'I could never even be attracted to a man who would expect me to stop working. Telling me not to work is like telling a 747 not to fly.' That was why the Cubans were surprised that the character she played in the film *had* stopped working. That wasn't women's rights, was it?

She and Castro – 'Fidel' she called him – met and discussed the matter. He was convinced it *was* just a part. He was, she said, the only man she liked to be with when he was puffing a cigar – apart, that is, from Lew Grade, for whom she bore no hard feelings.

She had heard about the sex appeal that Castro was supposed to give out with every puff of that cigar. She saw him as having a kind of femininity. 'He has a soft, caressing demeanour with a gleam in his eye and a gentle voice. It's almost an emotionally romantic quality. I expected a man more solidly aggressive. But if you try to use feminine wiles with Fidel, it absolutely turns him off. He likes to talk about serious matters.'

Needless to say, there were critics of her visit – after all, Americans were still banned from smoking those Havanas themselves. Shirley had to confess she found him trustful. But then she added: 'If one had to trust Castro or the CIA there wouldn't be much in it, I suppose. But he has done just wonders for Cuba in education and medicine. They wiped out illiteracy in only one year.'

To some it seemed like China revisited.

America appreciated her too. One journalist pointed out that with she and Jane Fonda having their names above film titles, Hollywood had rediscovered American women. The two were the 1978 equals of Davis, Hepburn, Russell and Crawford. Which wasn't bad for the girl who was still wowing them in a pair of fishnet tights.

Having made *The Turning Point*, she was ready for another movie – one that was called *Loving Couples*, about a married woman having an affair with a younger man. Surprise, surprise.

'That sort of thing is going on all the time,' she said at the time. 'Surely you know that?' Most people pretended that yes, they did.

The New York Times would have preferred it to be left to real life. 'A flat, lifeless movie' said Janel Maslin in her review for the paper. She didn't like the sexy doctor played by Shirley, though Sally Kellerman was a lot better. Shirley seemed good only when she was supposed to look angry. Some people knew that about her already.

What few people did know was that she was allowed to dictate terms that would perhaps have seemed outrageous to

Hollywood of old – like being permitted to arrive on the set at 11.30 in the morning. She was a night person and this gave her the opportunity not to suffer for it.

What was that? She needed more sleep than she used to? No, that wasn't it at all. Until four o'clock in the morning, she was busy writing her next book.

And if she didn't have Pete to cuddle up to after that? Well, she was still the best of friends with all the men who had been in her life, and she couldn't understand why other women didn't feel that way, too. If a man had been satisfactory enough to go to bed with, why should he seem so abhorrent now they were no longer lovers?

And Steve was still there, wasn't he? Despite the earlier reports of their being separated – with a capital 'S' – she was still claiming in 1979: 'I have the most marvellous relationship with him. We have come to an agreement of friendship. We like each other. And that's even more important than loving each other in my view. Liking has longevity to it. Love is intense and can burn itself out.'

It seemed that the live audience's love affair with Shirley MacLaine was as strong as ever. By February 1979 when she appeared in Las Vegas yet again, she was an established figure there. As with Sinatra and Martin, it was her own territory and she was guaranteed Standing Room Only – SRO were the most exciting initials in show-biz – whenever she appeared on The Strip.

'Why should I do a love scene with Robert Redford when I could be up here busting my ass in this fashion?' she asked. Few could guess the answer, but they loved the question.

Like many another woman she was trying to work out why her brother Warren hadn't married. A man such as he who needed women in his bed the way other people needed butter on their bread or sugar in their coffee, seemed a perfect candidate for the altar. But no. She thought she knew the answer. He was, she said, looking for another Shirley MacLaine, someone like his sister to whom he could relate.

If that sounded vaguely incestuous, she was soon to compound the felony. She wouldn't mind doing a love scene with brother Warren – just to find out what all the fuss was about. As she said, she hadn't seen him in the nude since he was six years old.

223

She wanted to go to a New York 'swingers' bar with him, but accepted his advice that it wouldn't be a good move. They'd be recognised.

She made a new TV spectacular, *Shirley in Paris*, and did another concert tour from coast to coast. In case anyone thought she was taking things too easy, there was another film, too.

Being There had her co-starring with Peter Sellers, just weeks before he died in London.

It was their first film together since *Woman Times Seven* and work on it coincided with rumours that the two were locked in a new affair. Both denied it, although she suspected he desperately wanted to get her to bed and sensed as much on the set of the film – the story of a wealthy woman (Shirley) who elevates her simple gardener to a greatness beyond both his imagination and his abilities. Banal words about his garden were taken as superb judgments on the world situation. He didn't have the brain to take the reactions of other people any more seriously than Shirley herself took his imagined love for her.

It was a superb Sellers performance. Shirley's own part may have seemed more restrained – except that she played the most graphic masturbation scene in modern movies. It was severely cut, which she has gone down on record as saying she thought was a mistake, because it was funny and honest. Laurence Olivier didn't, however – which is why he turned down the role of Shirley's aged husband and Melvin Douglas stepped in in his stead.

But it was Peter's film and she was always conscious that his health might not hold out for long.

Shirley was sitting in a car with him, shooting a scene on the Goldwyn lot, when he clutched his chest and grabbed her arm. It was the same lot where he had his first heart attack in 1964. Then he felt his heart being massaged back to life after it had stopped. It was as close to a real reincarnation as she had come across. But there would be another.

In *Out on a Limb*, Shirley describes Peter's role in *Being There* as the greatest in his career. She is not wrong.

Afterwards, he went back to Europe. She was standing talking to a couple of friends in her home in Malibu in July 1980, when she stopped still and froze. 'I've just had the feeling that something's wrong with Peter,' she told them.

Two minutes later, the phone rang. It was a newspaperman, telling her that he had died. It took a long time to get over that, though she tried.

The marriage with Steve finally ended officially with divorce in 1982. She wouldn't have said it was a failure, just a symptom of her freedom.

Shirley went back to thinking about the man she called Gerry. She indulged in seances and became convinced that she and Gerry had been made for each other once in another lifespan.

In 1983, the world got to hear about Gerry. But who was he? And who was the man called David she mentioned in *Out on a Limb*, the one who got her involved in meditation and reincarnation and who was not interested in her body?

So much of Shirley's book was dedicated to the subject of reincarnation that Warren Beatty said he saw it almost as a follow-up to his own movie *Heaven Can Wait*.

It was an important metaphysical part of her life. She agreed that she was something of a missionary – the charge she had once made about George McGovern – but in her case with no place for God. The old folks from Virginia wouldn't have been pleased to know that.

Gerry was the one who intrigued most people. She wasn't going to reveal his name. She wasn't going to incriminate him. Then came that business about his being a composite figure.

No, her Gerry was not standing at the coming General Election, she admitted. But the speculation grew – in the process far outgrowing the publicity hype which the publishers generated and for which she showed no little reluctance herself.

'It is amazing,' she said, 'that there are so many people who are more concerned about my in-body experiences than my out-of-body experiences. And that the affairs of state are not more important to them than the state of my affairs.' If she really were amazed, it would be . . . amazing. It was, though, a nice turn of phrase.

The 'Britishness' of Gerry was part of the composite nature of the characterisation, she said.

Speculation ran rife in the popular press. David Owen, Peter Shore and Tony Benn were mentioned as being possible candidates for the original Gerry – if only because their hair flopped over their foreheads. Even Michael Foot, the elderly Leader of the Opposition, was suggested. There was no evidence that he had lost the top of a finger like 'Gerry' but he had the same birthday, July 23.

They all denied it – the kind of denial that betrayed a sense of flattery; which is not surprising. To be even suspected of being the man with whom Shirley MacLaine was in love was very flattering indeed.

But who was he? She wasn't saying. Nothing would drag the name from her. Could he have been a member of the mother of parliaments? He almost certainly was not. And for a very simple reason – it is not the kind of place that holds secrets very well.

More than one senior political career has foundered because of a married MP's indiscretions with another woman. I once talked to a deserted wife who told me how she had watched unbelieving as a senior minister sat in the House restaurant with his hand on the knee of a woman who was not his wife – and then sat in frozen fascination, seeing the man's hand creep under the woman's skirt, and so high up her thighs that what happened next was open to public gaze.

One Labour MP put it to me like this: 'It would just be impossible for it to be one of us without everyone knowing. Nobody keeps a secret in this place for more than a couple of weeks – unless he is some kind of superman.' And even Shirley wasn't claiming 'Gerry' to be a superman.

Australia's Opposition Leader Andrew Peacock was mentioned, and they *had* been seen in each other's company and were known to be friends, but the suggestion was not taken seriously by anyone.

In Britain the speculation continued. Michael Foot said he was upset about being mentioned. Stan Newens was mentioned. So was Roderick MacFarquhar. Andrew Faulds, another Labour MP, said he knew the man's identity, but doubts remained. If the man existed, could he have broken that secrets barrier? Unlikely. Gerald Kaufman, Labour's Shadow Home Secretary, plainly enjoyed the greeting he received at a party meeting: 'Here comes Gerry.' Yes, but Shirley's Gerry? No. Perhaps he was the Prime Minister of Sweden, Olof Palme?

Well, that was an interesting idea, but it did not seem to

226

square with Shirley's stories of listening to him speaking in a British Commons debate, to say nothing of enjoying the telephones in the House at the expense of the British taxpayer.

My own feeling is that the whole affair was a grand hoax by a woman who knew what made news and what the newspapers would make of that news.

She was on somewhat safer ground discussing American politics. Yes, she would support Edward Kennedy if he showed any interest in running for President. It wasn't what people wanted to hear, but she wasn't giving away any more clues about Gerry.

Could he have been one of her characters from her reincarnated past? One guess was as good as another.

The constant references to a past life worried people. Shirley didn't know whether readers could take it either, so she did her own form of market research. She started holding small parties, at which she would gently broach the subject. The parties convinced her – people *could* take it.

Was *Out on a Limb* the novel she had been promising for so long? If it were, it was a good move. In hardback, 176,000 copies were sold, with another 12 million in paperback. She doesn't mention Steve, not even Sachi.

She would describe herself as reclusive. Which wasn't at all the way she was. She had just made another film called *Change of Seasons*. Bo Derek was her co-star. Shirley said she was 'sweet', even though the part Bo played was taking away Shirley's husband.

In fact 'sweet' was the term Shirley used all the time to describe Miss Derek who, much to the delight of most men, usually spent more time exposing her breasts than opening her mouth. In *Seasons*, Bo had her clothes on during most of the movie.

But she wasn't all that easy for the rest of the company. Sweet she may have been, but she is generally held responsible for the change of directors in the course of shooting – from Noel Black to Richard Lang.

Shirley was asked by *Playgirl* if Bo posed her many questions. Miss MacLaine answered: 'She doesn't know enough to know what to ask.'

Warren said he admired Shirley's screen acting. She didn't

'come on' or load it with a lot of 'fake, superficial, coy frilly sugar'.

In the new film, as in *Loving Couples*, she herself has an affair with a younger man. She understood those women. 'Young men are less demanding,' she said. 'They have different concepts of life and fun. They're more emotionally expressive.'

Vincent Canby, the veteran *New York Times* critic, said: 'The only appealing performance is Miss MacLaine's and she's too good to be true. A *Change of Seasons* does prove one thing, though. A farce about characters who've been freed of their conventional obligations quickly becomes aimless.'

But then, Shirley had always enjoyed scandalising people. Never more than when in July 1983, she and Debbie Reynolds danced for an audience of 1,000 at a San Francisco charity function and did a striptease.

The audience were mainly homosexuals. Debbie exposed a bare bottom. Shirley removed the top part of her dress and her bra, and let the audience see her breasts as she pranced topless on stage. Why? It, too, was a means of expressing herself, letting it all hang out.

Sachi, she would admit, wasn't at all like that. She thought that a lot of the things Shirley did and said were very unfeminine. Shirley said she knows Sachi was her mother in a previous life. As for herself, she is convinced she was both a madame and a dancer. And then there was that prostitute who existed at some other time and the court jester – a man – who was beheaded by King Louis XV. She had been them, too.

Whether knowing that helped her adjust to life in the 1980s she couldn't be sure. It certainly didn't stop her enjoying both life and love.

One of her lovers of this period was Andre Mikhalkov-Konchalovsky, a Soviet director. 'Shirley,' he was to declare, 'is a missile with a self-correction of trajectory and a powerful engine. If you get in her way, she doesn't explode, she just goes through, and maybe you'll have a hole.'

(She tells a lovely story of how Andre managed to get hold of a drug taken by Russian cosmonauts. Marlon Brando spotted the Russian characters on the label and drank the whole bottle – without knowing whether it was vodka or rat poison.)

What is sure is that no one man could make her happy. She

said it loud and clear: '*I* am the only one who can make me completely happy.' She wasn't unhappy or lonely. But if she could find a man who was just like her, she'd be doubly content.

There had been three brief affairs after Pete Hamill, but nothing long enough to be satisfying.

That might explain why she and Warren were, basically, so very different. 'We didn't meet in any of our previous lives,' she said seriously, uncomplicatedly.

Nor, as far as anyone knows, did Shirley meet Aurora Greenway. Aurora was the character she played in *Terms of Endearment*, the film that was to win her her first Oscar in March 1984.

This wasn't a typical MacLaine role either. But then things were happening to her. She was 49 years old and the part seemed the perfect recognition of the fact: the sort of recognition she had looked for herself on that 49th birthday when she took off for New Mexico and climbed a mountain. It seemed a significant thing to do as she contemplated a significant year. What would 1984 bring?

It was one mountain she wasn't going to fall off.

Chapter Fourteen

SHIRLEY WAS TALKED into the idea of *Terms of Endearment* by director Jim Brooks, who had previously worked on TV series like *Taxi* and *The Mary Tyler Moore Show*. Now he was going to produce and write the screenplay as well as direct the picture. He was nervous and desperately wanted her to star in his film. For days, he virtually parked himself on her doorstep till she agreed to take the role.

Completing the deal was a good move on both their parts.

This was no wealthy woman inveigling a young man to her bed. In a way, it was more like *The Turning Point*. Once again, she was a mother with a daughter – except this one wasn't a ballerina but simply a girl dying of cancer.

Instead of a juvenile lover, she took Jack Nicholson. For the second time – the first had been with Shirley's brother Warren in *Reds* – he was playing a supporting role, which, as they say in Hollywood, real stars ought not to do.

Nicholson played her next-door neighbour, a former astronaut – which showed just how far the world had come by 1983 – who had run to fat and to seed. Both of them put on a lot of weight for the movie; when they got into bed, stomachs bulging, their love-making had to be from memory.

The poignant role of the mother (of Debra Winger) was one of the great moments in Shirley's career. She really seemed to have found a turning point. There would be no more pot-boilers, no more strange ideas, just as there certainly would be no more cheques on the dressing-table.

It was a moving story, which six studios had turned down as utterly uncommercial. It occasionally sank into a pit of banality, but then managed to lift itself up out of the mire before the

231

damage went any further.

The film was a co-winner – with *Betrayal* – of the National Board of Review of Motion Pictures award for the best picture of the year. But that was nothing compared with what happened at that year's Academy Awards ceremony.

Shirley's Oscar as best actress was one of what became a virtual sweep that night. James Brooks took the award for the best director as well as that for best screenplay and then another for best film. Jack Nicholson won the Oscar for best supporting actor.

In the car on the way to the ceremony, Shirley was handed a package. It was a present from Warren, a complicated assortment of many parts. Shirley said that she was only able to figure out five of those parts, but because it was so complicated, she burst into tears. It was, she said, the most caring gift she had ever had – from the brother who would describe their relationship as 'complicated'. It was a very emotional evening.

When she went up to the podium to collect the award, Shirley tried to feign ease, but it didn't last long. 'I'm gonna cry,' she said before too long, 'because this show has been as long as my career. I have wondered for 26 years what this would feel like.'

Later, she told reporters, 'I deserve this.' It was generally agreed that she did.

She was soon back at work in Las Vegas. The auditorium seemed even more crowded than usual. 'I know why you're all here,' she said, 'you couldn't get in for *Terms of Endearment*.' It was a good line. The good actress was still a good comedienne.

The critics seemed to like the film. Margaret Hinxman, writing in the London *Daily Mail*, said she thought the story seemed to be a bit like a 'soap', which was now the current derisory expression. But she added – and nobody disagreed – that Shirley's performance had been stunning. 'Shirley MacLaine achieves unquestionably her finest hour on the screen. And Debra Winger matches her all the way. . . . It's an enormously skilful movie, often witty, always surprising and shrewdly observant about how poorly equipped most of us are in our modern society to confront the awesome tragedy of somebody else's terminal illness. Maybe I just expected too much.'

Shirley has never had any real doubts about the role. She loved Aurora Greenway probably more than any other she played. As she has said, it never occurred to her that Aurora might be the viper some other people saw her as.

In addition to her Best Actress award, Shirley was being honoured as befitted her years in show business. In May 1984, Hunter College, New York's premier educational establishment for women, gave her an honorary doctorate, one of three women honoured as 'Symbols of Freedom'. Shirley joked that she got it for 'recognition that I did it the hard way, without an education'. The college preferred to say that the award was for her 'proud independence, lifelong quest into philosophy and metaphysics' and her 'support of those who champion the victims of discrimination, particularly women'.

She was introduced by Bella Abzug, now out of the House of Representatives, but not absent from the political movement or Shirley's heart.

It was not the first such award. In 1973, she had received an honorary degree of Doctor of Letters from Dartmouth College for her 'deep concern about the problems of mankind'.

There were plans for the future – lots of them.

She still hadn't made the Amelia Earhart film, but one day she would, she declared. When she did make a movie in 1984, she took it no more seriously than did anyone else, for which much praise. If anyone were taking *Cannonball II* to heart, he would have to conclude that it was by far, without any question, the worst picture she has ever made. But it came and went and people blamed her for it no more than they would blame Laurence Olivier for making *The Jazz Singer* or *The Betsy*. She had the pre-assured comfort of knowing nobody would remember her for this story, which ostensibly starred Burt Reynolds as a racing-car driver.

More significantly, it was a reunion of the 'Clan'. Frank Sinatra, Dean Martin and Sammy Davis Jnr were in the film, too, and Shirley said she did it only to be with her old friends again. She didn't even bother to read the script – such as it was – before jumping at the opportunity to make the film. When she did try to read the script, she said she couldn't understand it, but made the film just the same. In fact, she insists none of the cast read the words in advance, but they all had a good time.

That said a very great deal about her and where she had got to. She was not concerned about posterity – it was just one of her passing lives anyway; the next one might be more important – she wanted to enjoy herself. It was simply a compartment; one of the many that made up the complex personality called Shirley MacLaine. It had no more to do with her artistic cinema compartment than it did with her political niche.

The one thing that bothered her was that whenever there was a script for a woman aged between 32 and 60, none of them excited her.

Television was becoming more and more her medium. One spectacle, *Shirley MacLaine, Every Little Movement*, was followed by another called *Illusions*. They were produced by her own company, Shirley MacLaine Enterprises.

By the time she celebrated her 50th birthday in 1984, Shirley was recognised as the elder stateswoman of American show business – which wasn't bad for a gal who still looked great in a pair of fishnets.

She also looked pretty nifty wearing a gold chain holding a collection of diamonds – each one given by a lover. She wasn't interested in 'things' for the sake of having them, which was why she only now had one house, in Malibu, and had given up her Rolls-Royce and three mink coats.

Biology naturally was catching up with her to some degree. As she said, she might one day have plastic surgery – she didn't need it – but she wouldn't consider herself for a remake of *Saturday Night Fever*. She had her own hot flushes.

When she opened in her show at the Gershwin Theater, New York, in the spring of 1984, there was not the slightest doubt that the Oscar *had* attracted people to the theatre. But it was Shirley MacLaine who had kept them there.

Time magazine again made her their cover feature – although incredibly for an article of its length, only in the United States edition.

Its sister magazine *People* did the same thing. Shirley MacLaine was big business – and she recognised the genius of others, too. On the night of the Academy Awards presentation, she had met veteran screen-writer Julius Epstein – who had won his own Oscar for *Casablanca*, a credit indeed. 'You're an inspiration to us all,' she said.

'I liked that,' he told me. 'I was 74, she was 50. I suppose that had something to do with it.'

The show took in a gross of $475,000 a week.

'Life is a feast for me,' she said when she reached her 51st birthday in 1985. Sometimes she went hungry, sometimes not.

No longer did she find it necessary to pick up a suitcase and just take off. Now she only had to go into a room and contemplate a flower.

Ask about her own personality and she will admit that it isn't easy to analyse. She said she seemed to be constantly unsettling her life while other people were getting theirs in a nice apple-pie order.

She has become even more committed than ever to the theory of reincarnation – although to her it is much more than a theory.

She sees it as an explanation for everything good – like her various lovers – and bad – like the serious illness of her mother to whom she seemed to be growing very much closer.

Reincarnation – and her love for her Russian film director – became the focus of yet another book published in the States in the autumn of 1985 called *Dancing in the Light*. Shirley meanwhile was dancing with a greater satisfaction than ever before.

She even played herself in a TV film being made of *Out on a Limb*. Charles Dance played the mythical Gerry and Shirley tried to show how she escaped detection by smothering her face in a mass of scarves.

She once said that a star could be a star one moment, but the next would suffer from a fickle public that had changed its collective mind. 'The public doesn't get tired of toothpaste, the public needs toothpaste.' Probably her great success was that, after all these years, she had achieved the status of toothpaste.

Another time she put it rather more succinctly: 'Being a film star is what I do, not what I am.' It was nice and modest, which film stars usually are not. Since Shirley MacLaine had no reason to feign modesty, there was good reason to believe her.

Always there was that feeling of something very special just about to happen – as at that night at the Wilshire Theater in Los Angeles where this story began.

If life was a feast, what kind of food would she be served in the future? She wasn't aiming for a banquet. Indeed, the long, rambling story she told on the stage in that 1984 show probably said a great deal. It was about the time she tramped for days up the Himalayas to meet a guru. Finally, he gives her his message.

'Life,' he says, 'is . . . just a bowl of cherries.' A cue for
There was always a cue for a song – and always people
wondered about this phenomenon called Shirley MacLaine. .
they wouldn't wonder – if they could see her now.